STAY CALM
Stay Healthy

Anyone can hold the helm when the sea is calm.

Publilius Syrus
Latin writer of maxims, 1st century BC

Expert contributors

writers

Susan Balfour Cert CT Psych
Stress management counsellor and psychotherapist
CHAPTERS 1, 3, 4, 5, 7, 9 and Introduction

Dr Chris Idzikowski BSc PhD CPsychol FBPsS
Director, The Edinburgh Sleep Centre
& The Sleep Assessment and Advisory Service
CHAPTER 2

Dr Susan Kersley MB BCh D Obst RCOG
Doctor (retd), life coach and NLP practitioner
CHAPTERS 8 and 10

Sheena Meredith MB BS MPhil
Consultant/writer (consumer law and medicine)
CHAPTER 6

consultant

Linda Blair MPhil CSci CPsychol
Clinical psychologist

STAY CALM
Stay Healthy

Defend yourself against stress
and improve your health

Published by The Reader's Digest Association, Inc.

London • New York • Sydney • Montreal

Contents

About this book

Calmness, health – and happiness – are closely linked. Studies also show that the most successful people are those who have learned how to manage their lives in a way that minimises stress and anxiety, and maximises optimism and creativity. This book will show you how to do the same.

In *Stay Calm Stay Healthy* you will be introduced to practical, down-to-earth, easily achievable ways of creating and maintaining a calmer and more enjoyable life. You'll find hundreds of useful suggestions, ideas and tips for tackling everyday stresses and strains, as well as strategies for boosting your confidence and self-esteem, and developing an optimistic outlook, so that you can handle difficulties from a more positive perspective.

PRACTICAL GUIDE FOR LIFE

This book is both a personal stress management guide and a pragmatic problem-solver in the areas that affect us most: home, family, relationships and social life, consumer and legal issues, nutrition and sleep, as well as physical and mental health. It draws on up-to-date expert advice from a range of specialists, including doctors, psychologists, nutritionists, stress counsellors, lawyers – and even interior designers. Rather than dwelling on the problems, the emphasis is on finding solutions.

By helping you to understand your personality type and your own reactions to everyday irritations, this book can help improve your working, social and family life, your parenting skills and the way in which you manage and cope with the world around you. The information is clearly divided into different sections, making it easy to find the advice you need. Helpful hints on every page, along with numerous boxes and side panels featuring fascinating facts, practical techniques and expert opinions, ensure that the explanations, suggestions and tips are easily accessible and straightforward to follow. There are also a number of case studies illustrating how others have coped with a variety of stressful life experiences.

POSITIVE APPROACH

This book is positive. From the start you will find helpful suggestions for getting more out of life: for preventing or alleviating stress-related problems, and for introducing more relaxation, harmony and fun into everyday living. *Stay Calm Stay Healthy* is designed to help you identify what upsets you most – your stress triggers – as well as presenting a vast range of ways to gain control over worries and anxieties before they end up controlling you and damaging your health and emotional wellbeing.

ADVICE FOR EVERYONE

While it was once thought that stress affected only a small number of people in certain extreme circumstances, it is clear that in today's world most people experience it in one way or another. Increasing numbers of people are succumbing to anxiety disorders such as panic attacks, sleep problems, hyperventilation and debilitating tension, as well as more serious mental health disorders. Emotional breakdowns, depression and other psychological problems are now relatively commonplace– even among children.

   Stay Calm Stay Healthy is a book for our times, offering hundreds of ingenious ways to defend yourself against life's pressures and strains and reset your life onto a calmer, healthier course. Featuring the latest scientific, medical and psychological thinking on stress management – both physical and emotional – this book shows you how to take back control and protect yourself against the many health problems that stress can cause, whether you're young or old, male or female, and whatever your walk of life.

Introduction

There's nothing worse than feeling that life's out of control, and few things worse for your health. Yet, in today's world, in spite of all the technological advances that were supposed to make life easier, many of us end up feeling overwhelmed by everyday pressures. A 2010 survey by the online market research company One Poll found that Britons now have 8.5 hours less 'me-time' a week than they did five years ago, with women grabbing an average of 50 minutes to themselves a day, compared to 1 hour 15 minutes for men. Of the people surveyed who worked a full five-day week, almost half admitted to taking their work home. As Fiona Fyfe, from Microsoft's Windows Live Hotmail, which commissioned the survey, commented: 'Juggling careers, family, relationships, household chores and financial admin is leaving Brits with little time to spend on themselves. The fact that free time has decreased by 8 hours a week over the last five years is testament to how much busier today's lifestyles are.'

Now, more than ever before, we need to find ways to manage and control the constant demands created by tight deadlines and overloaded schedules – trying to juggle work, home and family life. Not to mention the incessant barrage of information from the media and the frustrations when essential technology breaks down. Today's problems need up-to-date solutions to help us all cope better and to introduce some calm into our busy lives.

KNOW YOUR LIMITS

It's important to recognise that stress is not always bad for you. It helps motivate people to progress through life and accomplish their goals – after all, nothing is achieved without some pressure and effort. The key is how much stress you experience, and for how long. Unrelieved stress affects both mental and physical health, so it's vital to recognise when you're pushing yourself beyond the limits of your resources.

According to the European Agency for Safety and Health at Work, nearly one in four workers in the EU is affected by work-related stress, now thought to be responsible for 50–60 per cent of all lost working days. A 2009 survey by the American Psychological Association revealed similar findings in the USA, with nearly a quarter of adults experiencing high stress levels, while just over half reported moderate stress.

Nowadays, we are often expected to process vast amounts of information, as a result of increased media coverage from around the globe, the internet and other information technology. This has undoubted benefits, but can also place a huge demand on our minds and emotions; recent research suggests that technology is contributing to a workaholic culture, with staff working up to ten extra days a year because they can't bring themselves to switch off their mobile phones. When this is coupled with everyday irritations and frustrations, we tend to feel overwhelmed. In reaction to this demand, the body's stress responses may be activated far too frequently, which can have a detrimental effect on health.

FINDING THE BALANCE

In order to maintain good physical and mental health, it is necessary to find a balance between the different areas of life. This book shows you how. Finding the right rhythm between doing and resting – between 'using' and 'restoring' yourself – is crucial, as is learning not to overwork any one aspect of yourself: intellectual, logical pursuits, for example, need the counterbalance of creative activities.

Stay Calm Stay Healthy explains how to manage the day-to-day to your advantage – how you can find ways to tailor tasks and shape events to minimise pressures and reap the positive benefits that will follow. Discover the rewards of leading a life that is organised, serene and fun; of having more energy to pursue your ambitions and achieve your goals; of maintaining and enhancing relationships with family and friends; and of getting more from your leisure time and feeling a great deal happier, healthier and more positive.

SWITCHING OFF THE STRESS RESPONSE

The stress response is an automatic reaction, usually triggered before you realise what is happening. When the brain registers what it perceives as a threat – an emergency situation, a huge workload, an important interview or exam, or something that angers or upsets you, for example – it sends out chemical 'messengers' to gear up the body for what is known as 'fight or flight'. In other words, the brain alerts the body that extra physical effort will be needed to cope with whatever you are facing, and this brings about chemical changes within the body's systems and organs to assist in this demand.

The problem is that many of the events that activate the stress response today are emotional or intellectual threats that cannot be resolved in a physical way. As a result, the stress response – only designed to be activated for short

EXPERT VIEW

HAPPINESS IS THE KEY

Happiness, rather than just working hard, is the key to success, says Professor Sonja Lyubomirsky from the University of California, Riverside. Her team's study showed that happy people tend to earn more, and that their happiness came first – before their good fortune. She adds: 'There's strong evidence that happiness leads people to be more sociable and more generous, more productive at work, to make more money and to have stronger immune systems. These people are also better able to cope with stress and likely to be healthier and live longer.'

periods, to handle an emergency – may be switched on for hours, or even days, at a time. Unless the response is immediately defused by physical exertion, as nature intended, the chemical changes can put a great strain on the body's systems, and may eventually lead to exhaustion and a mental or physical breakdown. Learning to 'switch off' this response is a key part of staying calm and healthy, and you'll find plenty of advice on how to do this in chapter 3 – and throughout this book – along with more detailed information on the changes that occur in the body while the response is activated.

CONTROLLING YOUR REACTIONS

Learning to moderate your reaction to life's worries can minimise the physical and mental effects of stress. For, while it's not always possible to control what's going on around you, you *can* learn to adjust your response to whatever life throws at you. Many everyday problems that cause stress or anxiety are readily solvable with the right approach; sometimes it can be helpful simply to change the way you look at things. This book shows you how.

We all have our own unique way of reacting to life's pressures.
For example:
● Are you the type who bottles things up, or do you let everyone know what's bothering you?
● Are you very sensitive, inclined to react more intensely than someone who is thicker-skinned?
● Are you logical, tending to push emotional problems into the background, often storing up trouble for yourself at a later date?
● Are you imaginative, perhaps envisaging all the things that could go wrong with a situation, an event or a relationship before it's even begun?

You can't transform your personality, but knowing and understanding yourself can be a great defence against unexpected crises. Being aware of your stress triggers can help you avoid being caught off balance. In chapter 1 you will discover your personality type and associated traits that you may need to adapt to work better for you, thereby safeguarding your health.

YOUR DIY GUIDE TO HEALTH AND HAPPINESS

In these pages you will discover effective solutions to a wide range of emotional and practical problems. The advice is designed to help you get more out of life and put you back in control. All aspects of everyday life are covered, from building your defences and boosting your mood using diet, exercise and a variety of relaxation techniques, to discovering the secrets of good sleep, developing a positive attitude and the key to creating happy relationships, as well as learning how to cope on your own. You'll even find advice on consumer rights and legal issues, such as what to do about faulty goods or noisy neighbours, along with strategies for dealing with financial worries – one of the most common causes of stress today. The book also includes details of organisations you can turn to for support, should you find you need a helping hand along the way.

It's a manual for our times. The book explains in a lucid and accessible way why people act as they do, and then outlines dozens of different strategies for counteracting pressure, defusing conflict, feeling better and living life to the full. Staying calm – and staying healthy – is the key to enjoyment, and the way to a healthier, happier you.

Susan Balfour Cert CT Psych

1 know yourself

Some people thrive on pressure, while others prefer to avoid it at all costs. But too much stress, whether caused by overwork, unhappy relationships or a personal crisis, is mentally unsettling and produces adverse physical effects. How much an individual can tolerate is closely linked to personality traits – some people handle crises much better than others. This chapter helps you to understand your personality type and explains how, if necessary, you can modify your consequent behaviour to develop a healthier response to potentially stressful situations.

How do you react?

Are you a natural worrier? Do you create stress for yourself by setting unrealistic self-imposed goals? Or, conversely, are you able to stay calm, regardless of what life throws at you? And what kind of impact does all this have on your health?

Everyone deals with problems and challenges in different ways, according to their personal make-up. Stress, if handled badly, can have damaging physical – as well as psychological – effects. Learning to recognise your strengths and play to them, and how to control your reaction to stress, is key in safeguarding your health.

are you stressed?

Stress affects more people than you may think. A 2008/09 Health and Safety Executive survey reported that almost half a million working people in Britain believed they were experiencing work-related stress at a level that was making them ill. Stress, depression or anxiety accounted for an estimated 11.4 million lost working days during the same time period.

Austro-Hungarian endocrinologist Dr Hans Selye (1907–1982) was the first doctor to demonstrate the existence of biological stress and how it affects the body. He showed that it is a physical reaction to a stressor – some form of stimulus from your outer environment or inner thoughts and emotions that upsets the body's normal rhythm and compels it to adapt or adjust in some way. For example, if you are very cold, your body will begin to shiver in an effort to warm you up; in this case, cold is the stressor that causes an adjustment in the way that your body functions.

Warning signs

While a certain amount of stress and tension is necessary in order to achieve your goals, it's important to recognise how much pressure you can handle at any one time. When even small changes or demands make you feel overwhelmed or anxious, this could be a warning that you are handling too much change or pressure. Physical symptoms can alert you to stress.

Check how many of the following signs and symptoms apply to you:

- Sleeplessness (difficulty getting to sleep at night, or waking in the early hours)
- Being easily irritated
- Difficulty making decisions
- Always in a rush
- Feeling tired all the time/having no energy
- Resistance to change
- Feeling threatened by life's demands and other people
- Loss of a sense of perspective (inability to distinguish between the essential and the non-essential)
- Feeling indispensable/working to exhaustion
- Loss of sense of humour

- Digestive disorders (indigestion or loss of appetite)
- Stomach churning (feeling sick or 'butterflies' in the stomach)
- Pounding heart or palpitations
- Excessive sweating, or feeling shivery
- Dry mouth and throat
- Headaches
- Eliminatory problems (frequent visits to the bathroom or constipation)
- Reduced resistance to illness (succumbing regularly to colds, coughs and chest infections)
- Aching muscles
- Impaired memory and forgetfulness
- Drinking more alcohol than usual/needing alcohol to relax
- Smoking more than usual
- Eating too much or too little
- Using caffeine to keep going
- Tearfulness
- Feeling unable to cope, even with things that used to feel easy
- Loss of interest in other people

If you ticked more than five boxes you may be suffering from too much stress. These symptoms are warnings that you need to reassess the areas of your life that are producing the most stress. They also reveal the types of behaviour and aspects of personality that contribute to problems and difficulties.

Do you use caffeine to keep going?

WHAT THIS MEANS FOR YOUR HEALTH

Dr Selye found that, to maintain good health, the body must keep itself in a fairly constant internal state (homeostasis). If it deviates too far from its limits – for example, if body temperature, heart rate or blood pressure rise or drop beyond a certain point – then the person is putting themselves in danger. The body responds in the same way to all kinds of stressors, whether excessive heat, cold, injury, disease, anger or any other negative emotion or perceived threat, as well as extreme elation, excitement and joy, although positive stressors tend to be less damaging. How you deal with that stress, Dr Selye claimed, ultimately determines how successfully you adapt to change. This means it may not be the external stress that causes the problem, but rather the way in which an individual interprets the 'stressful' event and the importance they ascribe to it.

Health problems arise when the body is stressed too much, or for too long, and can't return to healthy homeostasis. Excessive stress has consequently been implicated in common health disorders from psoriasis, eczema, diabetes and hypertension to more serious illnesses such as cancer, heart attacks and strokes. If you can counter stress and handle life calmly, you are potentially protecting your body against disease, so learning to control your reaction to stress is vital. Discovering how you can modify your behaviour when necessary, as well as incorporating strategies such as relaxation techniques into your lifestyle (see chapter 3), will all help to bring the body back to normal functioning.

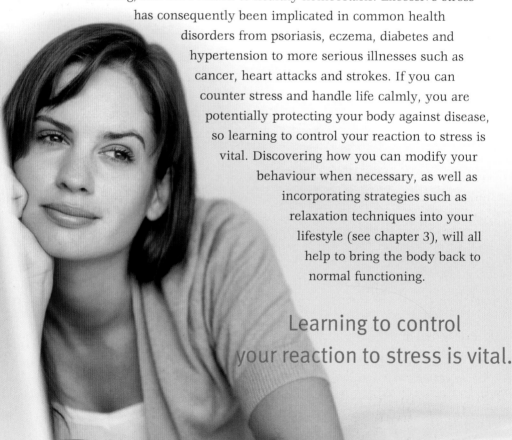

Learning to control your reaction to stress is vital.

STAYING IN CONTROL

One of our most basic needs is to feel in control of ourselves and our lives. According to medical research studies, knowing that you have a satisfactory level of control over the world around you is good for the immune system and the heart. Feeling out of control – or without sufficient control – is one of the major triggers of stress.

Not allowing outside influences to dictate one's inner state of body or mind – or, at least, not for too long – is therefore vital for staying in control. Some personalities find it easier than others to keep calm when faced with a crisis, but *everyone* can learn ways to better manage all of life's challenges, problems or anxieties. And throughout this book you will find numerous strategies and suggestions for doing just that – ways to handle the everyday stresses of life to help you stay calm, and so stay healthy.

When everything seems too much to cope with – even the things you previously found easy – this is a warning sign that you are handling too much stress and strain, and have crossed the boundary from positive, motivating adrenaline to negative, harmful stress (see chapter 3 for more on the physiological changes that occur during the 'stress response'). Take the test on page 17 to see if the stress you face is producing adverse effects.

Take the test on page 17

EXPERT VIEW

CONTROL IS GOOD FOR YOUR HEALTH

According to the Whitehall Study, an in-depth health study of civil servants carried out by University College London, higher-status employees have lower levels of heart disease. While it had been anticipated that the top executives would be suffering from 'executive stress', expected to induce heart-health problems, heart disease was found to be three times higher among junior office workers; heart health deteriorated in direct relationship with the lowest levels of autonomy and control. Giving people more say in decisions about their work may thus reduce stress and improve cardiovascular health.

Your personality type

Do you easily become emotionally fraught? Or worry about what *might* happen, rather than what is actually happening? Most of the things we worry about never happen, and many of the things people fret over resolve themselves in time. Perhaps your personality is making life more stressful for you than it needs to be. Some personality traits are inherited, but some behaviour patterns are learned from our parents and may need to be rethought.

always in a rush?

In the mid 1950s two significant underlying aspects of personality type became apparent, adding a further dimension to the understanding of how the way we approach life determines, to a high degree, how much stress or tranquillity we experience, and often the kinds of health problems we encounter. These personality types are called Type A and Type B, and were first observed in the consulting room of American cardiologist Dr Meyer Friedman – but not, in fact, by the doctor himself.

BODY-LANGUAGE CLUES

Dr Friedman's furniture upholsterer noticed that the fabric of the chair used by the patients was only worn out across the front edge of the seat; the back of the seat had clearly not been used at all. When the upholsterer asked what type of patients he treated, Dr Friedman realised that all his patients exhibited a similar pattern of behaviour. Rather than relaxing back in the chair, they all sat, keyed up, on the edge – and they demonstrated a generalised keyed-up attitude to life, too. They were always watching the clock, in a constant, self-imposed battle with time, always struggling to achieve more in less time – a trait that has become known as Type A 'hurry sickness'.

TYPE As AND STRESS

Dr Friedman's book, *Type A Behaviour and Your Heart* (published in 1974 with colleague Dr Ray H. Rosenman), provided crucial insight into the connection between Type A personalities and heart-health problems. Individuals exhibiting Type A behaviour generate a great deal of

EXPERT VIEW

TYPE A BEHAVIOUR AND HEART ATTACKS

A research study carried out by Friedman and Rosenman in the 1970s followed 1,013 heart-attack survivors for four and a half years to determine the effects of altering Type A coronary-prone behaviour patterns. The results indicated that behavioural counselling reduced rates of heart-attack recurrence from 21 per cent or higher to 13 per cent. The study showed that altering Type A behaviour significantly reduces cardiac morbidity and mortality in post-infarction patients.

In a more recent ten year study carried out in the USA, Type A personalities were found to be three times more likely to suffer from coronary heart disease. Type A behaviour was found to be more important than other factors – including family history, cholesterol levels and smoking – in predicting who was going to have a heart attack.

Are you an **A** or a **B?**

Read through all the statements listed below. One end of the scale represents extreme Type A behaviour, and the other end Type B. Circle the number that best represents how you behave in day-to-day life. For instance, if you're generally quite impatient, circle one of the higher numbers (7–10), whereas if you're patient, circle one of the lower numbers (1–4). If you don't lean strongly either way, go for a 5 or a 6.

When you have circled a number for each statement, add up the total score and refer to the scoring section below.

TYPE A											TYPE B
Always feels under pressure	10	9	8	7	6	5	4	3	2	1	Never feels under pressure
Extremely competitive	10	9	8	7	6	5	4	3	2	1	Not at all competitive
Always on time	10	9	8	7	6	5	4	3	2	1	Bad at timekeeping
Interrupts others	10	9	8	7	6	5	4	3	2	1	Good listener
Impatient	10	9	8	7	6	5	4	3	2	1	Patient
Very ambitious	10	9	8	7	6	5	4	3	2	1	Unambitious
Tries to do lots of things at once	10	9	8	7	6	5	4	3	2	1	Takes one thing at a time
Talks loudly and quickly	10	9	8	7	6	5	4	3	2	1	Takes time talking
Wants good job/seeks approval from peers	10	9	8	7	6	5	4	3	2	1	Cares about satisfying self/ others' approval unimportant
Fast at doing things	10	9	8	7	6	5	4	3	2	1	Does things slowly and steadily
Pushes oneself and others	10	9	8	7	6	5	4	3	2	1	Relaxed and easygoing
Hides feelings	10	9	8	7	6	5	4	3	2	1	Expresses feelings
Workaholic tendencies	10	9	8	7	6	5	4	3	2	1	Lots of hobbies and interests outside work
Eager to get things done	10	9	8	7	6	5	4	3	2	1	Doesn't rush at everything head first

Score

Your total score will be somewhere between 14 and 140. A score of 140 signifies an extreme Type A personality, while a score of 14 signifies extreme Type B. While there are no absolute divisions between Type A and Type B, most people lean towards one type more than the other.

The average score is 77. If your score is higher, this means you exhibit Type A characteristics, and if it's lower, then you tend more towards Type B. The higher or lower the score, the more extreme the tendencies. If you scored above 77 (and especially if your total is significantly higher), try and modify your behaviour to get more Type B responses into your life (see page 23).

stress for themselves and those around them, as well as constantly triggering the body's stress, or fight-or-flight, response, which is very wearing for the body (see also chapter 3).

A medically accepted definition of stress is: rate of wear and tear on the body's systems. Type As tend to wear themselves out quicker than their Type B counterparts, who are more relaxed and easygoing. This is measured in the kinds of illness they develop, as well as their longevity.

better health for Bs

Driven Type A behaviour can often lead to success; former prime minister Margaret Thatcher is a good example, as are many top executives. Some people welcome potentially stressful situations as challenges. But Dr Friedman emphasised that Type B behaviour also can – and does – achieve equal success but with the added advantage of improved quality of life, as well as better health.

You cannot transform your personality type, but you can try to modify your most undesirable attributes and self-defeating behaviour traits. Dr Friedman used to characterise himself as a 'recovering Type A', and, after having suffered two heart attacks at a comparatively young age, he made a determined effort to change his approach to life. He reportedly succeeded in adopting Type B behaviour and lived to the age of 90, demonstrating the efficacy of his transition.

HELPING YOURSELF

Everyone faces a large number of external stressors in everyday life. What you don't need is unnecessary self-induced stress on top of this. So if you recognise many of the Type A characteristics in yourself, try the following tips to get more Type B behaviour into your life. You'll be the calmer and the healthier for it.

TRY THIS!

COUNT IT OUT

Thomas Jefferson famously said: 'When angry, count to ten before you speak. If very angry, a hundred.' This is still good advice, according to Dan Johnston, assistant professor of psychiatry and behavioural science at Mercer University School of Medicine, Georgia, USA. Counting to ten before taking action works because it emphasises the key elements of anger management: time and distraction. This method becomes even more effective if you take a slow, deep breath between each number, as this helps counteract the fight-or-flight reaction in the body underlying the anger. The next time you feel yourself getting wound up, give it a try. (See chapter 10 for more advice on managing anger.)

- Avoid other Type As as much as possible. If you can't avoid them (perhaps you're married to one), try to bite your tongue more often and curb your tendency to compete and win at all costs. Allow others to win occasionally (you can pat yourself on the back for being magnanimous).
- Try to compliment and help those around you instead of always trying to outdo them.
- Consider the value of 'being' more, rather than 'having' more.
- Recognise that delegating doesn't mean you are failing. Allow others to help you; they will feel valuable as a result.
- When out driving, deliberately allow other drivers to overtake you or start off before you at traffic lights.
- If someone cuts you up on the road, wave them on with a smile – and then chuckle to yourself as you remember how many times you've behaved like that in the past.
- If you're standing in a slow-moving queue, let a couple of people push in front of you without seething with anger.
- Take up a leisurely outdoor activity such as cycling, fishing or rambling.
- Join a painting, pottery or woodwork class, or take up embroidery or upholstery; anything that requires patient concentration will calm your temperament as well as your heart.
- Sit still and read an absorbing book. Don't skip pages or turn to the end until you get there. And only read one book at a time.

HELPING HAND

DO YOU SUFFER FROM ANXIETY?

Generalised anxiety disorder (GAD) is a long-term condition – lasting six months or more – where you constantly feel anxious without really knowing why. Because you don't know what's triggering your anxiety, this can escalate and make you more anxious, as you worry about the reasons for your anxiety. GAD is thought to affect about 1.5 per cent of people in Britain. If you think you may be suffering from GAD, visit your GP for advice, or refer to the Resources section (see page 242) for details of organisations that can help.

Read a book – but don't skip pages or turn to the end until you get there.

Always have a jigsaw puzzle on the go.

PUZZLE POWER

Have a permanent jigsaw puzzle on the go, on a sideboard or on a tray that can be moved about, which you can turn to from time to time as an aid to calming down, and as a creative distraction from overworking your logical, left brain.

LISTEN TO THE DOCTOR

Dr Friedman advised his Type A patients to read the classics to strengthen the right brain, the creative hemisphere, which he maintained atrophied in Type A personalities. He also advised his patients to concentrate on smiling more, as they normally had a hostile grimace. He told them: 'Sweetness is not weakness', and quoted one of Hamlet's famous speeches: 'Assume the virtue even if you have it not, for its use almost can change the stamp of nature'.

This is sound advice for anyone wanting to change their personality in some way. In psychology it is called 'acting As If ...'. You act as if you have already become whatever you wish to be, and by acting it you slowly absorb the behaviour until it becomes part of you.

identify your stressors

Most of life's crises, of course, are not self-imposed, so understanding why you react badly to some things – or some people – and not others, is also key to dealing successfully with everyday life. People react to problems and challenges in differing ways, so it's crucial to identify your own specific stressors – the things that cause *you* the most distress.

The best way to do this is to carry a small notebook around with you, and note down each event, person or situation that triggers feelings of stress or anxiety, or makes you feel upset in any way. Against each entry write how it made you feel, and also how you reacted. Then, when you've had time to recover and reflect, go back and note down how you would have *liked* to have reacted, if different from your reaction at the time.

Identifying your stressors in this way gives you the opportunity to see yourself more clearly. Writing down how you would have liked to react is a step towards taking more control of your personal agenda, rather than simply reacting to outside influences. Often the only control we can have in any situation is how we choose to respond.

Jung's personality types

The psychiatrist Carl Gustav Jung's work on personality types helps shed further light on why we all react differently to life's day-to-day hassles – and how we can take steps to modify our reactions. Jung was the first to develop modern-day thinking on personality types, and in the 1920s coined the terms 'extrovert' and 'introvert' – terms still widely used to this day. Extroverts relate easily to the outer world of people and activity, and introverts tend to focus on the inner world of ideas and impressions. Jung realised, however, that this was too simplistic a categorisation, and after many years of observation maintained that people could be further classified into four fundamental personality types within the extrovert/introvert categories, depending on how they orientate themselves and perceive the world.

modes of perception

Jung called his personality typology the four 'functions', functions meaning modes of perception, or approaches to life. He maintained that there are four distinct ways of perceiving and orientating oneself to life: thinking, feeling, intuition and sensation (that is, using the five senses).

● **THE 'FEELING' TYPE** experiences people and situations subjectively, feels the atmosphere and the emotions of others. Feeling types are caring, warm and responsive, but can also be petulant and moody.

Which type **are you?**

Our predominant way of reacting is not thought out, but is an instinctive first response. Read the questions below and tick the answers that best apply, then check your score to find out your predominant personality type.

1 **You're faced with a number of demanding tasks. Do you:**

☐ **A** Get in a panic and jump from one thing to another without focus?

☐ **B** Systematically start on one task and forget the others until you've finished the first one?

☐ **C** Stand back for a while and work out which is the most important and which the least?

☐ **D** Imagine what each process requires before you start working on the one that most inspires you?

2 **You hear that someone has been criticising you behind your back. Do you:**

☐ **A** Churn away inside, feeling devastated, and try to avoid seeing that person?

☐ **B** Take no notice, but plan to take any chance that presents itself to criticise that person in return?

☐ **C** Analyse why the criticism was made, and then decide to confront the person?

☐ **D** Take a philosophical attitude; we're all guilty of criticising others, so it's no big deal?

3 **You're late for an appointment and get stuck in a traffic jam. Do you:**

☐ **A** Become upset, tense up in your shoulders, grit your teeth and grip the steering wheel harder?

☐ **B** Get out a map, or street plan and work out where you can turn off and take an alternative route?

☐ **C** Think about alternative routes but, after assessing how much longer they would take, decide to stay put, feeling angry with yourself for not starting out earlier?

☐ **D** Decide there's nothing you can do, so switch on the radio – you might as well relax and make the best of the time?

4 **A friend asks your opinion about a marital problem. Do you:**

☐ **A** Take their side, not wanting to upset them, then tell them about the relationship problems you've had in the past?

☐ **B** Point out that surely they must have anticipated this sort of problem; they knew what their partner was like before getting married, after all?

☐ **C** Respond in an abstract, factual way about statistical evidence proving that all marriages go through difficult periods, and so problems shouldn't be taken too seriously?

☐ **D** Remind them of all their positive qualities and what you love about them, sensing that they really just need a confidence boost?

Score

Mostly As: you have a predominantly emotional (feeling type) personality.

Mostly Bs: you have a predominantly practical (sensation type) personality.

Mostly Cs: you have a predominantly logical (thinking type) personality.

Mostly Ds: you have a predominantly intuitive (intuitive type) personality.

When you feel stressed or overwhelmed, it may help to change your way of reacting. If you tend to react emotionally, for example, try considering matters from a more objective and logical point of view. Equally, a totally practical approach may not be the best thing in situations involving relationship issues, where a more emotional, feeling response would work better. Most people are a mixture of types, but tend to lean one way or another, and it can be beneficial from time to time to adopt a different approach.

- **THE 'SENSATION' TYPE** experiences things predominantly through the senses. The outer world is considered to be much more important than the inner world of ideas, or vague notions of the imagination. Sensation types are interested in what exists in the present and value concrete facts and details. These people are pragmatic, at ease in all practical activities and very down to earth – the exact opposite of the intuitive type.
- **THE 'THINKING' TYPE** perceives things from a logical, objective, analytical and factual point of view. Thinking types tend to stand back and review a situation, then base their decisions on objective analysis of cause and effect.
- **THE 'INTUITIVE' TYPE** perceives the inner aspects of things and senses what's going on under the surface, values ideas and the imagination, has flashes of insight about how to make something happen, how to motivate someone and what makes people tick. Intuitive types are often visionary in that they can see the future possibilities of things and make connections others don't see.

poles apart

Jung devised a simple diagram to illustrate his hypothesis of the four functions. He recognised that if one function is dominant or uppermost,

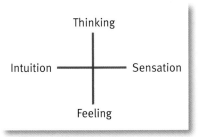

then the function at the opposite pole will be the weakest area for that person. Therefore, a thinking type will be underdeveloped in his or her feeling function, and an intuitive type will be weak in the sensation (or practical) function, and vice versa.

THE DOMINANT APPROACH

Today's greatest stresses are often encountered in interpersonal relationships, both at home and at work. Misunderstandings can lead to conflict and a breakdown in communication, but often they simply arise because the other person sees things from the opposite perspective to our own, or explains themselves in a way determined by their dominant function, to which we may be blind or may simply not understand. In these instances, the two remaining functions, or approaches, are available to be used as back-up, but will not be our first way of viewing things.

BROADEN YOUR PERSPECTIVE

The next time you feel particularly stressed, try not to react as you usually do. Instead, do your best to connect more strongly with one of the less dominant sides of your personality – your 'back-up' functions – as this will give you a different perspective on the problem. Looking at something from another angle will always shed new light on how to tackle it, and thus increase your options.

Think of how some people are right-handed and others left-handed, for example. We have two hands, and can use both, but there is always a preference of one over the other: the dominant approach.

THAT EXPLAINS IT

Applying Jung's theory may help you understand why you react to things the way you do, and why perhaps some of your communications and attempts to relate to others seem to miss the mark, or don't connect in the way you intended. It may also help you realise why certain activities or tasks never seem to go well for you, or appear to be more difficult for you than for someone

By understanding other personality traits you are less likely to be upset or stressed by others ...

else – because they are activating your weakest side, or because you are attempting to undertake something that is not your strong point.

In fact, people are not solely one type to the exclusion of the others; we are all a mixture of types, but with one type more dominant and another our weakest point. Two people of the same dominant type will have a satisfying rapport, and will feel less irritation and frustration with each other than they would with their polar opposite. But they may miss the opportunity to develop a broader view, or to discover alternative ways of handling situations that can only be learned from seeing the strengths of another personality type.

By understanding other personality traits you are less likely to be upset or stressed by other people's actions or reactions to you. Equally, you may be able to ease tension in a situation by explaining more clearly why you acted in a particular way.

Early influences

Being true to yourself is crucial for maintaining good mental and emotional health. People are often diverted away from their true selves by outside influences, especially those experienced early in life. The psychiatrist Dr Alfred Adler, a contemporary of Freud and Jung, maintained that people form a distinct view of the world by the time they are five years old. This picture is created by everything that surrounded us in those early years: people, attitudes, atmosphere, feelings (happiness, laughter, fear, sadness) and rules and traditions (dos and don'ts). This becomes the 'norm' by which we measure the rest of our lives.

The behaviour, thoughts and assumptions someone unconsciously absorbs from early conditioning can cause a great deal of stress – and distress – if they don't support that person in becoming a fully rounded, mature and unique individual. In other words, if you are not functioning independently as a result of your own feelings and thought processes, you may always feel at odds with the world and uncomfortable in your skin. It takes courage to be true to yourself, but not doing so also carries a price. As Dr Selye notes in *The Stress of Life*: 'Psychology has shown that knowledge about oneself has a curative value.'

Often the behaviour learned in our early years is no longer appropriate or helpful, so reassessing how we act and react to today's problems – and why – can provide solutions to managing stresses and difficulties (see questionnaire overleaf).

The pressures of life

Of course, not all behavioural traits come from the past. Perhaps the pressures of a current stressful situation – having to care for a sick child or an elderly parent, or a partner being made redundant or retiring – are placing too many demands on your energy and causing you to behave out of character, in ways you don't understand. Experiencing too many changes in your life all at once can make you feel overwhelmed.

If you feel uncharacteristically irritable, have trouble sleeping or begin to suffer health problems such as dizziness or headaches, you are probably overstretched and under too much stress. You need to reassess how you are managing your life.

Continued on p32 ➤

Are childhood influences still affecting you?

To find out how far your early conditioning may still be influencing your actions today, answer the following questions (write down your answers, if you prefer) and then refer to the section opposite, to discover how these influences may have affected your personality. Shedding light on why you react the way you do can help you to take positive steps to modify your behaviour, if necessary.

Of course, not all the advice given here will be true for everyone, so if something doesn't apply to you see if it triggers any other childhood memories that you can trace back to having influenced your behaviour.

1 What was your position in your early family? Were you:

☐ **A** The eldest child?

☐ **B** A middle child of three?

☐ **C** The youngest child?

☐ **D** One among more than two other siblings?

☐ **E** An only child?

2 If you had brothers and/or sisters, who was the 'boss' among you?

3 What were your family's rules (dos and don'ts)?

4 If there was a problem in the family, was it dealt with by your mother or father?

5 How did your parents (or carers) cope with stress? What sort of behaviour did they demonstrate when facing difficulties?

6 If you behaved badly, or were considered naughty, were you given a verbal telling-off, sent to your room or deprived of a special treat? Or were you made to feel guilty with no specific punishment?

7 Is there a particular incident you recall from your early childhood that upset you greatly, shocked you or frightened you?

8 What made you feel most happy as a child?

Effect on personality

1 **A** You may still feel like the most important person in a room, and perhaps wonder why no one else sees you this way. First-borns are most likely to be self-assured, assertive, competitive and natural leaders.

B You may feel you always have to compete with others to be noticed; the second-born has to compete with the more advanced and assured older sibling.

C You may feel you should be given special consideration, be 'babied', or expect to be taken care of, or may look to others to take responsibility or sort out problems. The youngest child is often the most unconventional and adventurous.

D You may feel most comfortable being part of a group and perhaps find it hard to function well if you're alone too much, or too isolated, when there's no one else against whom to measure yourself.

E You may be happiest doing things alone, or find it hard to ask for help or include others in your decisions. Others may get angry at what they see as your lack of team spirit.

2 Are you still behaving like the 'boss', expecting to be obeyed by others – or, conversely, still taking orders, finding it hard to be assertive and stand up for yourself?

3 Are these the basic principles by which you still live? Much of your stress may derive from still trying to fit into someone else's idea of what's right and wrong, or trying to live up to others' expectations. You need to act according to values that you truly believe in.

4 If it was your father, perhaps you assume that men are the ones who should sort things out? Or, if your mother, do you expect it to be women who deal with life's problems? Either of these assumptions may need rethinking or balancing out a little.

5 Do you automatically react as your parents did when faced with stressful problems, rather than deciding for yourself the best way to react? Just because your parents handled things in a particular way doesn't mean that you have to as well. You can adopt healthier ways of reacting that don't raise your blood pressure and cause the release of stress chemicals in your body.

6 Do you punish yourself in similar ways in your present life, withholding enjoyment or treats from yourself, or withdrawing from life when you feel guilty about something? Or perhaps you just carry a feeling of non-specific guilt a lot of the time? Punishment and guilt are not the best way to deal with mistakes you may have made. You need to learn the lesson, forgive yourself and move on. We all make mistakes, but in every mistake is the potential for growth. If we can learn from the experience, we grow and become wiser.

7 Are there any similarities with this early experience and the things that upset you now or cause you the most stress and anxiety? Remind yourself: that was then, and this is now. As adults, we have many more options open to us – we have more power, more control – yet we are often thrown back into feeling small and powerless, regressing into the child that we used to be. Affirming your power and acknowledging that you can take control to change things is the first step in overcoming any difficulty or anxiety.

8 Do you give yourself enough time for the things that make you happy now? Making yourself happy isn't self-indulgent – it's sensible life-management, because it refreshes and renews you. After all, 'recreation' means to 're-create'; if you don't have sufficient recreation time, you become dispirited and de-energised, and life can seem dull.

the stress **of change**

All change is stressful – even pleasant change, such as going on holiday – precisely because it requires some adaptation to new circumstances. But people often fail to recognise the amount of pressure they face. Try to gauge the degree of change you are facing and how much it is forcing you to adapt at any one time. Is it too much, or just enough to be interesting and stimulating, and to stretch you comfortably?

THE HOLMES AND RAHE STRESS SCALE

Demanding life events – such as getting married, moving house, changing jobs, having a baby, bereavement and so on – often cluster at the same time. And, because none of us has unlimited adaptation energy (see page 16), it is imperative we take good care of ourselves when dealing with a high number of life changes simultaneously.

This fact is well documented in medical literature. Research carried out by Dr Thomas Holmes and Dr Richard Rahe at the University of Washington School of Medicine in the 1970s, and largely undisputed by subsequent research, found a definite correlation with health problems and too many life event changes. They developed the Social Readjustment Rating Scale, also called the Life Events Chart or, more commonly, the Stress Scale, which identifies the life events that pose the most strain. Each event is ascribed a numerical value, 100 being the most stressful, grading downwards to the least stressful, with a value of 11.

HIGH SCORE, HIGH RISK

Their research found that anyone experiencing a total score of 300 points or more in any one year (that is, the total score obtained from adding the values of all the life changes that have affected you) has a 90 per cent chance of developing a significant illness. A score of 150 or more would make your chances of illness or a health change roughly 50:50. Ideally, the score needs to stay well below 150 in each twelve month period, and if you cannot avoid too many high-scoring life changes in one year, try and ensure that the following twelve month period is as restful and stress-free as possible. In addition, if you are facing a number of high-scoring changes in one or two areas of your life, attempt to keep things as stable as possible in other areas – don't make any unnecessary changes. (See also *The Wheel of Life* in chapter 8, for a good way to assess how balanced the different areas of your life are.)

Continued on p36 ➤

Your life events
stress score

Take a look at the chart below and tick any events that apply for the previous twelve month period, then add up your total score. If your score is more than 300, it's vital that you take steps to reduce the levels of stress in your life, using the advice given throughout this book, or you may be putting your health at risk. If your score is between 150 and 299, you still have a moderate risk of developing an illness, so you need to watch how much stress you are placing yourself under.

LIFE EVENT	VALUE		
☐ Death of a spouse or child	100	☐ Son or daughter leaving home	29
☐ Divorce	73	☐ Trouble with in-laws	29
☐ Marital separation	65	☐ Outstanding personal achievement	28
☐ Jail term	63	☐ Spouse begins or stops work	26
☐ Death of a close family member	63	☐ Starting or finishing school	26
☐ Personal injury or illness	53	☐ Change in living conditions	25
☐ Marriage	50	☐ Revision of personal habits	24
☐ Redundancy	47	☐ Trouble with boss	23
☐ Marital reconciliation	45	☐ Change in work hours/conditions	20
☐ Retirement	45	☐ Change in residence	20
☐ Change in family member's health	44	☐ Change in school	20
☐ Pregnancy	40	☐ Change in recreational habits	19
☐ Sexual difficulties	39	☐ Change in church activities	19
☐ Addition to family	39	☐ Change in social activities	18
☐ Business readjustment	39	☐ Small to moderate mortgage or loan	17
☐ Change in financial status	38	☐ Change in sleeping habits	16
☐ Death of a close friend	37	☐ Change in number of family gatherings	15
☐ Change to different type of work	36	☐ Change in eating habits	15
☐ Change in number of arguments with spouse	35	☐ Vacation	13
☐ Large mortgage or loan	31	☐ Christmas season	12
☐ Foreclosure of mortgage or loan	30	☐ Minor violations of the law	11
☐ Change in work responsibilities	29		

Christmas can be a stressful time of the year.

A THERAPIST'S NOTES

Richard, a successful bond trader, came to see me because he was confused and worried about his personal life, and had also just been passed over for promotion.

Despite having the trappings of success, Richard wasn't happy. He told me he felt an almost constant anxiety, which he tried to hold at bay by keeping manically busy. His way of dealing with problems was to push harder, to use more force, exert more energy. Married for seven years, with two young sons, he complained that his wife didn't understand the long hours he had to work, adding: 'She doesn't seem to make the connection between my working hard and the fact that she has a fabulous house and a great lifestyle.' When I suggested that perhaps his wife just wanted to spend more time with him, he said she did nothing but nag him when he was at home, criticising how he behaved with the boys and claiming that he bullied them.

Richard didn't have any close relationships in his life other than with his wife and sons. He'd lost touch with old friends and didn't believe in socialising with his team at work in case it undermined his authority. He wasn't worried about being popular, but went on to say: 'I used to love my job and competing to see who could get the best results, but that buzz isn't there any more; I feel a kind of emptiness inside.' He confessed that he'd been told his management style was too aggressive, and that some members of his team had complained that he refused to listen to their opinions or concerns.

Early conditioning

Richard explained that he had been sent away to boarding school at a young age and grown up in a strict environment, and had always tried to live up to the principles set out for him. Consequently he became a high achiever academically, and carried this inherent competitiveness into adulthood. Earnest, serious and extremely ambitious, Richard was clearly a driven man, but his lifestyle was taking its toll on his health: he revealed he suffered from high blood pressure and high cholesterol.

Realising the truth

Richard began to realise that he had been striving hard all his life to prove himself – to feel 'good enough'. As a result, he pushed himself – and others – too hard, including his two young sons. He was exhibiting typical extrovert Type A behaviour, and reluctantly admitted that he needed to slow down but didn't know how.

I suggested he invite his wife, Jill, to a session. It soon became apparent that Richard didn't listen to her, frequently jumping in to interrupt or correct her. I asked her how she felt about him constantly cutting her off, at which point she broke down in tears, saying he made her feel that her opinions were insignificant and stupid. She felt undermined in everything she tried to do, especially where the boys were concerned. Jill also revealed that the boys were frightened of their father because he was so demanding and shouted at them too much.

Richard felt his wife was not appreciating him, and that sense of not being 'acceptable' took him straight back to his childhood, when he'd assumed he couldn't be worth much as his mother had sent him away to boarding school. In fact, he didn't consider Jill intellectually inferior; rather, he admired her gentle, caring nature – the opposite of his mother's temperament, and what he'd longed for all his life. He finally admitted that he felt jealous of his sons being given loving attention from their mother – something he had never received.

He was essentially a very caring man who had never been shown how to express his emotions, and so they came out negatively. As a child he'd been taught that self-control was everything. He was carrying a great deal of suppressed anger, which was projected onto anyone in his current life who he felt didn't appreciate him or value his efforts.

A change in behaviour

Richard worked on relaxing a little more, trying to take a back seat when his wife was dealing with the boys, and he used his fierce self-discipline to hold himself back whenever he wanted to take over. I convinced him that slowing down didn't mean that he was slacking, but that sometimes it was the best strategy. This insight spilled over into his work life, where he realised he had been suppressing his team's initiative, as they dare not risk his anger if they made mistakes. He gave them more responsibility and started joining them in the pub occasionally on a Friday night. He also taught himself to be more of a team player, achieving a more harmonious atmosphere at work through encouragement rather than criticism.

As Richard got more in touch with his feelings, he was able to take life more slowly and enjoy the moment, instead of always rushing towards some future goal. Above all, he realised the benefit of spending time with his young sons just for the pleasure of it, instead of having to push them to excel at whatever they were doing.

He began to accept that his behaviour was the cause of most of his problems, so he worked hard to change himself and curb his inherent tendencies, recognising how unhealthy it is to be fired up all the time. He took up running to release tension and work off any residual frustrations. His blood pressure dropped to normal and he lost weight; but, equally importantly, he lost his 'free-floating hostility', which is a sign of excessive stress.

Subsequent research has found that how you interpret any of these life events also plays a significant part in how they impact on your health. If a divorce, for instance, is more of a relief than an agony, it won't take such a toll, although the practical changes involved – moving house or a reduced income, say – will still have an impact on your adaptive energy.

principles for life

Try some – or all – of the following suggestions. Even taking small steps like these can help to make you feel calmer and less stressed.

● **Make time for the things you enjoy.** Unsurprisingly, research has found that people who are in a state of contented happiness (not extreme excitement) have lower blood pressure and lower levels of the stress hormones adrenaline and cortisol, which means a much healthier internal body state. Thus both mind and body benefit.

● **Take time each day for yourself** – just to reflect, or read something uplifting; to listen to some soothing music, or soak in a long, warm bath with your favourite bath oils. It's essential to take regular time out from daily mundane concerns. Think of this time as recharging your batteries.

● **Go for a walk** in a park, or around the block or just down to the end of the garden, with no other intention than to give yourself space to drift and connect to the right ('creative') hemisphere of the brain.

● **Write down the things about yourself that make you feel anxious** – things you consider you don't do well enough, or aspects of your personality that you dislike. Then consider whether these spring from trying to be like someone else – from attempting to act against your own personality.

● **Try to see the positive** in aspects of yourself that you dislike. Most things have a positive as well as a negative side. If you don't focus on the negative, it will automatically become less of a concern.

● **Encourage yourself.** Give yourself praise for anything you achieve, no matter how small, and for any good deed you do, any task you complete and any problem you overcome. People often become their own worst critic, so encouraging yourself, or imagining a friend motivating you, can make all the difference.

Take time each day for yourself ...
listen to some music.

● **Laugh as often as possible.** Laughter cuts things down to size and puts problems into context. Research shows that laughing has beneficial effects on the body, too: according to ongoing studies at Loma Linda University Medical Center in California, not only does it elevate mood, but also lowers blood pressure, reduces stress, increases muscle relaxation and boosts the immune system (see also chapter 4). Laughter also exercises the muscles, nerves and organs of the abdomen, and helps us breathe more deeply, which is relaxing.

● **Mentally run through your daily accomplishments** each night, before you go to sleep, and tell yourself that you are OK.

Go with the flow

Another factor to consider as you begin to understand and work with your personality is your own individual body-clock. Everything in the universe has its own natural rhythm, and the more you're in tune with your unique rhythm of high and low energy, the more effective you'll be. Determining your best time to be active and your best time to relax and rest can help you to play to your natural strengths and make your day-to-day life less stressful.

get the timing right

Which is your best time of day? If you know you're not at your best in the morning, for example (an 'owl'), try to schedule important meetings and tasks for later in the day. But if you're at your most energised in the morning (a 'lark'), that's the time to deal with demanding matters. (For more on larks and owls, and associated sleep patterns, see chapter 2.)

10 TIPS FOR STAYING CALM

1 Don't be forced to accept schedules and deadlines that you can't achieve without putting yourself under undue pressure.

2 Don't always say 'yes'.

3 Don't overfill your day; be realistic.

4 Don't leave your own needs out of your daily planning.

5 Don't allow work to encroach on your leisure and pleasure time.

6 Don't feel guilty about relaxing, resting and taking some 'me' time.

7 Don't forget to praise yourself.

8 Don't neglect your relationships: they give you support and security.

9 Don't get overtired, as this makes problems seem greater than they really are.

10 Don't lose your sense of humour: it gives you a sense of perspective.

Don't work against yourself. This is a crucial part of taking more control of your agenda, so that you don't feel pushed around by other people or outside circumstances. Of course, there will be times when a degree of give and take is required, so you will need to be flexible too, but don't automatically acquiesce to other people's preferred timing, if there's a compromise that can be reached to suit all parties involved.

TAKE A STEP BACK

If you're in a state because something isn't being done fast enough, stand back, take a slow, deep breath, and remind yourself that everything has its own timing. Things can't always be hurried. Don't let yourself be oppressed by deadlines or timetables that are unrealistic or haven't been thought through – especially if you set them in the first place. You can't keep up the same speed and intensity all the time. Find your own energy pattern and try to work with it, not against it, as much as you can.

protecting yourself

A little introspection and analysis is useful, because that self-knowledge can help to protect you against external and internal pressures which cause stress and can damage health. In addition, understanding both your own and others' inherent personalities is also the key to greater tolerance, thus conserving your energy and helping you to stay calm.

The chapters that follow will show you not only how to reduce the amount of stress in your life, but also what you can do to safeguard your health – and consequently change your life for the better.

2 sleep tight

When you sleep well, you wake feeling bright and alert. By contrast, the effects of poor sleep include fatigue, memory lapses and poor concentration. Whether prompted by worries, noise, illness or a disorder, lack of sleep is a common cause of stress. Conversely, stress often leads to sleeplessness. Soon you're caught in a vicious cycle of sleepless nights and anxious days. You're not alone, though – it's estimated that 30–45 per cent of people worldwide suffer from insomnia. But thanks to scientific advances, a good night's sleep has become a much more achievable goal.

What is sleep?

Scientific understanding of sleep and sleep disorders has grown enormously since the middle of the 20th century. Yet statistics suggest that lack of sleep remains a common problem. Data from the British Household Panel Survey revealed that almost 20 per cent of those questioned felt they had lost 'more sleep than usual' due to worry – with the figure increasing to nearly 25 per cent among women.

But what is sleep? It is key to our physical and mental wellbeing, but there is still much to be learned about this crucial human function.

sleep mechanisms

Our current understanding of the nature of sleep owes much to the work of Austrian neurologist Constantin Von Economo (1876–1931), who discovered that the brain had clusters of nerves that controlled either sleep or wakefulness. This led to the realisation that sleep is not just the brain 'shutting down' like a piece of machinery; rather, it is a time when the activity of the brain's 'sleep centres' is enhanced while the workings of its 'wakefulness centres' are suppressed.

The need and pressure for sleep increases the longer we are awake and the more physical and mental exercise that we do. Scientists still don't know how many chemicals are involved in making us sleepy, but adenosine, which is also associated with carrying 'energy' to cells, is thought to be among the most significant. When we sleep, our adenosine levels are reduced (and our energy stores are replenished).

As we become sleepier, the sleep centres determine which areas rest and which remain active. For example, during REM (dreaming) sleep, the rational parts of the brain shut down but those that process visual information stay active – hence the illogical but visual nature of dreams. During normal sleep, the sleep centres are in control and the wakefulness centres are inactive, but in people suffering from sleep disorders, stress or discomfort, the wakefulness centres are active. This can either prevent them from falling asleep or make their sleep unsettled and unrefreshing.

SLEEP STAGES AND CYCLES

Further developments in the 1950s revealed the sleep process to be much more complex than previously thought, including different states and regular brief periods of wakefulness, lasting only seconds to a few minutes. While many of us sleep through these periods undisturbed, those susceptible to problems may become fully awake. This discovery was all part of the work of two American doctors, William C. Dement and Nathaniel Kleitman, who found that by using machines that measured brainwaves they could identify when someone was dreaming – they had uncovered Rapid Eye Movement (REM) sleep. People who are woken during REM sleep will invariably report that they were dreaming.

For the first time it was possible to identify mental states using external objective methods. Using these techniques, researchers ascertained that sleep is not a single state but composed of three main states: light sleep, deep sleep and REM sleep. They also established that adult sleep has a 90 minute cycle – that is, we go into REM sleep roughly every 90 minutes. At the beginning of the night these REM episodes are quite short, but they get longer as the night progresses (see overleaf).

Are you
clocking up enough sleep?

Many of us don't get enough sleep for various reasons. If you agree with the following five statements, you're definitely one of them:

- I get fewer than 5.5 hours of sleep most nights of the week.
- I sometimes unintentionally nod off at awkward or embarrassing times.
- I find that I sleep more when I'm not working, for example, during holidays or at weekends.
- I get up feeling dreadful more days of the week than not.
- It's generally impossible for me to watch television in the evening without falling asleep.

The more yes answers you give, the more likely it is that you're not getting enough sleep and need to review your whole sleep routine.

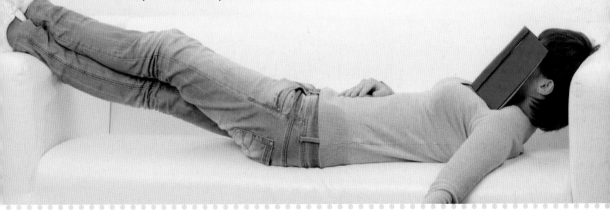

REM–REM cycle and wakefulness in normal sleepers

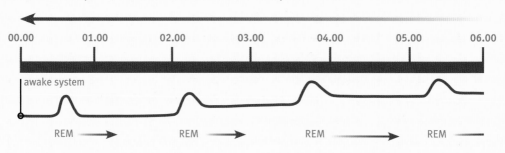

As these REM episodes begin, there is often a brief period of wakefulness. Young, fit, healthy people sleeping in optimal conditions don't notice these periods, so their sleep is not disturbed. But if you are experiencing any discomfort, whether physical or mental, this wakefulness may register and can lead to sufficient anxiety to awaken you fully.

OUR 24 HOUR BIOLOGICAL RHYTHMS

It's not just sleep that causes us to wake up in the morning feeling bright, fresh and alert. The brain's 24 hour biological clock is also responsible. Our 24 hour, or circadian, clock consists of about 60,000 nerve cells deep in the brain and its function is to manage our 24 hour rhythms.

On the whole, human beings are not nocturnal; we are diurnal and work best during the day. The biological clock ensures that we are physically and mentally at our most efficient in daytime and enables

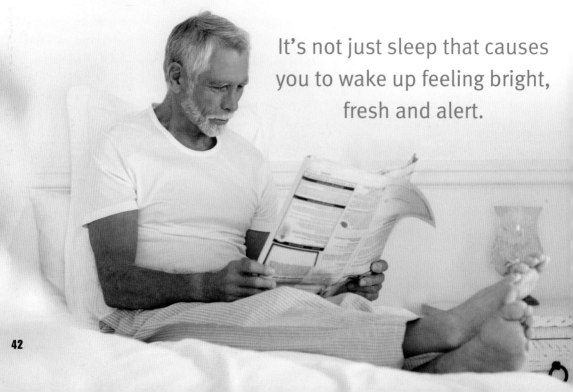

It's not just sleep that causes you to wake up feeling bright, fresh and alert.

recovery during the night. It helps to make our sleep more restful, for example, by preventing an accumulation of water in the bladder, thus reducing the number of times we need to go to the toilet. Fewer digestive juices, enzymes and acid are produced in our stomachs during the night, as they are not necessary. In fact, various adjustments to how our bodies and minds work ensure that everything runs as efficiently as possible.

Of course, you can sleep during the day in the same way that you can be awake during the night – the clock does not prevent this from happening. Instead, our biological clocks optimise conditions so that our best sleep takes place during the night and we are most awake during the day.

why do we **need sleep?**

We need sleep to keep ourselves in peak condition, both mentally and physically. If you've ever suffered from periods of sleeplessness you know how hard it can be to overcome, and that it can become a major cause of stress. Poor sleep also has health implications: for instance, restricted or disturbed sleep has been associated with obesity.

Research shows, too, that minor sleep disturbances, where you don't even wake up, can cause your daytime performance to suffer. But lack of sleep isn't just stressful in itself – it can lead to poor concentration and lapses in memory, and can adversely affect logical thinking and risk-taking, which in turn can lead to accidents. People returning home from work late at night, for example, are more likely to be involved in a road-traffic accident.

Despite all the research, there is no clear answer as to what sleep actually does. But it is clear that sleep deprivation, for whatever reason, affects mainly the mind and less so the body.

HELPING HAND

HOW TO NAP

Here are four simple rules to ensure your naps don't interfere with your night-time sleep. Studies show that even 'shut-eye' without sleep helps.

● The ideal conditions are the same as for night-time sleep, but, if that's not possible, comfort and safety are key.
● Get the timing right: a mid-afternoon siesta is ideal because our natural 12 hour sleep cycle means we're extra sleepy at this time.
● Nap length should be 20–30 minutes or roughly 90 minutes (the length of one sleep cycle), plus the time it takes to fall asleep (allow 10 minutes). The shorter naps prevent you from feeling groggy when you wake up.
● Allow 20–30 minutes after a nap before doing anything that requires attention, as your mental performance will be poor for a while (a condition called 'sleep inertia').

What happens
when we can't sleep

Sleep experts often refer to poor-quality sleep, which means sleep that is sufficiently disturbed to disrupt the deep-sleep stages but not disturbed enough to cause wakefulness. This leads not only to tiredness, fatigue and difficulty concentrating, but also to problems with appetite control and glucose metabolism. This may result in obesity, high blood pressure, diabetes and, eventually, an increased chance of having a stroke or heart attack. Obese people also have a higher risk of developing obstructive sleep apnoea (OSA), a condition in which the person doesn't breathe properly during the night (see page 55), and this in turn causes poor-quality sleep, which feeds back into this vicious cycle.

Those who regularly sleep badly are also more likely to complain of body aches and memory loss, according to the UK-based Future Foundation, a think-tank that analyses and forecasts social and consumer trends. And 49 per cent of people say they feel depressed or unhappy following or during a period of insomnia. This is backed up by research from the European Social Survey, whose data shows that people who frequently have restless sleep are more likely to feel sad, anxious or depressed.

A condition called 'tired all the time' (TATT) is also becoming more common. This is not a diagnosis but a symptom, and the preferred term is 'chronic fatigue'. TATT is characterised by unexplained fatigue and feelings of being unable to cope during the day for a period of a month or more. The first thing to do is look for a cause – check the information on *Sleep disorders* (see pages 51–58) and *How to get a good night's sleep* (see pages 59–61) – and assess your mental state, then address any issues (see also *Resources* on page 242 for sources of more information).

women and sleep

Men and women's sleep varies, and these differences emerge as we get older. Generally, women suffer from insomnia more often than men, possibly because there are more times in a woman's life when her sleep may be disturbed (see overleaf). Men, on the other hand, are more likely to experience objectively measurable sleep disorders than women, yet are less likely to report problems.

Avoid stressful TV just before bed.

Assess your 'sleep pressure'

Sleep experts use the term 'sleep pressure' to help them determine the causes of poor-quality sleep. Answer the four questions below to find out what forces might be influencing your sleep pattern – that is, compelling you to stay awake – then find out what you can do about it. Answer yes or no to each question.

HIGH WAKE PRESSURE

1 Do you find that you can easily fall asleep on the sofa watching TV, but as soon as you go to bed your mind starts to race?

If yes, this suggests that your pressure for wakefulness is too high. Perhaps daytime anxieties have returned to your mind or previous periods of sleeplessness in bed have triggered worries about a sleepless night? Practising deep breathing or autohypnosis (see Resources on page 242) may help.

2 Do you find watching emotionally charged films or reading exciting books causes sleeplessness?

If yes, these have activated your wakefulness centres, making it difficult for you to 'switch off'. Avoid them and introduce more calming pre-bed rituals, such as having a warm bath or meditating.

LOW SLEEP PRESSURE

3 Do you nap during the day, then find that you cannot sleep at night for as long as you'd like to?

If yes, you have reduced the pressure for sleep, and the pressure for wakefulness is too high for sleep to occur. Revise when you nap and the duration of your sleep – see the box on page 43, which explains how to nap without it interfering with your night-time sleep.

4 Are you in a sedentary job and take little exercise?

If yes, sleep may be a problem for you because physical (as well as mental) exercise is required to create a pressure for sleep. To help you sleep well, aim to exercise at least three times a week, preferably for 30 minutes at a stretch (see also chapter 3).

How we deal with sleep problems also varies. The Future Foundation found that, although insomnia sufferers in general were as likely to turn to friends and family for help as they were to go to their GP, women tended to seek the help of friends and family, while men preferred discussing things with their GP (or self-diagnosing via the internet).

Why is insomnia such a problem for women? Pregnancy (see below) and the menstrual cycle play a part. A mother may also develop insomnia if her children interrupt her sleep; mothers learn to be vigilant at night and some can never properly relax and switch off.

SLEEP DURING THE MENOPAUSE

During the menopause, hot flushes and night-time sweating often cause insomnia, which may persist into later life. Sleep-related breathing problems also increase after the menopause. Decreasing levels of progesterone may be responsible; the hormone is thought to increase respiratory muscle control, protecting against snoring in earlier life.

It used to be thought that hormone replacement therapy (HRT) was the best treatment for menopause-related symptoms, but for some women it increases the risk of breast cancer, heart disease and stroke. Dietary isoflavones (plant-derived oestrogen), found in foods such as soya, red clover and tofu, may help alleviate some symptoms. Relaxation therapies are also helpful.

WHY YOU CAN'T SLEEP DURING PREGNANCY

Almost all women have trouble sleeping during pregnancy. Initially, progesterone, secreted from the placenta, is likely to cause fatigue and sleepiness. And progesterone can cause a rise in body temperature, which disturbs sleep. Body changes, morning sickness and nausea can also affect sleep in the early hours.

During the second trimester, things start to look up. Women often experience less tiredness and sleep disruption, although heartburn may now become a problem because of the increasing size of the baby.

Almost all women have trouble sleeping during pregnancy.

Three-quarters of mothers also have frightening dreams or nightmares, which may involve the baby – often a distortion of daytime concerns.

By the end of the pregnancy most women wake up an average of three times a night. Pain resulting from the softening of the ligaments between the pelvic bones, loosening in preparation for the birth, and the extra weight of the baby all add to sleep problems.

Later in the pregnancy, try to have a nap during the day (see *How to nap* on page 43), and at night place a pillow between your knees, with your knees and hips bent, to reduce the pressure on your back. Most women find sleeping on their side is usually the most comfortable position.

About 30 per cent of pregnant women snore because of nasal congestion coupled with the womb and foetus pressing on the diaphragm. If breath pauses (apnoea) are also experienced, it can lead to increased blood pressure, especially in women who suffer from headaches and swollen legs. More than 30 per cent of pregnant women are also affected by restless legs syndrome (see page 59), particularly in the third trimester.

EXPERT VIEW

ARE YOU A LONG SLEEPER?

The International Classification of Sleep Disorders recognises that some people are long sleepers. Long sleepers are those who sleep for 10 hours or more daily and who are excessively tired if they sleep for a shorter period.

But what about adolescents and young adults, a group who often seem to need more sleep than others? They may experience a form of 'sleep delay syndrome' (see page 51) rather than being genuine long sleepers. This is first seen as a tendency to stay up later at weekends, followed by weekdays, then a difficulty getting up in the mornings (or being tired during the day if they do manage to get up). It's not clear why this happens – it could be that staying in bed too long in the first place resets the internal clock to a socially inconvenient time.

trying too hard

Some people become obsessed with sleep. They may be trying too hard to sleep when sleep's not really the problem, or they may be worrying about the amount of sleep they're getting – and, paradoxically, this adversely affects the amount of sleep they get.

SHORT AND LONG SLEEPERS

Most of us sleep for between 5.5 and 9.5 hours, and that's what we need to function well. The general advice, though, is that 8 hours' sleep is the optimal amount. This creates problems for both short sleepers and long sleepers, two groups who need the 'extremes' to be at their best.

Long sleepers, for example, often have to deal with the fact that others may not accept that they really do need extra sleep time. This can also interfere with work requirements. Short sleepers, on the other hand, who generally sleep for fewer than 5 hours a night, break into two groups: those who thrive on their shortened-sleep need, and those who try to achieve the goal of the 'required' 8 hours, which results in stress. The latter group may end up being classed as insomniacs because they are unable to sleep for longer. If the time in bed is spent lying awake worrying, eventually the brain becomes conditioned into remaining awake in bed, and this may further prevent sleep.

Two additional factors can damage sleep, though neither may actually have immediate or direct effects:

● Fatigue that has other causes (see *The 5 Most Common Causes of Fatigue*, page 53), rather than insufficient or poor-quality sleep.
● Burn-out (physical and mental) caused by a stressful lifestyle. Trying to get more sleep to combat fatigue when the problem isn't sleep can make the insomnia worse. In these cases, the root causes need to be addressed.

Is stress the problem?

G enerally, you can be said to be stressed if you are trying to work beyond your physical and mental capacities. You may not even be aware that you're not coping. Stress can cause poor sleep, and the poor sleep can add to problems with functioning, so it's important to tackle both the source of the stress and to optimise your sleep conditions to make sure sleep comes more easily.

According to Future Foundation research in 2009, stress about financial matters was the top reason cited for lack of sleep, especially among people aged 16 to 44. Other causes of worry-induced insomnia were work and family, with 15 per cent of respondents saying they didn't know what caused their insomnia and had always suffered from it.

controlling stress

If you want to get a better night's sleep, take control of any causes of anxiety in your life, starting with work and chores at home. Follow these simple time-management steps to put yourself back in charge.

Keep a **sleep diary**

Your sleep can vary a lot, particularly if you have periods of insomnia. Some nights may be good, others bad, and you're more likely to remember the bad nights than the good ones. A sleep diary is useful not only for enabling you to get some sense of perspective. It can also help you to establish a regime that will improve your sleep.

The variable nature of sleep means that it's best to keep a diary for at least two weeks, though four weeks is better. It should note:

● When you go to bed.

● When you turn off the lights to go to sleep.

● The approximate times and durations of any periods of wakefulness during the night (including getting up to attend to children or to go to the bathroom, for instance).

● The time when you finally wake up.

● The time when you get up.

Your diary can include details of what happened during the day that may aid your understanding of the following night (if you've had a nap, for example, or done some exercise). It is also useful to keep a note of how awake, rested and refreshed you feel when you get out of bed, on a scale of 1 to 10. By calculating the average time when you fall asleep and the average time when you wake up, you may be able to choose better bedtimes and getting-up times (this works best if you are sleeping for at least 5 hours a night).

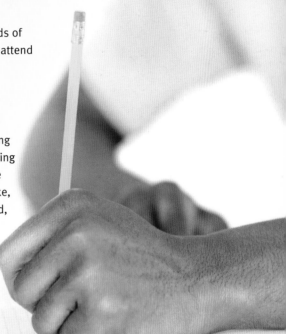

● Define your role in life. Be sure you understand your own role and responsibilities, at home and at work.

● Don't take on more than you have to. Learn to say no.

● Do the important and urgent tasks first.

● Concentrate on the task in hand – whatever it may be – so that you do it right first time.

● Don't procrastinate. Tackle anything that needs to be done and is making you anxious – don't look for excuses not to start.

● Limit your time on email.

● Prioritise your work. Don't overwhelm yourself with a long to-do list.

● Delegate tasks if you can (at home and at work).

Are you drinking
more alcohol to relax?

Is stress causing you
sleep problems?

The quiz below will help you to assess whether stress is the main factor in your sleep problems. Run through the following questions and tick any that apply, then check the results at the end.

☐ Are you putting on more weight around your middle?

☐ Do you find that you have a 'short fuse', are more sensitive, irritable or easily frustrated than you used to be?

☐ Do you have a general feeling of being overwhelmed by everything you're dealing with right now?

☐ Do you find yourself always feeling overtired or exhausted?

☐ Have you experienced weight gain or weight loss recently?

☐ Do you feel muscle tension, especially in your neck, back and jaw?

☐ Do you find that you are ill more often than usual?

☐ Do you find it more difficult to make decisions and concentrate, and do you forget things more often?

☐ Do you often feel anxious about things you can't control?

☐ Has your libido decreased, or are you often just too tired for sex?

☐ Do you experience tension headaches?

☐ Do you find yourself eating to cope with annoyances, or craving sweet or salty food more often than usual?

☐ Do you find yourself drinking more alcohol to relax, smoking to deal with stress, or becoming dependent on illegal drugs or prescribed medication?

If you have ticked more than three questions, stress may be affecting your sleep. Continued stress can lead to anxiety, depression and sleep problems, so tackling the causes of your stress should be a priority. For example, consider ways to improve your time management if your main problem is that you never have enough time to do everything in your busy life. Can you enlist more resources or cut out unnecessary time-wasting activities? Increased muscle tension, decreased libido, weight gain or loss are all indications that your brain is getting into a state where it cannot manage its response to stress any longer. If it's simply not possible to reduce or remove the causes of your stress, try to manage your sleep in the ways described in this chapter, as better sleep can improve your ability to cope.

● Deal with clutter. If you haven't looked at a piece of paper in more than a year, throw it out – or, if it's an important document, file it away (see chapter 9 for more on dealing with clutter).

● Save the boring chores for later – they could be the beginning of your wind-down routines for the day.

Sleep disorders

Sleep disorders come in many different forms. Some sleep problems result from other underlying issues or factors; for example, biological clock disorders can appear to be insomnia. Late-to-bed 'owls' invariably take a long time to fall asleep if they go to bed early, and similarly 'larks' can't help but wake up early (see panel overleaf). Both traits can be mistaken for insomnia. People's sleep patterns can also be erratic, so a sleep diary is helpful in assessing the average (see page 49).

is your biological clock out of sync?

Normally, our natural 'lark' or 'owl' tendencies don't produce any untoward effects, but sometimes they can be more extreme. Phase advance syndrome is when the larkish tendency is pronounced; for example, the person goes to bed at 8pm and wakes up very early. Similarly, phase delay occurs when the owlish tendencies are antisocial at the other end of the scale – the person goes to bed at, say, 3am and gets up at 11am or even midday. Being asleep when the rest of society expects you to be awake can create social problems. People may resort to excessive amounts of alcohol, nicotine or drugs to help them fit in with society's demands, then suffer the consequences over time.

It can help to introduce bright light, either in the morning to advance your biological clock or in the evening to delay your clock. The type of light boxes used to treat seasonal affective disorder (see chapter 10) are effective, as are dawn-simulation light alarm clocks (made by Philips, NatureBright and Lumie, among others). Medical treatment may be given alongside light therapy in the form of melatonin (although use is controlled in the UK) and possibly sleeping pills (see page 62).

Are you a lark or an owl?

Are you an early bird or a night owl? Answer these simple questions for a quick assessment based on your natural tendencies.

DO YOU FIND:

- You're sleepy by 9pm?
- It's easy to get out of bed by 6am?
- It's hard to stay up until 11pm?
- You naturally consider yourself a morning person?

If you answered yes to three or more of the above questions, then you can consider yourself a 'lark'.

DO YOU FIND:

- You're still wide awake after 9pm?
- It's hard to get out of bed before 10am?
- It's easy to stay up after 11pm?
- You naturally consider yourself an evening person?

If you answered yes to three or more of the above questions, then you can consider yourself an 'owl'.

THE EFFECTS OF LIGHT

In recent years, some surprising discoveries have been made relating to the biological clock. Scientists have found that our brains know it's light and time to wake up before we even perceive it – thanks to our ganglion cells. The light-sensitive part of the eye is called the retina. It consists of:

- Rods that are sensitive in the dark.
- Cones that are colour-sensitive.
- Ganglion cells.

The rods, cones and ganglion cells all feed into the optic nerve. Most of the optic nerve relays signals to the brain's visual perception areas, but a small branch breaks away and leads directly into the middle depths of the brain and the 'biological clock'. Some of the ganglion cells are light-sensitive, and their output feeds directly into the biological clock. The ganglion cells are in front of the rods and cones, which is why the biological clock knows if it's light or dark before we're aware of it.

These ganglion cells are also particularly sensitive to blue – the kind of deep blue you see on a clear summer's day. One implication of this is that light enriched with blue frequencies or orange-tinted glasses that block blue light may be used to speed up or slow down the biological clock. New treatments for jet lag, also using light, are now being investigated, as light is the main synchroniser for the biological clock.

JET LAG

Jet lag is caused by two factors:
- Moving so rapidly into a new time zone, either 3 hours east or west from the point of departure, that the brain's biological clock can't adapt.
- The effects of 'travel fatigue', caused by the general hassles of travelling, early or late departure times, the stress of queues, and so on.

General travel fatigue should be handled in the same way as any sleep disturbance. For example, charge up your 'sleep battery' by extending your sleep prior to departure. Also try to nap while travelling – getting as much sleep as you can, whenever possible, is the best antidote for all fatigue. If you have to perform, you can turn to coffee for a boost, but don't rely on it, especially not for extended periods of driving. Keeping the routines and rituals associated with sleep at your destination helps you to re-establish your sleep.

Here are some tips for overcoming jet lag caused by the mismatch between local time and the brain's biological clock:
- If your journey crosses two or three time zones, either east or west, it's best to allow your body to adjust to the new time zone by itself.

DID YOU KNOW? ?

THE 5 MOST COMMON CAUSES OF FATIGUE

Although poor sleep can lead to tiredness and fatigue, there may be other, medical causes underlying these symptoms. If you haven't been able to resolve your sleep problems, visit your GP, who may test your blood or suggest other diagnostic tests. The most common causes of fatigue, apart from insufficient or poor sleep, are:

1 Lack of minerals (such as iron).
2 Hormonal disturbances: these may be related to the thyroid or the adrenal glands or to diabetes.
3 Recurring infections/lowered immunity.
4 Gluten intolerance and coeliac disease.
5 Heart, lung and neurological disorders.

- If your journey crosses more than three time zones westwards, stay up as late as possible on the first and second day of arrival.
- If your journey crosses more than three zones eastwards, get out in the light in the late afternoon and early evening to help you adjust.
- Get some exercise in the late afternoon and early evening.
- If melatonin is available where you are, you can take a low dose (1–3mg) at bedtime to speed up your adaptation (check with your GP before you travel, if you're worried about taking it).

Light is the most important factor in adapting to a new time zone. But its effect is not uniform, so you might find it useful to consult a jet lag calculator (which may cost a small fee) to help you work out your optimum exposure to – and avoidance of – light (see *Resources* on page 242).

other types of insomnia

Specialists often classify insomnia according to certain characteristics. For example, you may be said to have adjustment insomnia if you can't sleep because of a particular, identifiable reason, such as relationship difficulties, bereavement or work problems. Your insomnia should go away when the issue is resolved, or when you adapt to the stress. Idiopathic insomnia, on the other hand, also known as childhood-onset insomnia, starts at an early age and is difficult to overcome. You may find behavioural or cognitive treatment helpful, and sleeping pills are an option (see page 63). It is estimated that as many as 600,000 people in the UK may suffer from this form of insomnia.

Another chronic form of insomnia is called psychophysiological, or conditioned, insomnia. It may come on quickly or gradually and can last for many years, often needing expert help. As well as having a 'racing mind', sufferers often 'learn' sleep-prevention behaviour; for example, they usually focus on their inability to sleep, which creates a vicious cycle of poor sleep, daytime irritability and poor concentration.

If you have this form of insomnia, ask your GP about cognitive behavioural therapy for insomnia (CBT-I), as this is now recognised as a very useful treatment. You may also find keeping a sleep diary helpful, especially if guided by a sleep specialist. Another tried and tested technique is the (Bootzin) '20 minute rule': you can remain in bed only if you are asleep within 20 minutes, at any time of the night. Any longer and you have to get up and leave the bedroom, not returning until you feel sleepy again.

SLEEPING WELL AS YOU AGE

You may find that you experience more sleep issues the older you get, particularly as more and more problems interfere with your ability to sleep through the night – for example, having to go to the toilet, pain from arthritic joints, or problems with flexibility or tinnitus.

The main rules for improving sleep still apply. Remember that the average sleep cycle is approximately 90 minutes (see page 41), so if you wake up to go to the toilet or because you're in pain, it's probably at one of these times. Sleep will soon follow, so just get the job done (go to the bathroom, massage the affected area or change position, for instance) and allow yourself to go back to sleep.

You can also experiment with napping (see *How to nap*, page 43). A short nap may give you more energy, which will enable you to take more exercise. If you don't get enough energy you'll become sleepy but won't be able to sleep. Exercise promotes sleep and helps you maintain flexibility. Swimming is particularly good if you can't sleep because of sore joints and weak muscles.

Other tips for a good night's sleep are:
● Minimise your liquid intake prior to sleep, and avoid big meals and alcohol just before bedtime.
● Stop smoking – it's associated with lung and other cancers as well as bronchitis, which causes breathing difficulties during the night. In the short term, nicotine withdrawal can cause wakefulness, but this will pass.

Minimise your liquid intake just before bedtime, for a good night's sleep.

sleep-related
breathing disorders

Some people experience sleep problems that are caused by interruptions in their breathing while they sleep. Such problems are relatively common and affect people more after the age of 40, and men more than women. There are two main types:

● **OBSTRUCTIVE SLEEP APNOEA (OSA)** It's estimated that 3.5 per cent of men and 1.5 per cent of women in the UK have OSA, and obesity is a major cause. It occurs when the muscles of the throat relax and either cause a total blockage (apnoea) or a partial blockage (hypopnoea) in the throat. This leads to a lack of oxygen, which causes the person to come out of a deep sleep into a lighter sleep or to wake briefly, resulting in

tiredness during the day. If you have OSA, your partner may be the first to notice, because loud snoring is often a sign – he or she may observe a change in your breathing, or hear you gasping or choking. Alcohol always makes OSA worse, and high blood pressure is common.

If you suspect you have OSA, see your GP. The recommended treatment for severe OSA is nasal CPAP (Continuous Positive Airway Pressure). A mask is worn either over the nose or nose and mouth; this is connected to a small device that gently blows air into the mask and through the airways so that an obstruction doesn't develop. Snoring is also prevented. Nasal CPAP is now so common that airlines may allow use during long flights.

● **CENTRAL SLEEP APNOEA (CSA)** This form of sleep apnoea occurs when the brain's control of breathing weakens. It occurs most often in men aged over 60 who have suffered some form of heart failure. Nasal CPAP (see above) and other types of respiratory aid are used to treat the condition.

SPECIALIST SLEEP CENTRES

If sleep problems are having a serious impact on your life, you may benefit from attending a specialist sleep centre. These special clinics monitor and assess sleep disorders such as insomnia, snoring, restless legs syndrome, narcolepsy and sleep apnoea. You may be referred by your GP, or you can sometimes book an appointment yourself; treatment is often offered through the NHS as well as privately.

At the centre, your sleeping problems will be addressed by an expert or team of experts, who will try to get to the bottom of any underlying physical or psychological issues, although most sleep centres focus on respiratory-related sleep

HELPING HAND

ARE YOU A SNORER?

Snoring occurs when air does not move smoothly through your air passages while you sleep, causing tissues in your mouth, nose and throat to vibrate. It can cause havoc in your personal relationships and may be a symptom of OSA (see page 55). Being overweight makes you more likely to snore, but the problem also becomes more common with age, as the throat muscles become weaker. People often find that losing weight, stopping smoking, sleeping on one side and avoiding alcohol before bedtime reduce their snoring.

If your snoring is caused by allergic or respiratory congestion, it may be relieved by using decongestants, and some people find nasal strips attached to the outside of the nose and Brez internal nasal strips effective. If snoring is severely affecting your quality of life, and you have exhausted all other remedies with no success, there are also surgical options you can consider. Consult your GP for more information.

Snoring can cause havoc in your personal relationships.

disorders such as sleep apnoea. Sleep-related respiratory disorders may
be diagnosed using home-monitoring equipment, which can, for example,
measure nasal airflow, chest movement and oxygen levels. Overnight
recordings taken in a sleep centre bedroom, however, provide more
accurate measurement and assessment. Usually, electrodes are attached
to measure your brainwaves, eye movement, chin muscle tone, nasal
airflow, snoring, chest and abdominal movement, heart activity and
leg movements.

narcolepsy

Narcolepsy is a relatively rare chronic sleep disorder. Estimates vary, as
it often goes undiagnosed, but it's thought that anywhere between 18,000
and 30,000 people in the UK, or possibly more, may have the condition.
People with narcolepsy become excessively sleepy or may actually fall
asleep during the day. They sometimes also experience a complete loss
of muscle tone as they fall asleep, called cataplexy, which can cause
them to collapse; this can be brought on by sudden shocks, emotional
responses or even laughter. Other symptoms include hallucinations and
sleep paralysis – that is, remaining 'paralysed' after waking. If you have
narcolepsy, or think you may have it, see your GP. You may be treated
with stimulants such as methylphenidate and modafinil.

sleepwalking and night terrors

Sleepwalking – somnambulism – occurs during periods of deep sleep, when the rational parts of our brains are not functioning. Children are more likely to sleepwalk than adults, especially around the age of 12; around 15 per cent of children sleepwalk regularly, compared with 2–4 per cent of adults. Stress, overtiredness, alcohol and any condition that prevents the brain from awakening easily are all associated with adult sleepwalking. If you or someone you live with is a sleepwalker, adopt a good sleep routine (see page 61) and make sure that your sleeping environment is safe (for example, free from tripping hazards, especially around stairs). If you sleepwalk a lot, it's worth seeing your GP, as medication is available that can help.

Confusional arousal is the term sleep experts use for confusion and movement that occurs if a sleepwalker is awakened from a deep sleep; the person's ensuing behaviour may be aggressive or even violent. If you need to deal with someone who is sleepwalking, it's best to tell the person to return to bed rather than physically engaging with them.

Children are more likely to sleepwalk than adults.

Another form of 'sleepwalking', REM Behaviour Disorder (REMBD), occurs during REM sleep. Normally during REM sleep the muscles are paralysed, presumably to prevent dreams from being acted out. In REMBD the muscles are not paralysed and sleepers 'act out' their dreams (for example, someone dreaming about football may actually run and kick in their dreams). The disorder can be treated using clonazepam. People suffering from Parkinson's disease often also have REMBD, and unfortunately REMBD is also associated with the development of Parkinson's.

Night terrors is a less common condition that causes the person to scream loudly and intensely. This is more frightening for carers and friends, as the screamer usually does not recall the event.

How to get a good night's sleep

Some people sleep well regardless of where they are or what they do. Shift workers, flight attendants and night-time carers, for example, can often sleep whenever they need to, while others cannot tolerate any disruption. Many of us are somewhere in between: we can manage for a while, but if our sleep patterns get worse this may ultimately turn into a sleep disorder that needs treatment.

So how can you avoid developing a 'sleep disorder'? Take defensive measures. Learning and practising the techniques outlined in this chapter will help you to feel calmer and more positive during the day, and that's vital for good health. The best advice is to keep a regular routine. Going to bed and getting up at roughly the same time every day is crucial for keeping your sleep/wakefulness cycles synchronised with your biological clock. Although developing routines and rituals prior to bed is helpful, prevention starts long before bedtime.

EXPERT VIEW

RESTLESS LEGS SYNDROME

People suffering from RLS (also known as Ekbom's disease) experience creepy-crawly sensations in their legs (and sometimes arms), coupled with the irresistible urge to move them. About 5–10 per cent of adults in the UK will develop it. Julian Spinks, a British RLS specialist, has described it as 'like trying to eat a doughnut without licking your lips'.

The sensations usually occur late at night and are almost certainly caused by low iron levels. The neurotransmitter dopamine is also implicated, and there is a genetic link. Pregnant women may suffer from RLS due to poor iron absorption, and vegetarians and people on renal dialysis machines can also suffer. Taking iron supplements may help.

lifestyle pressures

Our lifestyles nowadays are so busy that a new form of sleep loss has been identified: 'voluntary sleep loss' or 'sleep restriction'. We can cope with some sleep loss, even over a period of a few years – having and looking after children is a common cause. But long term, a lifestyle that squeezes out sleep, and shift work (most shift workers sleep 2–3 hours less than the rest of the population) can contribute to future health problems. If this affects you, for your health's sake try to reorganise your life and make sleep more of a priority.

exercise

Physical activity is a great stress-reliever, and getting enough exercise – ideally three to five 30 minute sessions weekly – is associated with better sleep (although over-exercising can also lead to sleeplessness).

Getting exercise doesn't mean you have to go to a gym – just keeping active is the important thing (see chapter 3). Dance, for example, is a great way of maintaining fitness, relieving anxiety and promoting sleep; any anxiety tends to dissipate as you focus on getting the steps right. Gentler forms of exercise that help to promote sleep include:

● **YOGA** The stretches involved in yoga promote flexibility (if you have to toss and turn during the night, you can do so more easily), while learning to control your breathing helps to reduce anxiety and focus the mind. The more energetic Ashtanga yoga (power yoga) also has an aerobic component that burns extra calories. Yoga is above all about mind control, and it is this that helps most to promote sleep, as it reduces intrusive, disturbing thoughts.

● **TAI CHI** This ancient Chinese martial art consists of slow circular movements, breath control and concentration or mindfulness. It is a low-impact, moderate-intensity aerobic exercise. Studies of the effect of tai chi practice have shown improvements in participants' immune function, balance and strength.

● **PILATES** In developing his physical fitness method, Joseph Pilates combined the breathing and mind control aspects of yoga with the physicality of gymnastics. His method consists of centring, concentration, control, precision, flow and breath.

Getting exercise doesn't mean you have to go to the gym ...

Getting your
sleep conditions right

The International Classification of Sleep Disorders (ICSD) catalogues more than 80 different disorders, including 'inadequate sleep hygiene' – a lack of awareness of what promotes sleep and what impairs it. Routine is vital if you want to sleep well. Your biological clock and your sleep and wakefulness centres cooperate to maximise good sleep, and changing your routine – or not having any kind of routine in the first place – knocks them off balance.

The crucial 'sleep hygiene' factors include your physical environment and physical and mental condition. Review your sleeping situation against the top ten ingredients for a good night's sleep:

1 ASSESS THE LIGHT Your bedroom should be dark at the beginning of the night (to allow the release of melatonin; see page 62) and light at dawn (to reset your 24 hour clock).

2 SET YOUR TEMPERATURE You need to be warm immediately prior to sleep to allow the blood vessels of your hands, face and feet to open up; it then needs to be cooler through the night to allow your body temperature to drop. A hot bath or a massage will help with this, or use a hot water bottle (as this will cool during the night).

3 LOSE THE GADGETS Don't have televisions, computer games, and so on, in the bedroom. Your sleeping room should be reserved for sleep and restful activities, not ones that keep you awake and alert.

4 BLOCK OUT NOISE For most people, the bedroom should be generally quiet, although some people prefer background noise to mask any intrusive sounds, such as central heating pipes creaking or traffic noise.

5 CHOOSE YOUR MATTRESS This depends on your physical condition. Generally, use your own judgment, though if you have back problems ask your GP or back specialist for advice. Mattress toppers can be used to alter the level of support; some differ on each side, ideal for couples with different preferences. Air your mattress daily, turn it frequently and replace every ten years.

6 TIME YOUR EXERCISE Avoid taking exercise for 3 hours prior to going to bed.

7 DON'T EAT TOO LATE Steer clear of heavy food, for at least an hour before bedtime, as well as caffeine-containing drinks, and nicotine. Eating small, regularly spaced meals throughout the day may help you to sleep, as may a warm milky drink at bedtime.

8 PERFECT YOUR WIND-DOWN ROUTINES Allow yourself a period of time to settle down prior to going to bed. Try a breathing or relaxation exercise (see pages 62 and 84), or have a warm bath.

9 MAKE YOUR HOME A SANCTUARY Your home has to feel safe. Take sensible precautionary measures before going to bed to avoid worrying about what might happen if intruders were to gain entry or if there were a fire. Keep your home secure (see also chapter 6) and make sure you have adequate, working smoke alarms.

10 CLEAR YOUR MIND Leave the worries of the day behind and don't take them into the bedroom (see also chapter 4). If you're a worrier, sit down half an hour before bedtime and write a list of everything that's making you anxious, and also consider briefly what you might do about it. Leave the list outside the bedroom. If you're still worrying in bed, write your worries on another list beside the bed or just visualise yourself writing the list, then throw it in your mental dustbin.

Supplements and sleeping pills

When one of your nerve cells is stimulated, it releases one or more brain chemicals near the nerve cell to which it 'connects'. We have many brain chemicals, some of which are now quite familiar to us – for example, serotonin, adrenaline and histamine. Health-food shops often store supplements that may boost the levels of these chemicals.

SEROTONIN

Serotonin is regarded by many as a 'happiness' chemical and a sleep promoter, but this is an over-simplification. Serotonin affects our sleep, sexual behaviour, risk-taking, aggression, motivation, temperature regulation, exploratory behaviour and eating (to name just a few).

The amino acids tryptophan and 5-OH tryptophan are the building blocks for serotonin, as well as melatonin (see below). Tryptophan is abundant in meat, poultry and milk (see chapter 5), and taking tryptophan supplements may increase brain levels of serotonin, though other factors have an impact. For example, reduced oestrogen levels after the menopause may reduce serotonin synthesis. Availability of tryptophan supplements varies from country to country. Its use is controlled in the UK, but 5-OH tryptophan, which has similar effects, is generally available (for example, in capsule form as 5 HTP).

MELATONIN

There has been considerable research conducted on melatonin and, while all sources agree that it improves sleep, how it does so is still not clear. Here's what we do know:
- Melatonin is secreted by the brain's pineal gland.
- Less is produced the older we get.

TRY THIS!

ABDOMINAL BREATHING

Anxiety and tension are associated with fast, shallow breathing. So as part of your winding-down routine try this exercise to focus your mind and provide feedback to your brain that you're relaxed and everything's OK. Lie down with a light book on your chest, to check that your muscles are moving up and down correctly. Practise for a few minutes.
- Inhale slowly through your nose.
- Feel the book on your chest rise.
- When the breath reaches your stomach, push your abdomen upwards, letting your abdomen rise slightly higher than the book (due to the diaphragm expanding).
- Hold for 1 second, then reverse the process. Exhale and allow your muscles to relax, and let the air out of your chest and nostrils. Relax your jaw as you exhale.

● Its release can be stopped by beta blockers (a type of medication that controls blood pressure).

● It is secreted only during the night and even this release can be blocked if light is present.

Certainly, melatonin has an effect on our biological clock, and in some cases it is soporific – that is, it makes us feel sleepy. It is also very good for controlling jet lag. Again, rules vary: in the USA it's available at pharmacies, while in the UK its use is strictly controlled – mainly because it has yet to undergo extensive pharmaceutical testing. A formulation of melatonin called Circadin has now been licensed for the over-55s in the UK, but for no longer than three weeks (see also overleaf).

sleeping pills

Sleeping pills – manufactured chemicals that are used as sleep aids – may help if you take them for short periods and in certain situations. They fall into two main classes: prescribed and non-prescribed.

NON-PRESCRIPTION SLEEP AIDS

Over-the-counter sleep aids consist of antihistamines (the chemical names of the most common are diphenhydramine and promethazine). Generally, the body's metabolic breakdown of these drugs is slow (meaning it takes the body many hours to break them down), so if you take them you may experience considerable 'hangover' effects the morning after. These products have been around for decades and were originally used for allergic reactions. It is unclear whether people who take them as sleep aids build up a tolerance to them, as happens when they are used as antihistamines. It is not advisable to use them routinely; consult your GP if you think you need a regular sleeping aid.

PRESCRIPTION DRUGS

Prescribed sleep medications fall roughly into three classes:

● **MELATONIN** (or melatonin-like drugs) may be prescribed by GPs in the UK only under special circumstances (see page 63). Chemical dependence is rare, and, as it's rapidly metabolised, a hangover effect is unlikely.

● **SEDATING ANTIDEPRESSANTS** are often prescribed as a sleep aid rather than for their antidepressant effects. Amitriptyline and dosulepin are the two most commonly prescribed by GPs, though medicines such as mirtazapine may also be prescribed, as their combined anti-anxiety and soporific effects improve sleep greatly. Some people may develop a dependence, and hangover effects may occur; always follow the directions of the prescribing doctor.

● **GABA DRUGS** (GABA is a neurotransmitter in the brain) consist of benzodiazepines and what are now called 'z-drugs' (zopiclone, zolpidem, zaleplon). The 'z-drugs' are thought to have fewer of the undesirable effects associated with benzodiazepines, such as dependence, hangover, rebound insomnia and tolerance, though it is generally recommended that they are used intermittently. Each 'z-drug' has pros and cons, so your GP will need to advise what's best for you.

herbal supplements

Herbal treatments also act on the brain, and many users find them effective in the treatment of anxiety, stress, depression and sleep disorders, though as yet there is no scientific basis for this. Herbal medicines are often regarded as 'safe' because they are 'natural', but care must be exercised before taking any supplement. If you have been prescribed any medications, consult your doctor before taking herbal preparations as they can interact with prescribed medicines.

HERBAL SLEEP AIDS

The following herbs are commonly found in herbal supplements available from health-food shops. It's worthwhile visiting a herbalist first, however, as he or she can recommend the best herb or combination of herbs for your needs.

● **Camomile, garden** (*Anthemus nobile*) and **camomile, German** (*Matricaria chamomilla*). The flowers of both plants are reputed to be mild sedatives that can ease anxiety and insomnia. Camomile extract is readily available as a tea.

Peppermint can help you sleep when you've got a cold.

- **Hops** (*Humulus lupulus*). The flowers are used for the treatment of sleeplessness; for some people, hops induce sleep more rapidly than valerian. Hops should be avoided if you are suffering from depression (they act as a mild depressive on the higher nerve centres, and may accentuate symptoms).
- **Lady's slipper** (*Cypripedium pubescens*). This root is traditionally recommended for treatment of sleeplessness associated with anxiety, as it is thought to calm the mind.
- **Lavender** (*Lavendula officinalis*). Opinion is divided, but it is claimed that the flowers have antidepressant effects and may help to improve sleep. Lavender bags or pillows may be soothing.
- **Passion flower** (*Passiflora incarnata*). Passiflora are grown mainly in the temperate and tropical regions of the world. The medicinal parts of the plant are thought to relieve anxiety and insomnia.
- **Peppermint** (*Mentha* x *piperita*). There is modest evidence that peppermint reduces sleeplessness, particularly for those suffering from a common cold, because of its decongestant properties.
- **Skullcap** (*Scutellaria lateriflora*). This herb is often used as a remedy for sleeplessness and is thought to relax nervous tension and relieve anxiety, so may be especially useful during stressful periods.
- **St John's wort** (*Hypericum perforatum*). This herb has similar properties to prescribed antidepressants, and takes 2–4 weeks to exert its effects. Tell your GP if you are taking it, as it can interact with prescribed medicines.

TRY THIS! ✔

AROMATHERAPY OILS

Many people swear by aromatherapy as a sleep aid. Certainly, lavender and geranium oils may have soporific qualities, and using them to promote sleep associations may be effective. Sleep associations work by fooling your brain into associating certain elements or routines with the need for sleep. For example, if you have trouble sleeping when you're away from home, try sprinkling geranium oil (or a scent that you find soothing) on your pillow at home for a week before a trip. Take the oil with you and sprinkle it on the pillow in the unfamiliar bedroom. You should find that sleep comes easier because your brain associates the smell of the geranium (or other) oil with sleeping.

Once your brain and body
settle down, good sleep
should follow.

- **Valerian** (*Valeriana officinalis*). Valerian is the most widely recognised herbal sedative; the roots have been used for centuries in infusions to reduce sleeplessness and promote sleep.
- **Wild lettuce** (*Lactuca virosa*). This herb has been used as an aid for sleep disorders since Roman times.

Taking control

Although sleep problems can vary from simple sleeplessness to chronic insomnia, and even one disturbed night may sometimes have crippling effects the following day, the good news is that there's much that can be done to overturn the problem and underlying causes. The first step is not to panic, but to let your brain and body settle down. This will generally happen naturally or by following some of the simple advice on good 'sleep hygiene' in this chapter. But if not, and there are underlying anatomical or psychological reasons for your sleep problems, you can get help from a specialist sleep centre. Don't let sleep – or, rather, lack of it – ruin your life.

3 get physical

Staying calm doesn't mean you have to sit meditating all day. Physical activity, in fact, is one of the best ways to achieve a peaceful sense of inner wellbeing. Think how you feel after a walk in the countryside or along a beach in winter, pushing forward through bracing winds and breathing in healthy ionised sea breezes. We were born to move. This chapter shows you how easy it is to be more active in your daily life, and how simple calming, breathing and relaxation exercises can help during a busy day.

Be more active ...
every day

Lifestyles today often involve long periods of sitting down – at computers, in front of the TV, in the car or in sedentary jobs. This isn't good for our bodies, as we are not using them in the way they were designed to be used, and this can make us feel irritable, fidgety and generally 'un-calm'. The body was built to be in movement, and movement encourages a healthy body.

The saying 'What you don't use, you lose' is undoubtedly true of the human body. Muscles go flabby when people are inactive. And the under-used body also affects our mental state, and can cause us to feel depressed, tired and lethargic, or unable to think clearly.

movement matters

Watch how much activity a healthy young child packs into a day – then compare that to the average adult. It's almost impossible to keep children still, as they respond instinctively to the body's desire to move and consequently have supple, tension-free bodies.

You may not enjoy organised exercise, or like the idea of going to the gym. But any physical activity – be it walking briskly, running, dancing, vigorous housework, weeding the garden or mowing the lawn – can work wonders on your inner feelings, and is one of the best ways to release tension when you feel stressed or anxious.

Research shows that walking 10,000 steps a day can significantly improve health, boosting stamina, helping with weight loss and strengthening the heart, among other benefits. Yet most people take only between 3,000 and 4,000 steps in an average day. Although 10,000 steps may sound excessive, it's worth

DID YOU KNOW? ?

GREEN FINGERS

Recent studies carried out at Kansas State University have shown that gardening two or three times a week is equivalent to a moderate workout in the gym and burns up just as many calories. It also strengthens the fingers, enabling them to grab and grip items more robustly, and increases strength in the arm, shoulder and chest muscles – vital for maintaining balance, strength and coordination as we age.

considering that 1,000 steps is equivalent to only around 10 minutes of brisk walking. So you can see that getting closer to that healthy target is probably much easier than you think.

LIFESTYLES NOW AND THEN

In the not too distant past, everyday life involved far more physical effort: washing clothes and other household items was done by hand, floors were swept and carpets beaten, wood for fires had to be chopped and stacked ...

Nowadays, machines do much of the hard work. Although to be welcomed in many ways, this has also made people more passive and inactive; adults today burn up to 800kcal fewer per day than they did in the 1950s. General daily activity should account for around 30 per cent of the calories we consume each day, but this figure can drop to as low as 15 per cent in those with sedentary lifestyles, which leads to weight gain and other health problems.

Instead of harvesting our own vegetables, or walking to the local shops for our basic foods, most people get into the car, drive to the supermarket and take a short stroll round the aisles. Then it's back into the car and home, to sit down at the computer or in front of the TV. But it doesn't have to be this way (see *Daily workouts* overleaf, for easy ways to build exercise into everyday life).

TAKE A WALK

The car undoubtedly encourages sedentary living and one easy change most of us could make is simply to leave it at home more often and walk or cycle instead. And, while jogging on hard surfaces is generally not recommended, as it can jar the spine and place undue strain on joints, walking on unyielding surfaces such as pavements actually strengthens the bones in the legs and hips. This sort of exercise becomes increasingly important as we get older.

Walking 10,000 steps a day can significantly improve your health.

Daily workouts

Exercising needn't be a chore. There are plenty of things you can do during your normal daily routine to help give your body a workout.

- Get off the train or bus one stop early and walk briskly the rest of the way to your destination.
- Walk upstairs whenever you can (or even run), instead of taking the lift or escalator.
- Stop halfway up the stairs, hold onto the banister to maintain your balance, and lift one leg onto the step two or three above the one you are standing on. Stretch out the muscles in the extended back leg, rocking gently forwards and backwards to gain the maximum stretch, then change to the other leg.

TRY THIS!

CHAIR-OBICS

If you've been sitting for a while, bend over sideways in your chair, keeping your spine straight and letting your arm hang down loosely towards the floor, lifting your other arm up over your head in an arc. Hold the bend for a few seconds, then repeat in the opposite direction. Feel the releasing stretch through your body. This exercise also helps if you have problems with balance when standing.

- Put on your favourite music when you're at home and dance to it for half an hour, or play music in the kitchen while you're cooking. Dance through all the movements you're making: from oven, to fridge, to larder, to table ... Just jig in time to the music and you'll enjoy the chore so much more.
- Every time you reach up into a cupboard, or towards a high shelf, turn this into a stretching exercise. Emphasise the stretch, and stretch out as many muscles as you can all through your body, especially through your middle area around the waist.
- When you bend down to pick something up from the floor, bend your knees and keep your back upright and straight. Always bend from the waist, keeping your back straight rather than curling your spine, to ensure you don't strain a muscle or suffer a slipped disc.
- Jog on the spot, or jump up and down on the spot if you feel angry; just get it out physically.
- If you're vacuuming, really exaggerate the movements so that you stretch your arm muscles, then change arms halfway through. Try to get into a regular rhythm.

Calming effect

Physical exercise makes us feel calmer because it induces beneficial physiological changes in the body. It releases the tension in the muscles, stretching and strengthening them, while allowing the blood to circulate more freely (tension causes the blood vessels to constrict). This increases the circulation of blood to all the cells of the body, bringing life-enhancing oxygen and nutrients, and carrying away toxic waste.

In addition, endorphins – the body's natural pain-relieving chemicals – are released when we push ourselves physically. Endorphins are natural opiates that work in a similar way to morphine, and are sometimes called 'feel-good' hormones, because they boost our mood and can make us feel quite 'high'. They are also released in situations involving acute physical stress – so that a soldier does not feel his wounds in battle, for example, or a mother in labour feels less of the pains of childbirth than she otherwise would.

Regular vigorous exercise also has the benefit of burning calories and keeping weight under control. Being overweight or obese is a risk factor in a number of health problems, such as Type 2 diabetes, where exercise forms an important part of the treatment. This condition is more common in people who are overweight. Sustained exercise helps to reduce weight and use up the excess blood sugar (glucose) in the body.

Physical activity combats the harmful effects of the stress chemicals that are produced by the 'fight-or-flight' response (see overleaf), too, bringing the body back into a state of equilibrium.

EXPERT VIEW

COMBATING TYPE 2 DIABETES

Strong evidence from American and Finnish studies (among others) indicates that moderate physical activity, combined with weight loss and a balanced diet, can bring about a 50–60 per cent reduction in the chance of developing diabetes among those already at high risk. According to research carried out at the University of Missouri, Columbia, as little as 15 minutes of strenuous exercise a day can help fight Type 2 diabetes.

> Endorphins are sometimes called 'feel-good' hormones, because they boost our mood and can make us feel quite 'high'.

Back in action

Yoga can help to keep your back strong and healthy. Back muscles often become weak and vulnerable due to inactivity and poor posture. Performing simple yoga exercises regularly will strengthen them and can help to alleviate common aches and pains. (NOTE: Start gently – give your muscles a chance to warm up – and don't strain. If you feel pain at any point, stop immediately.)

Exercise 1: THE CAT

Strengthens lower back muscles
and loosens pelvic region

REMEMBER: Breathe in as you hollow down, and breathe out as you arch up. If kneeling is difficult for you, you can practise these movements while sitting on a chair.

Kneel down on all fours, with your hands under your shoulders and your knees in line with your hips, keeping your arms straight. As you breathe in, hollow your back by pushing your stomach towards the floor. Hold for a few seconds, then, as you breathe out, push your back up so that your spine is arched like a cat when it perceives danger. Again, hold for a few seconds. Repeat the movements six to eight times in each direction.

Exercise 2: THE LOCUST

Strengthens lower back muscles and
stimulates abdominal region

Lie on your stomach on the floor, an exercise mat or your bed, with a small cushion or folded towel under your head and your arms by your sides. As you inhale, slowly lift up one leg as far as is comfortable, keeping the leg straight. Hold for a moment, then exhale as you bring your leg back down, and repeat with the other leg. Alternate, raising each leg about four times. Then, if you are able, lift both legs together four to six times.

• *Do not try this pose if you are pregnant or have a hernia.*

ADVANCED OPTION: If your muscles feel strong enough, try lifting your upper body at the same time as both legs and hold for a count of six. This will tone slack stomach muscles.

Fight or run?

The fight-or-flight, or stress, response is an automatic reaction programmed into the body's systems to help us deal with a perceived danger or threat to our survival. It is designed to help us fight or run for our lives, and sometimes this is exactly what is needed. If you absent-mindedly stepped out into the road in front of a car, for instance, you would react by jumping out of the way before you even had time to think. This response takes over when you have to act quickly to avoid danger.

SWITCHING IT OFF

These days most of the dangers we perceive are more likely to be threats to our emotions, our self-esteem or our psychological wellbeing. In such cases a physical reaction is not usually the answer, but the response gets switched on nevertheless. The chemical changes that take place in the body are geared towards helping us cope in an emergency, but they are only intended to be used in the short term. In the long term, if the stress response is constantly triggered or continues for hours on end, the changes can put a strain on the body's systems.

So, while the fight-or-flight reaction can be a lifesaver when physical danger threatens, when it is switched on by other everyday crises we need to learn how to turn it off, to safeguard our health. Relaxation is key.

what stress does to the body

Stress produces the following physical effects:

● **HEART RATE INCREASES** The heart rate speeds up in order to transport blood more quickly to the large muscles you would need for running fast or fighting off an aggressor, and also to supply the lungs with extra oxygen. This is ideal if you need to take action, but not much help if you're angry after being woken in the middle of the night by noisy neighbours, upset by a disparaging remark from a friend, or engaged in a heated argument with a colleague. A rapid heartbeat is not, in itself, dangerous to your health but, because it induces raised blood pressure, too much stress can lead to permanently high blood pressure when combined with poor lifestyle habits such as smoking, lack of exercise, unhealthy diet, high cholesterol levels, or a family history of heart problems such as angina.

● **BLOOD THICKENS** Extra clotting factors are released from the spleen to prevent excessive bleeding, were you to be injured. Again, this is necessary in a real battle or a physical accident, but not helpful in the day-to-day mental and emotional battles of ordinary life. If you have thick, sticky blood circulating around your body much of the time, it can cause blood clots to form, and the additional work involved in pumping the blood can cause your energy levels to decline. If you often feel anxious and stressed, drink plenty of water to help thin your blood (see chapter 5 for more information).

● **ADRENALINE IS BOOSTED** Extra adrenaline is pumped into the system to keep the fight-or-flight response going, and to give you extra strength. Although adrenaline makes you feel 'high' and supercharged at the time, it is actually physically taxing and exhausting over the long term.

Adrenaline is physically taxing and exhausting over the long term.

● **BLOOD SUGAR LEVELS INCREASE** The liver releases greater amounts of glucose to provide extra short-term energy to fight or flee from danger. If the glucose is not used to fuel physical activity the pancreas has to produce extra insulin to facilitate the sugar uptake by the body's cells. This can result in the malfunction of the pancreas, and some doctors believe that diabetes can be aggravated, or even caused, by this harmful effect of constant stress. When under stress you should therefore reduce your intake of sweet food and drink – unless you are making extra physical effort – as the body is already coping with excess sugar.

● **CORTISOL LEVEL INCREASES** Extra cortisol is released from the adrenal glands as a protection against inflammation, or allergic reactions. This may be helpful in the short term, but the long-term effect can suppress the immune system and so reduce resistance to illness. Excessive cortisol secretion also interferes with the liver's ability to regulate fats, resulting in higher levels of 'bad' cholesterol (LDL) and increased abdominal fat deposits. Together with adrenaline, it turns off the long-term building projects of the body, such as tissue repair, growth and bone recalcification, in favour of a short-term physical spurt.

How do you respond to stress?

When you feel wound-up, angry or stressed, how do you react? Do you:

- ☐ **A** Sound off to a friend?
- ☐ **B** Try to hide it and continue as normal?
- ☐ **C** Reach for a snack?
- ☐ **D** Pour yourself an alcoholic drink?
- ☐ **E** Indulge in a little retail therapy?
- ☐ **F** Go out for a walk?

Tick your most usual response or responses and see below for some expert analysis of how they may help or hinder your mood.

A Good idea. Talking over your problems can help you to distance yourself from them and look at them objectively. Even better, if you both have time, take a walk together – the exercise and company will help you to relax.

B A brave face is fine in some situations, and soldiering on may be the best response when, for instance, the source of stress is a tight deadline. But be careful that you're not bottling up tension, as that will make you feel depressed. Do something physical as soon as you can – even if it's just walking up and down the stairs in the office.

C Chocolate and other sugary snacks are particularly tempting when you're stressed and will provide a quick 'sugar high', but if it's your usual response you could end up piling on the pounds. Try to reach for a piece of fruit instead – if you don't have any to hand, take a quick stroll to your local store to buy some.

D Alcohol undoubtedly eases tension but it is also a depressant, so you could end up feeling even worse, particularly if you drink alone. So make it social, meet a friend and take a walk to your local bar or pub.

E Sometimes spoiling yourself is just what you need – as long as it doesn't become an expensive habit. But build in some physical exercise as well – walk to the shops and take the stairs if that's an option in the department store.

F Ideal, if you can. Or run, dance or take a cycle ride. Pure physical exercise boosts blood circulation to all parts of the body, including the brain, helping to clear the mind, so you can think through problems effectively. Exercise also boosts your endorphin levels, which gives you a natural mood lift.

Don't argue while you eat.

● **CHOLESTEROL LEVELS MAY INCREASE** The liver produces extra cholesterol to supply additional energy. When your stress levels are high, reduce the amount of saturated fat and high-fat dairy products you consume, to ensure you don't add to the cholesterol internally, inducing fatty deposits in your arteries (see also chapter 5).

● **DIGESTIVE SYSTEM SHUTS DOWN** This occurs either completely or partially. Your mouth goes dry and it's difficult to swallow, and you generally lose your appetite whenever you are anxious, upset or fearful. This is because the blood vessels to the stomach constrict so that the blood can be diverted elsewhere to supply the large muscles needed to run or fight. This can cause acute indigestion, stomach cramps and may eventually contribute to peptic ulcers.

● **MAY WORSEN IBS** Irritable bowel syndrome is a common condition causing episodes of abdominal pain and bowel disturbances – either constipation or diarrhoea. It is known to be exacerbated by stress. Regular periods of deep relaxation help most people with this problem, as does learning to be more relaxed in day-to-day life.

- **ENDORPHIN LEVELS FLUCTUATE** Initially, endorphin levels are increased, but if the stress response is activated for long periods without respite, levels of this powerful painkiller and mood enhancer have been found to diminish, causing pain thresholds to be lowered.
- **SWEATING INCREASES** Sweating is the body's cooling system, and when faced with any threat you sweat more to release the heat you would generate in a fight or while running for your life. But in a business or social situation this response is embarrassing, which just adds to your stress. Understanding why your palms are sweaty or your face glows when you are stressed may help you to control this reaction.
- **LIBIDO REDUCES** Again, the body's logic when facing a life-threatening situation is to switch off, or slow down, all the systems that are not immediately essential for staying alive. Procreating the human race, or indulging in sexual pleasure, are superfluous in an emergency. As a result, people who are stressed experience a decrease in libido – both in desire and performance – and decreased fertility. The stress response interferes with the production of sex hormones (testosterone in men and oestrogen and progesterone in women), altering the balance, and this is often the root cause of failure to conceive, when medical tests have revealed that nothing is physically wrong. Stress can also cause impotence in men. Learning to relax will switch off the fight-or-flight response, and restore normal body functions. (See also page 82 for more on this subject.)
- **MUSCLES TENSE UP** The muscles that would help you to fight for your life or run faster than you ever thought possible tense up automatically. Unrelieved tension is very tiring: it winds you up and

DON'T X

NO ARGUING AT THE TABLE

Don't argue while you eat. If you're stressed and agitated, you won't be able to digest your food properly, as your digestive system goes into fight-or-flight mode. Children, in particular, should be kept calm when eating a meal, otherwise they will – quite naturally – refuse to eat, as they instinctively know their body is in no fit state to receive food.

Sweating is the body's cooling system, and you sweat more to release the heat you would generate in a fight or while running for your life.

wears you out. This makes it all the more vital to take control of the tension inside, as you may not be able to control events around you (see *Tension is the enemy*, below).

STAY CALM AND RELAX

The most effective way to remain calm, conserve your energy and switch off the fight-or-flight response is to learn how to relax deeply. The step-by-step routine featured on pages 84–86 is a particularly effective way of achieving this, or try the breathing exercise on the opposite page.

When crises occur, often the only thing we can control is how we respond to them. By learning how to relax and control stress, you will protect your body – and probably lengthen your life.

Tension is the enemy

When we are stressed, pressured or upset, or feel threatened in some way, we automatically tense our muscles. You can observe it in others: the clenched jaw, the frowning forehead, the tight fist, hunched shoulders, and crossed legs and arms folded tightly across the body in a defensive posture. This is part of the stress response, which makes us feel protected or ready for action, but we need to recognise when we have tensed up unnecessarily because tension is very tiring. A tightly held muscle is a hard-working muscle, using oxygen and energy to no good purpose. People who are tense are usually also chronically tired, as a result. Sustained tension results in painful and aching muscles, too.

A tightly held muscle is a hard-working muscle, using oxygen and energy to no good purpose.

Our shoulders are one of the first places in the body to become tense when we feel stressed, anxious or upset, so check your shoulders when things start to feel difficult. If they're tense you are probably contracting all the muscles in this area and the tension will spread to your neck and head, often causing headaches.

How to breathe in a panic attack

Extreme emotion alters our natural breathing pattern, making us breathe shallowly, in the upper part of the chest. The following technique helps to return breathing to normal, and restores a sense of calm and ease. Use it if you suffer from panic attacks – which affect as many as one in ten people – or whenever you become stressed in any way.

- **First, breathe out.** Let your breath out in a slow sigh. Now breathe in slowly, feeling your diaphragm (just above your waist) expand outwards. Now breathe out again slowly, saying to yourself: 'let go'.

- **Breathe in again,** feeling your ribcage on either side of your body expand sideways. Now slowly exhale, making your out-breath a little longer and a little slower than your in-breath.

- **Repeat by inhaling slowly.** Think to yourself 'low and slow', and direct your breath low down into your diaphragm. Feel the middle of your body expanding and your ribs spreading sideways, as your lungs fill up with oxygen. Never hold your breath once you have inhaled – just let your breath out again in a slow sigh.

- **Pause for a second,** then breathe in again, feeling the expansion in the middle of your body. Now breathe out again slowly.

Persevere even if your breathing still feels too high in your chest. Your breathing will soon drop down to your diaphragm as you relax.

Continue this rhythm for a few minutes. Concentrate on breathing 'low and slow', and always let your out-breath be a little longer and slower than your in-breath. This is our natural breathing rhythm. Remember: it's the out-breath that relaxes you.

TRY THIS!

RELAX YOUR SHOULDERS

When you feel 'wound up', one quick way to release the tension is to drop your shoulders and breathe out in a long sigh. Then pull your shoulders down a little further towards your hips, breathing deeply into your abdomen at the same time. Hold your shoulders down for a second or two, then just let them go and breathe out slowly. Your shoulders will bounce back into their natural relaxed position, and your breathing should be calmer. Keep breathing slowly into your abdomen.

A THERAPIST'S NOTES

John, a successful lawyer, came to see me because he had begun to experience panic attacks, feelings of extreme anxiety and sleeplessness, and was worried that he wouldn't be able to hold down his demanding job.

After we had worked together for a few weeks, John revealed that he felt inadequate compared to many of his colleagues, who seemed to handle pressure better and appeared more confident and versatile than he was. He was anxious about being invited to play tennis or golf, or attend a social event, for fear of being 'shown up', and so kept himself to himself.

John told me that, as a young boy, he had loved art and music and was exceptionally good at sport, but these activities had been squeezed out of his timetable as he was made to focus on gaining good academic results and, ultimately, a law degree. I suggested he was constraining himself to such an extent that the energy from his unused talents was finding its outlet in worry and anxiety, and encouraged him to take up some artistic or sporting activities in his spare time, to restore some balance to his life.

Taking the plunge

Eventually John took my advice and, at the age of 42, he enrolled himself for piano and singing lessons, as well as tennis coaching. He gradually began to feel more like his 'old self', and was becoming calmer, happier and more in control, as he reconnected to his musical and sporting sides. He was quite surprised, and commented: 'I'm doing more, yet I've got more energy and enthusiasm than I had when I was doing less!'

As the new areas of his life increasingly stimulated him, the stresses of his job seemed less overwhelming. In addition, while concentrating on learning new skills John forgot about problems at work, and so returned to work mentally refreshed. The singing lessons helped him to breathe correctly and deeply, and relaxed many of the tense muscles in his chest and shoulders, and the piano playing brought him pure joy. His sleep difficulties also disappeared, because he was physically tired after playing tennis three times a week.

Balancing work and play

John says he feels more alive and contented, now that he has a more rounded life and gets greater enjoyment out of his free time. He has a new circle of friends at the tennis club, and met his girlfriend through the choir he joined. He even socialises more with his colleagues. He now feels his whole life is successful, rather than just one section of it.

As John discovered, the challenge for us all is to create a healthy balance between the different areas of our lives and the different aspects of ourselves. As Dr Hans Selye notes in his book *The Stress of Life*: 'If there is proportionately too much stress in any one part, you need diversion.' Whatever the pressures, recognising the need to look after your body and your inner self is the key to happiness and good health.

LETTING OFF STEAM

When life's events – or other people – wind you up, or you're feeling tense and frustrated, sometimes the best thing you can do is to let it out. Try one of the methods of release below – or come up with your own. You'll feel better afterwards.

● **Stamp your feet** vigorously and loudly into the floor, just like a toddler having a tantrum.

● **Run up and down the stairs** a few times, or go for a brisk walk around the block.

● **Write down** exactly what is upsetting or stressing you. This can be a positive way of getting it all out of body and mind, enabling you to gain a little distance and look at the problem more objectively.

● **Start a cleaning task** that you've been avoiding for ages, and really revel in being utterly miserable. You'll feel so much better once that chore is behind you.

● **Punch a pillow** or cushion to release pent-up tension, anger and frustration. If you're at work, go into the washroom and try some air boxing (in Japan, many companies provide a punchbag in a private room where employees can go to let off steam).

● **Shout into a cushion** or pillow, or turn up the music on your radio to drown out your shouts and screams. Alternatively, sing along loudly to the music. Just let it out for a while, and you'll find that you probably end up laughing.

Once you've let off steam, be sure to apply a relaxation technique or two to restore calm (for example, see the *Try This!* box and the breathing technique outlined on page 79), so that your body's functions can return to normal.

SHAKE IT OUT

Shake your arms and hands, the way you see swimmers and athletes loosening up before a race. Feel the shake going all the way up into your upper arm. This releases tension if you've had your arms in one position for a while – using a keyboard, holding a telephone or the steering wheel of the car, or even holding a book or newspaper for some time. After shaking your hands, stretch out your fingers and thumbs and hold for a few seconds – stretching will also help to relax them. Try to do this frequently throughout the day.

Run up and down the stairs, or go for a brisk walk.

don't neglect your sex life

We are programmed to enjoy sex, but we often give it low priority, so it simply doesn't happen. But this is to ignore one of nature's great relaxants and a joyful de-stressing activity which burns calories, too.

As mentioned earlier, however, when we are anxious or stressed our desire may be switched off, and we may need to give it a helping hand. Try to create a romantic atmosphere. Buy an oil burner, to produce a sensuous fragrance, and try giving each other a relaxing massage in a candlelit room, using aromatic oils such as jasmine, rose or bergamot. Put on soothing music, and take time to slow down. Enjoy being together with your partner in a relaxed and fun way.

Give as high a priority to this activity as you do to anything else in your life that you consider important. Research shows that being touched reduces stress – as well as alleviating pain and helping to heal injuries, according to Stanford University (see also chapter 7). Taking time for those intimate moments also soothes us, uplifts us (due to the release of those mood-enhancing endorphins), and gives a sense of belonging and security.

try deep relaxation

Deep relaxation isn't just a pleasant sensation – it's also vital in assisting the body with all the renewal and repair processes necessary to maintain health. It boosts the immune system, too.

Many of us don't relax sufficiently even when we're asleep, often grinding our teeth all night or simply not letting go of the tension in our muscles. As a result, we don't feel refreshed when we wake up. Learning deep relaxation (see *18 steps to total relaxation* overleaf) will help you add a restorative period of time to your day, and enable you to sleep better as you become more practised at letting go.

Exercise for you

All sporting activities are beneficial to our health, but so, too, is any activity that simply gets us moving. The absolute minimum of vigorous activity required for staying healthy is 30 minutes at least three times a week, but more is even better. Recent studies in the United States have revealed that cardiac function in 70-year-olds who have kept fit all their lives is actually better than in sedentary 20-year-olds. Do not rush straight into strenuous exercise if you're unfit, however; you will need to build up your exercise programme gradually. A visit to your GP for a general fitness check-up may be advisable if you are unsure of your condition.

Whatever activity you choose, it should be enjoyable and not seen as a chore – otherwise you won't want to do it. You can also break activities up into small slots: for instance, walk briskly for 15 minutes, and then later on in the day perhaps cycle for 15 minutes or skip or dance for short periods. Exercise doesn't have to take up huge amounts of your time, but it does need to be sustained.

ABOVE ALL, HAVE FUN!

Think back to the things you enjoyed doing as a child. Could you take them up again? Buy a bicycle, join a dance class, try ice-skating or go swimming. Learn yoga or tai chi, go horse-riding, join a ramblers association or take up a martial art. If time is at a premium, or you'd prefer an activity you can do at home, a simple solution is to buy a skipping rope and skip for 20 minutes a day. Or, if your lifestyle permits, why not consider getting a dog? Not only will this be rewarding and enjoyable in itself, helping you to relax, but it would also necessitate taking regular walks.

There are many excellent exercise DVDs around, which you could use at home if you're not keen on going to a gym. Inviting your partner, family members or close friends to join in your 'home workout' would encourage you to keep at it, and provide enjoyable social interaction as well. This could become a regular weekly meeting followed by a healthy meal to which everyone contributes, with benefits to all.

Continued on p87 ➤

18 steps to total relaxation

Practise this routine every day for about half an hour if you can and you'll soon become skilled at 'letting go'. Then use it whenever you're tense, when life feels overwhelming, when you can't sleep at night or simply to restore energy levels. Practising deep relaxation is especially helpful for anyone with high blood pressure as it slows the heart rate, helping to bring down blood pressure levels. (If you're short of time, try the 10 minute routine on page 88 instead.)

You might like to record these steps onto a Dictaphone or digital recorder, using a calm voice, so that you can play them back to guide you through the sequence. Or you could ask a friend or your partner to read them out to you as you practise. You'll soon become familiar enough with the steps to be able to work through them on your own.

1 Lie down on a firm surface, a bed or sofa, or on the floor on a mattress. Place a small cushion under your head and a large cushion or pillow under your thighs, to take the strain off your abdomen and ease the small of your back. Make sure you're warm – perhaps cover yourself with a blanket – as you can't relax completely if you get cold.

2 Focus your attention on your **shoulders** and pull them towards your feet – the opposite of shrugging. Hold them there for a few seconds, then let them go. Now feel as if your shoulders are tipping backwards towards the support you're lying on. Register having more relaxed shoulders.

3 Become aware of your **arms**. Move them slightly away from the sides of your body, and bend your elbows outwards a little. Let your hands rest apart from each other on your lower abdomen or on either side of your body. Now push your arms down into the support, hold for a moment, then stop pushing. Feel your arms sinking down more heavily into the support. Tell yourself to let go through all the muscles in your arms. Feel them being completely held by the support. Let go a little more.

4 Now move your attention to your **hands**. With your hands still supported, stretch out your fingers and thumbs. Hold the stretch for a few seconds, then let your fingers flop. Let them go limp – don't clasp them together – and register the feeling of still, relaxed hands. Feel just how calming it is to have completely relaxed hands.

5 Now be aware of your **legs**. Push them down into the support, hold them there for a few seconds, and then let go. Now let them fall apart a little more. Feel them sinking down more heavily into the support. Let go a little more and feel the relaxation flowing through all your leg muscles.

6 Now be aware of your **feet**. Stretch out your toes and hold for a moment, then let your feet flop out sideways. Feel your feet in contact with the support and register the complete relaxation you feel in all the muscles of the feet.

7 Now be aware of your **abdominal muscles** below the waist. As you breathe out, let these muscles feel loose, limp and easy – no holding in. Now feel your **buttock muscles** letting go. Feel the whole of your lower body being supported more fully and relaxing more completely.

Practise this routine for about half an hour a day and you'll soon become skilled at 'letting go'.

8 Now be aware of your **diaphragm**, just above your waist. Feel as if this part of you is expanding slightly. Let go all around your middle, and feel how you breathe naturally into your diaphragm area as you relax. Be aware of your middle expanding as you breathe in, and feel yourself letting go more completely as you breathe out. It is the out-breath that relaxes you. As you breathe out say to yourself 'let go', and feel this letting-go all through your body. Take a few moments to experience your calm, rhythmical breathing in the middle of your body, breathing out a little more slowly than you breathe in, and let go even more.

9 Now be aware of your **back**. Press down a little more heavily into the support, hold for a few seconds, then stop pushing and let go. Feel your whole body relaxing deeply.

10 Now be aware of your **mouth** and **jaw**. Make sure your top and bottom teeth are slightly apart, not clenched together. Let your tongue rest near the bottom of your mouth behind your lower teeth: this is the relaxed position for the tongue. Let your lips touch lightly. Register how it feels to have a relaxed mouth and jaw.

11 Now imagine a **smile** beginning in your mouth and slowly spreading out into your **cheeks**. Feel as if your cheeks are widening a little, so that the whole of your lower face feels relaxed and calm.

12 Now be aware of your **eyes**. Let your eyelids be lightly closed; let your eye muscles relax. Don't focus on anything. Just let your eyes rest, and become aware of how relaxing it is to shut out visual stimuli for a little while.

13 Now be aware of your **forehead**. Imagine that gentle fingers are smoothing it outwards from the centre to the temples. Feel as if it is widening out. Imagine all the worry lines being smoothed away. Now imagine it being gently smoothed upwards. Feel as if your forehead is becoming higher. Feel a sense of having a high, wide brow that is smooth and serene.

14 Now imagine those gentle hands smoothing up over your **head**, gently massaging your **scalp**. Feel as if your head is expanding a little, as you let go of any tension in your scalp. Imagine the tension floating away.

15 Now just enjoy the feeling of being deeply relaxed. Enjoy the feeling of ease. Rest in the calm that comes with letting go completely.

16 Stay in this relaxed feeling, and rest your mind by picturing a beautiful, peaceful place – somewhere you'd like to be right now, a place that feels safe and calm. Rest here for a few minutes – enjoy taking a little time away from the outside world. This is your inner sanctuary, where you can return for rest whenever you choose.

17 When you're in a state of deep relaxation, hold the awareness that all the repair mechanisms of the body are enhanced, and the immune system is boosted. By relaxing deeply, you are helping your body towards better health.

18 When you wish to come back to normal alertness, do so slowly and gently. First, wiggle your fingers and toes, then have a stretch. Stretch out your arms, hands and fingers, then stretch your legs, feet and toes. Push your heels away from you to stretch out your spine and body. Roll onto your side and, when you feel ready, sit up slowly and stay there for a few minutes, as you prepare to return to everyday living. Maintain the feeling of calm for as long as you can.

THE **10** WORST THINGS TO DO WHEN MENTALLY EXHAUSTED

- Flop in front of the TV every evening.
- Consume several glasses of alcohol.
- Overindulge in unhealthy foods, such as sweets, cakes, crisps, fry-ups.
- Overdose on caffeine to keep you going.
- Play video games that wind you up and give you an adrenaline rush.
- Drive your car before you've rested or refreshed yourself by taking some physical exercise in the fresh air to provide the brain with more oxygen.
- Enrol for an evening class where you'll be sitting still and overtaxing your tired brain.
- Chain-smoke: cigarettes are known to constrict blood vessels in the coronary arteries.
- Pick fights with the people closest to you.

- Spend all evening on the telephone, complaining about how tired you are.

Understandable as all these may be, they do nothing positive for your body. In today's world we tend to place undue importance on the mind and allow it to tyrannise the body, which eventually undermines the body's health.

Don't chain-smoke.

QUICK YOGA STRETCH

Lift both arms above your head and link your thumbs. Now pull upwards. Feel the stretch through the whole of your body, especially through your waist and abdomen and up each side of your body. Then let your arms flop down, and repeat the movement, but this time with the opposite thumb in front. Pull up again, with straight arms. Don't hold your breath – breathe normally but in tune with the movements: breathe in before you stretch, out on the stretch, and then in again when you release. You should always breathe out at the point of greatest strain, so that your breath assists you.

Stretch at every opportunity: first thing in the morning, between activities during the day, and – especially – after sitting still for any length of time. It will help you stay supple and relaxed.

FEEL THE BENEFIT

As well as the obvious physical and mental benefits of taking up an activity, there are plenty of other advantages to getting moving, such as:

● You meet new people and form new friendships – or even partnerships.

● You gain a sense of belonging to a community or club, counteracting feelings of loneliness and isolation.

● Concentrating on a sport offers a respite from work, as it takes the mind away from everyday concerns, which is in itself rejuvenating, and allows you to have fun.

● Many sporting pursuits get you out into the countryside. Looking at nature rather than concrete buildings is uplifting, and can also help your eyesight (particularly if you do a lot of close-up or screen work), as it allows eye muscles to stretch and focus out over longer distances.

● Indoor sports, such as bowling, table-tennis, squash and badminton, as well as dance or step classes, or specialist classes like yoga and tai chi, allow you to 'let go' and unleash the child in you that loves to play and move.

● Sports like swimming make you breathe deeply and fully, which is very relaxing. In fact, swimming exercises all the muscles of the body without the pull of gravity, thereby having a stronger unwinding, strengthening and toning effect.

● Sport can enhance your self-esteem, as you improve and master your chosen activity.

Relax in 10 minutes

This routine is ideal when you need a 'quick fix', and is easy to do when you're at work. Use it whenever you feel the need, to help you relax and regain a sense of calm.

1 Sit well back in an upright chair with your feet flat on the floor, letting the chair support your thighs and back. Pull your shoulders down towards your hips, hold for a moment, then release. Move your arms a little away from your sides, with your elbows slightly bent and your hands on your thighs. Feel your arms letting go of any tension: imagine the tension flowing out of your fingertips.

2 With your hands supported on your thighs, stretch out your fingers and thumbs. Hold for a moment, and then let your fingers flop – let them be limp and loose. Register the feeling of still, relaxed hands. Become aware of your thighs supported by the chair, and let go a little more into the support.

3 Slide your feet forwards a little, so that your knees are now only slightly bent. Be aware of your feet on the floor supporting your lower legs, and let go through all the muscles in your legs. Let go through your body, letting the seat of the chair take your weight. Push your back into the back of the chair and let go a little more.

4 Breathe slowly into your diaphragm, in the middle of your body. Feel your ribs expand outwards as you breathe in, then relax more

deeply as you breathe out, letting your out-breath be a little longer and a little slower than your in-breath. Register how your out-breath relaxes you.

5 Now be aware of your mouth. Make sure you're not clenching your teeth: let your top and bottom jaw fall a little apart, your tongue resting behind your lower teeth, and let your lips be just lightly touching. Close your eyes lightly and let your eye muscles relax. Enjoy the peace that comes from shutting out the visual world for a while. If you have time, picture a calming, peaceful place – somewhere you would like to be, such as by the sea or in the countryside or a beautiful garden.

Hold on to this relaxed feeling for as long as possible. If you can, use these positions in everyday situations, so that you avoid sitting on the edge of a chair, keyed up and tense, while you work.

Don't forget to take time at work to relax.

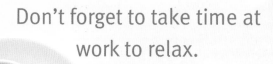

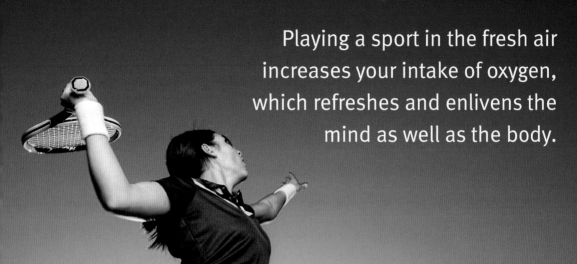

Playing a sport in the fresh air increases your intake of oxygen, which refreshes and enlivens the mind as well as the body.

● Playing a sport in the fresh air, such as tennis or golf, increases your intake of oxygen, which refreshes and enlivens the mind as well as the body.

● Most importantly, during exercise the body releases endorphins – natural opiates which can boost your mood (see page 71).

DID YOU KNOW?

JOGGING JOY

According to research carried out at Wakayama Medical University in Japan, regular jogging exercise has been found to significantly lift depression and combat stress, as well as improve physical fitness.

UNWIND IN AN INSTANT

Any sporting activity, whether a team sport or a solo pursuit, adds an extra dimension to our lives and widens our perspective, which always helps to put problems in their place. But when we're wound up it's not always possible to rush out onto a tennis court or take off for a swim, which is why it's vital to be able to unwind in the moment – at any moment – whether in the car or office, in a meeting, or even having a row at home. The exercises on the following pages, as well as all the techniques you've already learned in this chapter, will help you to do just that – to loosen up and restore calm when you need it most.

Making movement a part of our daily lives makes us fitter, healthier and more relaxed, and boosts our overall wellbeing. So get physical – and feel the difference.

Loosen up

Here are some simple loosening and unwinding movements that you can use daily, or whenever you feel the need, to restore a sense of calm and ease. Do them while waiting for the kettle to boil, or in between chores; while you're sitting at your desk or waiting for a lift; or on a bus, train or plane (the leg and ankle exercises are especially useful during air travel) or stuck in a traffic jam. Don't strain or push your body any further than is comfortable.

NECK STRETCH 1 ▶

Turn your head to the right, as if you're trying to see someone standing behind you. Hold for a count of six and feel the stretch on the opposite side. Now do the same to the left, looking over your left shoulder. Repeat about six times each side, always holding for a count of six. Keep your body facing forwards, and don't clench your teeth.

NECK STRETCH 2 ▶

Tip your head towards your left shoulder as if you were trying to touch your shoulder with your ear. Keep your head facing forwards and don't let your shoulders hunch up. Hold for a few seconds and feel the stretch in the opposite neck muscles. Now do the same to the right. Repeat about six times, or as many as you have time for.

◀ SHOULDER ROTATIONS

Circle your shoulders regularly to keep them supple and relaxed. Circle backwards for six rotations, and then forwards for six. End with a few backwards circles to leave the shoulders in a good position.

ARM RELEASE ▶

Stretch your arms out sideways, at right angles to your body, and then bend your wrists, pulling your hands backwards. This releases tension when you've had your arms and hands in fairly static positions for a long time, perhaps holding the telephone, using a keyboard, driving or gripping a pen for hours on end. This stretches out all the nerve fibres, as well as the muscles.

ARM ROTATIONS ▶

Stretch your arms out on either side of your body and circle them backwards eight times, then forwards eight times. This large, vigorous movement helps you to breathe more deeply – as though your breath has been released from tight bands constricting your middle. It also releases the upper back muscles, and helps prevent curvature of the spine caused by poor posture.

ARM SWING ▶

Swing your arms up to shoulder height in front of you and then let them drop – just let them go – registering the sensation of letting your arms drop down naturally. Keep swinging them for a few moments – up and drop, up and drop – and enjoy this carefree, rhythmical movement. This is very relaxing for the arms, where a great deal of tension accumulates during the day.

LEG STRETCH

Push your heels away from you and feel the releasing stretch in your calf muscles. Then point your toes downwards and stretch the shin muscles (if you suffer from cramp, don't hold this movement for too long). Do this when you've been sitting still for long periods.

ANKLE ROTATIONS

Circle your ankles and rotate your feet, first in one direction for a count of ten, and then the other. This improves the circulation in your legs when they have been still for some time. These movements are crucial for older people, who can develop leg ulcers if circulation becomes too sluggish.

BODY SWING ▲

Swing your shoulders round to the right and then the left several times, letting your arms flop and fold loosely around you as you swing. Don't use any effort to swing your arms – just let them go limp and loose, as if they were ribbons hanging from your shoulder joints. This childlike, carefree movement is excellent for releasing tension.

◄ LEG SHAKE

Stand up if possible, and shake your legs one at a time – the way you see swimmers and athletes limbering up before a race. Shake your legs vigorously and feel the wobble going all the way up into your thigh muscles.

4 think positive

Being able to see the positive aspects of any situation, even when you're confronted by difficulties, can be life-changing. It will help you develop a 'can-do' attitude, which in turn gives you a sense of power and of being in control. Conversely, feeling that you can't influence your circumstances leads to stress and anxiety. This chapter shows you how to unwind mentally, how to become more positive in your outlook and, when you're faced with trying situations, how to find coping strategies that suit your type of personality.

Assess your outlook on life

'Whether you think you can, or you can't, you're probably right,' observed the car manufacturer Henry Ford. In other words, people's thoughts tend to determine how well or how badly they function – a conclusion Ford had reached, no doubt, after assessing the attitudes of his workforce.

Successful people frequently state that having 'a positive attitude' is an essential component of their success. Psychological researchers have drawn a similar conclusion: that is to say, we are what we think.

Consider this: we're often more naturally attracted to happy, positive people than to those we perceive as negative, and we tend to avoid people who constantly complain, or who are always tense.

the benefits of positive thinking

People who think positively expect good and favourable results; they focus on thoughts, words and images that are conducive to growth, success and happiness – all of which enhances their energy.

Life coach Anthony Robbins highlights an important distinction between 'successful' and 'unsuccessful' people in his book *Awaken the Giant Within*. He states that the two groups interpret their past experiences in completely different ways. Successful people, he says, never dwell on past mistakes. They simply shrug them off as an aberration, an annoying 'blip' that isn't worth thinking about. They focus on the future and the next goal and expect to succeed, no matter what happened in the past. Unsuccessful people, on the other hand, hold on to the memory of the past mistake, often replaying it over and over in

DID YOU KNOW? ?

POSITIVE ASTHMA PROTECTION

Being able to look on the bright side may even help protect you from asthma. If you have a tendency to be anxious about everything, you're three times more likely to develop the condition, researchers at Heidelberg University in Germany have found. This may be because chronic worry can affect your hormone levels, which can inflame the airways.

BANISH NEGATIVE THINKING

These are the top ten examples of negative thinking. If you regularly find any of these going through your mind, it's time to take action.

1 When something goes wrong, it's usually my fault.

2 If I plan an outdoor party, it will probably rain.

3 If something could go wrong, it probably will.

4 I'll never get the job I really want.

5 I'm not interesting.

6 I'm hopeless with money.

7 I'm unlovable.

8 Some people have all the luck – I don't.

9 There's no point in trying too hard, as I'll never be successful.

10 I usually mess things up – I'm such a loser.

their imagination, and assume it will happen again. What's the difference between the two groups? It's very simple: attitude. If you want to be successful, you have to expect to be successful. You'll never be successful if you expect to fail. The right attitude is your most important asset.

If you frequently have negative thoughts and feel out of control, you can counteract this type of thinking by training yourself to look for the positive aspects, whatever your situation.

Be positive ...

You don't have to answer your phone every time it rings.

easing the pressure

Your natural personality will, to a certain extent, colour how you think about yourself and the world outside, as discussed in chapter 1, as will your upbringing and early experiences. But if you find it difficult to be positive, you may be caught in the stress response, in which every part of your mind and body is automatically geared up to save your life (see chapter 3, page 73, for more information on this).

When you're overloaded and under stress, your perspective automatically narrows; you block out everything that doesn't help you to escape from perceived danger. You become tunnel-visioned and lose sight of the bigger picture. Positive thinking feels expansive, negative thinking feels constricting. If you're normally positive, but find yourself losing this perspective, try to assess how much stress you're under and take steps to offload some of it.

DID YOU KNOW?

TURNING A CRISIS INTO AN OPPORTUNITY

The Chinese character for 'crisis' perceptively has two meanings: 'danger' and 'opportunity'. We can fall into the danger and find ourselves overwhelmed and unable to cope, or we can seize the opportunity. Every crisis presents us with an opportunity to rethink the status quo, and to make adjustments where necessary.

CUTTING DOWN ON STRESS

Adopting simple tactics to combat whatever causes you stress will also help you to think more clearly and positively:

● **Don't be a slave to the telephone.** You don't have to answer it every time it rings.

Are you an **optimist?**

This quick quiz will help you to identify your own thinking patterns. Ask yourself, 'Which answer would I give first?' – your initial reaction is the most telling one. Tick one answer in each case, then check the summary at the end.

1 If you woke up in the morning and saw that it was raining, would you think:

☐ **A** Oh good – I won't have to water the garden.

☐ **B** That's great; the plants and trees really need a good drink.

☐ **C** I'm glad I bought a new umbrella.

☐ **D** What a horrible day.

2 If a friend cancelled an arrangement at the last minute because he or she had an unexpected invitation to see a play, would you think:

☐ **A** That's good – now I can read the book I've been trying to find time for.

☐ **B** This is a good chance for me to get started on the tax return/work project/painting job that I've been postponing.

☐ **C** I'd do exactly the same if a sudden free visit to the theatre came my way.

☐ **D** How inconsiderate. My company is obviously not that important.

3 If your car didn't start in the morning, would you think:

☐ **A** Oh well, I suppose I'll have to walk, so I'll get more exercise.

☐ **B** This is an opportunity to visit the high street (or another place), where parking is impossible.

☐ **C** The car's overdue for a service anyway, so I can get that carried out while the problem is being repaired.

☐ **D** I bet this will be horribly expensive, or will take ages to fix, so I'll be without a car while it's in the garage.

4 If you were invited to a party where you knew almost no one, would you think:

☐ **A** This will be fun and I might meet some interesting people.

☐ **B** I should go, as it's the sort of challenge I need.

☐ **C** At the very least it'll be free food and drink and I might actually have an enjoyable evening.

☐ **D** I'm not good with strangers, and I probably won't have anything in common with anyone.

5 At work, if you were asked to take over a new project from a colleague, would you think:

☐ **A** This is an interesting challenge.

☐ **B** My boss must think I'm capable – I'll prove him or her right.

☐ **C** This could lead to the promotion I've been hoping for, and possibly more money.

☐ **D** I wonder if I'm up to it. If it was too difficult for him/her, then I can't imagine I'll find it easy. Maybe I'm just being left to clean up the mess.

Summary

A and B answers: demonstrate positive thinking. You have an optimistic slant on life, creating uplifting feelings and a happy frame of mind.

C answers: indicate sensible acceptance of the situation and the resolve to just 'get on with it'. This is a more neutral, essentially practical state of mind, without much emotion. This is good common sense, but you could be missing out on the energy boost that often comes from stronger positive thinking.

D answers: point to negative thinking. You tend to assume the worst-case scenario, or give a downbeat response rather than an upbeat one.

Follow up this exercise by being more aware of your thoughts and by trying to determine whether a negative thought always, or usually, appears in your mind before a positive one. Read on to learn how to train yourself to look for the positive aspects of every situation.

- **Learn to say 'no'** when that is honestly what you want to say. It's important to realise that saying 'no' is not always negative; it's a positive step if it frees you from demands that are too much to cope with, or if it gives you some rest and recuperation time. Practise saying 'no' with a lift at the end of the word, instead of with an aggressive, downbeat ending. If your 'no' sounds positive, you'll feel less guilty and others will not be offended or upset by your response.

- **Establish your boundaries.** Saying 'no' is the first step. You're not a vending machine that has to deliver every time someone pushes a button. Creating clear boundaries with others will make you feel more in control of your life, and will save you much unnecessary stress. Blurred boundaries are one of the greatest sources of discomfort and distress.

- **Manage your time.** Try to be clear about how much time you can realistically give to another person, a domestic task, a work or personal project or any event that uses your energy. Time management is an essential part of stress management; successful people are very careful about how they spend their time and energy.

TRY THIS!

FACE YOUR DEMONS

If you hate public speaking, perhaps it's because you always assume you'll do it badly and your audience will be hostile. Instead of seeing them as a group of critics, try to think of your listeners as enjoying your work and focus on what you can give them.

Changing your attitude in this way can be applied widely. Whatever you're trying to cope with – whether a traffic jam, endless questions from children, a nosy neighbour or writing a report – make it your friend, not your enemy, and you will relax and use less effort to deal with it. Questioning and adjusting the way you interpret the world has been developed into an increasingly popular training programme called neuro-linguistic programming, or NLP. NLP courses are run in many areas and can be sourced through the internet.

- **Control your personal space.** This is another boundary, which, when crossed, can cause a great amount of stress and distress. If you feel your space is being invaded, tackle it, whether it's your children, your partner, colleagues at work, or flatmates/housemates.

- **Don't take on too much** just to make others happy. Try to feel comfortable with making yourself happy.

- **Don't spend too long on one type of activity;** vary your activities during the day. If you've worked for several hours at your computer, do something physical such as gardening, walking to the shops, vacuuming, or just jogging on the spot to deepen your breathing and stimulate your circulation.

- **Don't feel guilty about taking a break** from your routine. Regular breaks enable us to be more creative and

Don't feel guilty about taking a break.

productive in the long run. It may be just 10 minutes spent having a cup of coffee while watching the news on TV, cycling to the local shop, or taking time to phone a friend or family member for a chat.

● **Try to have longer breaks away from home,** or from your usual routine, as often as possible. A weekend away or a short holiday can be wonderfully refreshing.

Change your view

It's well documented that whenever we feel particularly stressed or exhausted we tend to have negative and gloomy thoughts. Our bodies become tense and our mental outlook narrows. We develop feelings of hopelessness and think we can't cope, which eventually becomes the reality.

People who always expect the worst often claim that they're merely being realistic. But why is it realistic always to expect negative outcomes or the worst from others? By attempting to look at things from a different point of view, it's often possible to change our reality. That's because it's not so much events but how we interpret them that affects how we function and feel. And, as individuals, we can determine how we view a situation or another person.

For example, medical research has shown that if you tell patients to expect harmful side effects during treatment, they're more likely to experience them than patients who aren't warned about them. What's more, it seems that if you're told you're at a higher risk of developing a condition, you're more likely to develop it than those who are equally at risk but who are told they have a low risk.

In another eye-opening study, Harvard researchers explained to 44 hotel maids that their daily work constituted serious exercise. When the women were tested a month later they were found to have lowered their blood pressure, lost weight and improved their waist-to-hip ratio – without doing anything differently. Just thinking of themselves as regular exercisers did the trick. A control group who weren't given the same information didn't show the same health-improving results. This is further proof of the power of the mind. Yet how often do we challenge our thoughts and attitudes? These studies demonstrate that when we alter our thinking, our experiences change.

strengthening the positive

If you find that you're more inclined to have a negative rather than a positive thought, here is a simple but effective exercise in mental discipline to give you a more positive perspective.

Every time you catch yourself having a negative or critical thought, turn it round and formulate the exact opposite, then say it over and over in your mind. Do this even if an inner voice tells you that what you're thinking is ridiculous or just plain untrue. Saying positive things repeatedly allows them to sink down into your subconscious mind, from where they will influence your viewpoint as well as your behaviour. Get into the habit of practising this technique every day and you'll create more balance in your thinking.

LOOK FOR THE GOOD

When things seem impossibly difficult or 'bad', search for something 'good' in the situation. If you can find some good aspects in whatever you have to cope with, you're not denying the situation but merely bringing some equilibrium into circumstances that may have had you feeling off-balance and overwhelmed. It's not a question of deceiving yourself about problems or stressors; rather, it's disciplining yourself to look for ways to think positively, which will ultimately empower you.

Balance your thinking

This exercise can help you to recognise that there are different ways of looking at a situation and also understand how having a different perspective can bring about a calming or energising state of mind.

● Imagine living in a house where the front windows all look out onto a busy main road with a great deal of traffic. The constant movement of cars and people might be stimulating or upsetting but the view wouldn't make you feel peaceful,

● Next visualise the back windows of the house, which look out over fields stretching far into the distance, where mountains rise to meet the sky – a gentle, calming aspect.

● Now imagine a visitor arriving. If he or she couldn't see the view from the back windows, your visitor would assume you lived in a stressful environment. But if the person entered from the back of the house and glanced at the view through the back windows only, he or she would conclude that your surroundings were peaceful and harmonious.

The point is that, while both views are correct, each is in fact only a partial truth. It all depends on which set of windows you choose to look out from. How often does this happen to us in our real lives? How often do we see only half of the picture, or only one side of an argument?

This imaginary picture can be used to help you adjust and balance your thinking. When things feel difficult or overwhelming, call up an image of the house with the two different views, then make a conscious choice to visualise yourself looking out of whichever set of windows would help you most at that moment. There's always another way to look at things. When we recognise this, we can usually find more resources with which to cope.

Your imaginary picture can help you adjust your thinking when things feel difficult or overwhelming.

Looking for the positive certainly makes life easier and more joyful, so it's crucial to attempt to adjust your own thinking if it has turned negative. Negativity doesn't help anyone. It saps your energy. It's disabling. It doesn't lead to success in relationships, nor in any of life's endeavours.

balancing **left and right** brain

The left hemisphere of the brain is the logical, rational side of our thinking; it controls words, verbal communication, step-by-step logic, detail and analytical thinking. The right hemisphere is considered the creative side of the brain; it sees the whole picture rather than the details and is involved in spatial awareness. The right brain is activated when we listen to music or look at pictures and aesthetically pleasing objects, as well as when we draw, sculpt or paint or undertake any DIY or craft activity.

Because much of everyday activity is concerned with business and communication, we tend to overuse the left hemisphere, especially when operating under stress. If you find yourself churning over a problem, have a go at an activity that engages the right side of your brain. When you do so, solutions often appear. Don't neglect the creative side of yourself.

Try the following to create balance between your left and right brain:

● Listen to music as often as possible. Play uplifting music in the background when you're carrying our repetitive or boring chores.

● Practise positive visualisation: whenever you feel anxious, or before a difficult meeting, interview or exam, call to mind an inspiring image (a favourite beach or flower, for instance) and use this picture to help you feel calm and to remind yourself of the beauty and positive side of life.

● Dance and sing whenever possible – even if you do neither very well. Sing along, or dance, to your favourite music with a friend or on your own, and you'll discover new depths within yourself.

● Call up in your imagination a happy event, such as a wedding, a special birthday or a trip to a favourite holiday destination: this confirms the positive aspects of living.

● Keep a pad of paper and a jar of coloured crayons next to the phone, and doodle as you talk – especially if the conversation is stressful. Draw at other times – like you did as a child – for inspiration.

● Take up some regular artistic or creative activity – possibly something you used to enjoy when you were younger but have allowed to lapse.

EXPERT VIEW

BE NICE TO YOUR STAFF

The National Institute for Health and Clinical Excellence (NICE) reported in 2009 that the UK's annual bill for sick days due to stress-related problems – £28 billion – could be cut significantly if employers took simple steps such as giving positive feedback to workers, as well as allowing flexible working. Professor Cary Cooper, an expert in workplace psychology at Lancaster University, said, 'You cannot overestimate the importance of saying "Well done" to staff.'

The positive power of laughter

t's been observed that children laugh about 300 times a day, whereas adults
laugh, on average, only about five times each day. The more we laugh, the better our
perspective. Problems also seem to shrink, bringing an increased sense of energy. Over the
centuries it has been claimed that laughter is one of life's greatest medicines; as the Bible
says, 'a merry heart doeth good like a medicine' (Proverbs 17:22).

Laughter is sometimes described as 'inner jogging'. Research has shown that it can help to:

● Lower blood pressure.
● Reduce stress hormones.
● Boost immune function by raising levels of infection-fighting cells.
● Trigger the release of endorphins, the body's natural painkillers.
● Produce a general sense of wellbeing.

Modern humour therapy dates from the 1930s, when clowns were brought into American hospitals to cheer up children hospitalised with polio. More recently, the role of laughter as an aid to healing has been well documented in *Anatomy of an Illness as Perceived by the Patient*, by the American journalist, author and professor Norman Cousins, who created his own laughter-based, self-healing regime after being diagnosed with a degenerative disease. He suffered adverse reactions to most of the drugs he was given and decided, with the cooperation of his doctor, to take matters into his own hands. Cousins discontinued his medication and, as well as taking megadoses of vitamin C, spent his days watching Marx Brothers films and episodes of the TV comedy show *Candid Camera*, as well as reading humorous books. He claimed that 10 minutes of laughing gave him 2 hours of drug-free pain relief. In time he experienced a gradual withdrawal of symptoms and eventually regained most of his lost freedom of movement.

In India, Laughing Clubs, in which participants gather in the early morning for the sole purpose of laughing, are becoming increasingly popular, while in the UK, the psychologist and psychotherapist Robert Holden launched the country's first laughter clinics in 1991 with funding from the NHS. Demand was so great that he set up the Happiness Project in 1995. Information can be found in the Resources section on page 242.

Staying positive at exam time

Certain periods of our lives are more pressured than others; for most youngsters, exam time can be especially fraught. The anxieties about achieving good results can begin to affect the whole family, so it's particularly helpful at these times to ensure that humour, laughter and relaxing moments are not pushed aside by too much tension.

Strike a balance between working hard and taking regular relaxation breaks – to watch a favourite TV programme, go for a run or listen to music. Putting the books down and doing something you enjoy for a short while will keep you in a good mood and fresher and more alert for longer, so you'll learn more. Here are a few handy tips to help you stay positive at exam time:

● Keep your body relaxed to help reduce exam nerves. See the relaxation and loosening-up techniques described in chapter 3.

● Don't sit for too long in a static position studying, or staring at your computer screen. Introduce some movement every 2 hours; get up and walk about for a few minutes, stretch and yawn, and perhaps go outside and breathe in some fresh air.

● Practise calm, diaphragmatic breathing. Breathe gently into the middle of your body, feeling your ribs expanding outwards as your lungs fill up with oxygen. Then release your breath slowly, in a long, slow sigh. You cannot feel anxious and breathe calmly at the same time, so practising calm breathing is a foolproof way of calming your nerves. (See also chapter 3, page 79.)

Strike a balance between working hard and taking regular relaxation breaks.

- Don't deprive yourself of sleep by studying into the small hours; sleep deprivation can make everything look more difficult. Try to study at the best time for you (see chapter 2 for more on lark and owl tendencies).
- Eat well to nourish your body and brain (see chapter 5). Don't skip meals, as low blood sugar can cause feelings of anxiety.
- Eat a good breakfast on exam days (see chapter 5 for meal suggestions).
- Drink plenty of liquids (though avoid too much caffeine). Dehydration can adversely affect your memory.
- Be kind to yourself. Don't fret about things you haven't done. Make a mental list of four achievements that you're proud of.

If things become overwhelming for you, or a family member, consider seeking professional help. Stress-management courses may be available in your area, as well as personal counselling and help from other ancillary organisations. For more information, see chapter 10, *Helping Hands*.

HELPING HAND

SLEEP POSITIVELY

If you experience difficulty getting to sleep at night, run through all the things that day that have given you a sense of satisfaction – such as cooking an enjoyable meal, tidying a room or taking clothes to the charity shop. Then focus intensely on that pleasurable feeling and sense of pride. Experience a warm glow inside, and before you know it you'll have dropped into a peaceful sleep. (See chapter 2 for more tips on how to get a good night's sleep.)

The subconscious mind

Psychological research has discovered that the subconscious mind believes exactly what it's told. It doesn't discriminate or judge the truth of statements and concepts in the same way as the conscious part of our mind. Consequently, we have to be careful what we tell it. Although most of us don't give much thought to its workings, the effect of the subconscious mind is very powerful and it plays a significant part in controlling our behaviour.

If you constantly tell yourself, for example, that you're no good with money, your subconscious mind will ensure that you behave in ways that make the statement come true. You'll find yourself spending money when you know full well that you can't afford it. Somehow, without knowing quite why, you will perpetuate that behaviour and prove to yourself that you are indeed the spendthrift character you said you were.

Similarly, if you tell yourself that you're sexually undesirable, that message is fed into your subconscious mind as a fact. Then, when you do discover that someone finds you attractive, your subconscious sabotages the situation in order to confirm the original belief.

It may seem extraordinary that your subconscious should have this power. Although you might not deliberately ruin your chances of success or happiness, negative thinking tends to create negative experiences, just as positive thinking usually produces positive effects.

banishing self-criticism

If you're stressed, you may have a tendency to blame yourself when things go wrong, even if you weren't at fault. And it's easy, if you live alone, or work alone from home, to lose perspective and become too full of self-doubt. Boredom can also give you a negative self-image, as can being too introspective; both make it harder for you to get a clear picture of what's what.

Be kind and compassionate to yourself and recognise that no one is perfect, that everyone makes mistakes, but that our mistakes can be our greatest teachers if we're willing to learn from them. Don't dwell on them. Instead, remind yourself of all the things you've got right in the past and regularly call to mind your achievements.

IT'S GOOD TO TALK

If you spend a lot of time alone, try to meet up regularly with friends, or at least to talk to them on the phone. Exchanging emails is fun, but not quite the same as hearing someone's voice or being physically in their company. We need feedback from others, to hear another person's point of view, as it broadens the picture and can help put our own worries into perspective. Technology – so helpful in many ways – can cut us off from each other, and from the human contact that is essential to our wellbeing.

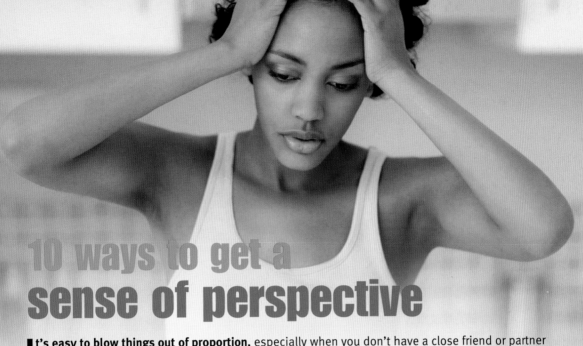

10 ways to get a
sense of perspective

It's easy to blow things out of proportion, especially when you don't have a close friend or partner with whom you can talk over your problems. Here are ten practical suggestions for seeing things from a fresh perspective:

1 When faced with any problem, try to look at the facts without emotion. Often it's our emotional reaction to a problem that creates the most distress. Be as objective as possible and you'll think more clearly and discover solutions that emotions can mask.

2 When something feels extremely difficult, ask yourself, 'Can I change anything?' If the answer is 'Yes', set about changing whatever you can; taking action, no matter how small, empowers you. But if the answer is 'No', ask yourself, 'Can I accept the situation?' When you decide to accept something, you stop using your energy to resist it and you start to relax. As a result, new solutions often reveal themselves.

3 Timing is always important. When nothing seems to be working, remind yourself that most things change with time. If you can relax and go with the flow, things may resolve themselves when the time is right.

4 Practise letting go. Churning over problems never helps, it just saps your energy. One useful technique is to visualise putting your worries or problems into a large wooden box, then firmly closing the lid and locking it with a large key. Try to do this each night before you enter your bedroom. Never take your worries to bed with you.

5 Distract yourself by watching a comedy film or DVD, or by reading a humorous book. Encourage yourself to see the funny side of things (see also page 103).

6 Listen to some happy, optimistic music. Music has an extraordinary power to change our mood and banish gloomy thoughts.

7 Feed your senses with positive and beautiful sights and sounds. Look at nature and listen to the sounds of birdsong or children's laughter. Walk through parks, take time to stare at magnificent buildings, or visit art galleries. 'We become that which we behold', as William Blake, the great artist and visionary, stated.

8 Take some exercise every day (see chapter 3). Exercising your body calms the mind and releases uplifting chemicals into your bloodstream.

9 Enhance your environment. Bring flowers into your living space, create a relaxing atmosphere with candles or low lighting, or burn calming incense or essential oils, such as jasmine, bergamot, rose or lavender.

10 Get enough sleep. A rested mind and body will produce creative solutions to whatever you face (see also chapter 2).

If you find yourself isolated, take part in a group activity.

If you're retired or find yourself isolated, take part in a group activity such as a yoga or creative-writing class, join a walking group or tackle a new skill such as Thai cookery or amateur dramatics. This will take you into a different environment, among potential new friends, as well as enabling you to discover fresh talents. Volunteering to help with community projects or a local charity is another good way to meet people, to tackle new challenges, and to feel useful and valuable (see chapter 8 for more information on activities).

In times of difficulty, seek out the people who love and accept you, and be strengthened by their support and their positive reactions to you. Don't be too proud to ask for help. When you turn to others to help you, you're showing them that they're important and valuable to you. Equally, when you're in the company of others, you're able to see that we all have problems and weaknesses – you're not the only one.

Be in the now

Most of us spend so much time thinking about past or future events that we're rarely completely in the present moment. But focusing on past regrets or upsets or worrying about what might happen expends huge amounts of emotional energy, which could be better used to enjoy the here and now.

Increasingly in Western society too many things compete simultaneously for our attention, and as a result we seldom concentrate on one thing at a time. But dividing our attention in this way can be very tiring.

Mindfulness training is now widely taught to address many of the problems arising from the fact that we don't have sufficient control of our minds. This Buddhist teaching says there is no other time but the present moment, and that we should try to be fully present in whatever we're doing or saying, giving our full attention to everything that we engage with. This premise is a helpful way to release ourselves from worry and anxiety. There is usually nothing worrying about the present moment – right now. It is our thoughts about the past and our fears for the future that cause us the most distress. But the past cannot be changed and there may be nothing immediate you can do to affect the future. Grasping this immense, and yet simple, truth is an important key to releasing yourself from all sorts of stress, worry and unhappiness.

MINDFULNESS TRAINING

In the USA, Dr Jon Kabat-Zinn at the University of Massachusetts Medical School has successfully developed the Mindfulness-Based Stress Reduction (MBSR) programme. It includes Transcendental Meditation techniques to calm the mind, yoga for physical suppleness and cognitive behavioural therapy to help people challenge negative thoughts. Those treated have reported lasting benefits, ranging from reduced stress and better health to clearer thinking and increased creativity.

In Britain, the Mental Health Foundation has called for mindfulness training to become more widely available on the NHS. To manage his own stress, Dr Jonty Heaversedge, a South London GP who starred in the BBC series *Street Doctors*, sought help from a Buddhist centre and learned to meditate. He believes that mindfulness training can help us all improve our physical and mental wellbeing in today's pressurised world.

GIVE IT A TRY

Here's an easy way to practise being in the now:
● Whenever you feel stressed, anxious or fearful, fix your attention on your immediate surroundings; be aware of your body and your breathing, and be completely focused on what's going on now.
● Tell yourself, 'I've only got to manage this moment.' When you discover you can do that, the next moment becomes manageable as well.

All you have to do is handle the present time. You cannot perform in the future – next week, next month, or even tomorrow; you can deal only with things that are here and now. Of course, you have to make plans and organise for the future, but it's only 'now' that anything really happens. Recognising this can help you to feel relaxed and calm.

THINK YOURSELF CALM

Find a quiet place and focus on relaxing your whole body with this step-by-step technique (see chapter 3 for more relaxation methods). Practise either sitting or lying down; you can even try it when you're on a bus or train, or sitting on a bench in the park. The key is to give your mind – and your senses – a rest from the outside world for a short period of time.

- Be aware of the rhythm of your breathing and focus on your out-breath, making it a little longer and a little slower than your in-breath.
- Close your eyes and picture yourself lying on a sun lounger on a beach. Imagine the sound of the sea gently lapping against the shore.
- The sun is shining. Be aware of the sun warming your body and a gentle breeze cooling your face.
- Be aware of the sunlight. Feel yourself surrounded by light. Imagine the light flowing into your body through the pores in your skin.
- Feel the light flowing around your body, lightening your feelings, lightening your body.
- Imagine the light flowing up through your body into your head, clearing and enlightening your thinking.
- Just rest in that peaceful state, with light all around you and a lighter feeling within you. When you feel ready, turn your attention outwards and listen to the sounds around you, open your eyes and take a few minutes to come back to the present moment and your actual surroundings.

Be happy and prosper

Research has long suggested that a positive outlook promotes good health. A new study reported in the *European Heart Journal* proves it more conclusively than ever. Dr Karina Davidson and her team at Columbia University Medical Center in New York tracked 1,739 healthy adults over ten years. They found that happy, positive people were 22 per cent less likely to develop heart disease than those with a negative outlook.

Although Dr Davidson stated that they could only speculate at this stage on the reasons for this result, she assumed it had something to do with happy people taking more relaxation time and recovering more quickly from stressors, so that they did not prolong the body's stress responses. She also assumed that positive, happy people don't spend time reliving stressful situations, but shrug them off and move on.

So even though it may not always come naturally, making a determined effort to banish negative thoughts and adopt a positive approach whenever possible – especially when things look difficult or problematic – will not only make day-to-day life feel a lot easier, but could also boost your present and future health and happiness.

food for thought

Changes in diet over the past fifty years are thought to be a significant factor in rising physical and mental ill health. Food is the fuel that provides our day-to-day energy, but it is also the raw material the body uses for renewal and repair. Food can even influence our moods, making us feel down in the dumps or, conversely, positive, calm and alert. This chapter reveals what to eat to benefit both body and mind, as part of a healthy, balanced diet. Find out which foods promote calm and ease sleep, which help to boost energy when dealing with pressures, anxieties and stress, and which foods should be avoided altogether.

Your daily food plate guide

A healthy, balanced diet consists of consuming foods from each of the six food groups: protein, carbohydrates, vitamins, minerals, fibre and fats. But working out what you need to eat each day can be difficult.

A useful guide for eating healthily is to picture a large plate containing everything you might eat in the course of a day. The 'eatwell' plate, devised by the UK Food Standards Agency, illustrates how to get the balance right, showing how much of each type of food you should ideally be eating. You don't have to worry about getting it exactly right at every meal, but if you aim to achieve the ideal balance over the course of a day, or even a week, you'll be on the right track.

THE EATWELL PLATE

Use the eatwell plate to help you get the balance right. It shows how much of what you eat should come from each food group.

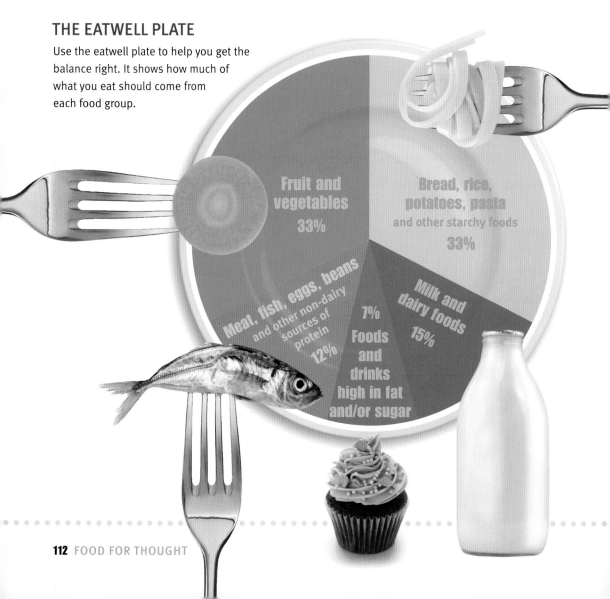

Fruit and vegetables
33%

Bread, rice, potatoes, pasta and other starchy foods
33%

Meat, fish, eggs, beans and other non-dairy sources of protein
12%

Foods and drinks high in fat and/or sugar
7%

Milk and dairy foods
15%

making a meal of it

Achieving a healthy balance isn't as hard as you may think. Here are some examples of how to get the balance right over the course of a day (for further meal suggestions, see pages 132–133):

● **BREAKFAST** Start the day with fruit, yoghurt, porridge or a whole-grain cereal with skimmed or semi-skimmed milk and little, or no, sugar (if using sugar, go for the unrefined, raw cane variety; see page 127 for more information). Or you could have wholemeal toast, perhaps accompanied by a boiled egg. Don't skip breakfast; this can cause you to feel weak or light-headed and very low in energy.

● **LUNCH** Ideally, one meal a day – preferably at lunchtime – should include a large salad containing as many uncooked vegetables as possible, as well as the usual salad ingredients. Try to include some seeds too, such as sunflower, poppy or sesame, and some alfalfa, if you can get hold of it. Accompany the salad with a jacket potato and a small amount of protein in the form of fish, lean meat or grated cheese on the potato.

If you're not keen on salad, replace it with two or three cooked vegetables, and on some days add nuts instead of meat or fish. This combination gives you a plentiful supply from each of the six food groups mentioned earlier, providing you with a good range of nutrients. If you have to return to work after lunch, this type of light meal is ideal, as it will give you energy but not make you feel sleepy in the way a heavier meal would.

If you usually eat a sandwich at lunchtime, try to make sure it contains some salad foods, such as tomato, lettuce, cucumber, watercress or avocado. If possible choose wholemeal rather than white bread, or whole-grain crispbreads. Whole grains provide slow-release energy as they take longer for your body to metabolise, which helps to keep blood sugar levels more stable. By contrast, refined

TRY THIS!

KEEP A FOOD DIARY

The best way to address your eating habits is to first gain a clear picture of exactly what you consume each day. Buy a small notebook and, at the end of every day for a fortnight – or even a month – write down everything you have eaten and drunk that day. Alternatively, take a picture: studies carried out at the University of Wisconsin-Madison in the USA found that photo diaries were especially effective in – literally – helping people watch what they were eating. Taking a photograph just before eating helped to trigger critical evaluation just at the right time, and the volunteers reported that they had to think more carefully about what they were eating because they had to take a picture of it.

Once you realise what you are actually consuming on a daily basis, you can then work out where adjustments need to be made, following the guidelines in this chapter.

Make sure you finish your evening meal in good time before bed.

carbohydrates – such as white-flour products or sugar – give you an immediate, but short-lived, energy boost, quickly followed by a dip in energy levels (for more on sugar, see page 126). To supplement your sandwiches at work, why not take along some extra salad ingredients and fruit in a food-bag or lunch box? A light lunch with foods containing a wide variety of vitamins will help you to avoid that sinking, sleepy feeling in the early afternoon.

● **DINNER** The early evening is when you could choose heavier foods such as pasta, curry and rich sauces, as well as occasional desserts, gateaux or pastries. The body has to work harder to digest richer foods so, if you eat an unusually large fried breakfast or a sumptuous feast in the middle of the day, you may feel drowsy as your digestive system handles this unexpected load.

It takes a number of hours to fully digest a meal; the body's digestive processes slow down when you're asleep, so try to make sure you finish your evening meal in good time before going to bed.

DID YOU KNOW?

HOLD THE SECOND HELPINGS

It takes about 20 minutes for your brain to register that you are full at the end of a meal, so when you're tempted to go back for seconds try waiting a little while first, to see if the urge to eat more disappears.

Comfort foods

At times of stress there is often an urge to turn to food and drink for comfort, but unfortunately 'comforter' foods tend to be high in sugar content and/or fatty in nature, and have no lasting emotional benefits. When we indulge in these 'goodies' we feel momentarily happy, because eating them stimulates the pleasure centre in the brain and may also trigger childhood memories of receiv ing sweets or chocolates as a reward for doing something well, or for good behaviour. But rewarding ourselves in this way is actually adding to the problem rather than solving it.

Crisps, chips, fry-ups, ice cream, sweets, chocolate bars, cakes, biscuits, sugary, fizzy drinks ... Low-quality food of this type provides insufficient quantities of the raw materials necessary for maintaining and rebuilding the body's organs and systems, and therefore puts the body under extra strain. It causes waste that cannot be utilised and which is often stored as fat in, or between, our muscles and other body tissues, making us feel run-down and low in energy – and so we're tempted to reach for another treat to lift us up again. This may produce a quick 'high', but it is not long-lasting, and is usually followed by a rebound sinking feeling. We then reach for more sugar to lift us up again, and the vicious cycle goes round and round, with soaring and dipping blood glucose levels, which are far from conducive to calm and good health.

Comfort foods don't do too much harm if you only indulge in them occasionally, but they don't provide the body with what it needs to withstand stress and stay healthy.

Comfort eating may help in the short term, but its effects are not long-lasting.

A THERAPIST'S NOTES

Vanessa came to see me when her boyfriend, Tim, insisted she face up to her eating disorder. Tim didn't know how to help her, and felt he couldn't cope alone any longer.

Vanessa was bulimic, fluctuating between almost starving herself and bingeing on huge amounts of food, after which she would feel dreadful remorse and make herself throw up. As we worked together for a number of sessions, the underlying factors began to emerge.

Vanessa had been the youngest child in her family, with two older brothers and a much older sister. She had always felt left out when the siblings played together, and during family discussions she felt dismissed. Her mother had looked after her physical needs, but Vanessa never felt they had an emotional attachment. She told me she had always had the feeling she wasn't really wanted, and felt unloved and a nuisance to everyone in her family. When asked what she felt when she binged, she replied: 'It's as if I have a huge hole inside me – an empty space. Sometimes I just can't bear it, so I try to fill it up with food, as though I'm trying to stuff the feeling down, to smother it.' As our sessions continued, Vanessa began to talk more and more about how she didn't feel important to anyone; that nobody thought she was special, or interesting.

Acknowledging the problem

I helped Vanessa to see that she was really trying to feed the baby she had been – the baby who, she felt, had never been given what she needed. The baby was starving for lack of the unconditional love that gives a child its sense of self – its sense of being acceptable. Vanessa was using food to suppress painful feelings, and to feel loved. If certain essential needs during babyhood – and childhood – are not met at the right time, there always remains a hunger for that important input. Many people, unconsciously, try to find a partner who will compensate for the things they never received; who will give them that unconditional love and acceptance, which only a parent can give.

Hope for the future

As Vanessa began to see what was driving her bulimia, she stopped blaming and hating herself. I encouraged her to take on responsibility by looking after herself in the way that a 'good' mother would. By giving herself the things that made her happy, and recognising that she deserved to feel proud of herself, she no longer needed to feel that she was unlovable.

Vanessa gradually became more confident and more interested in her possibilities for the future. The bulimia became a thing of the past, although she admitted she couldn't be certain it wouldn't return if she encountered too much stress or unhappiness. It takes a great deal of courage to tackle an eating disorder, and she remains quite fragile, but is eating regular, healthy meals and, as time passes, becoming increasingly stronger.

Instead of reaching for the chocolate, try to think of another way to give yourself a lift.

don't reach
for the chocolate

Comfort eating is frequently used as a way of dealing with difficult emotions. Some people have a complicated relationship with food, and – in extreme cases – eating disorders may develop as a result. (Some eating problems have deep-rooted underlying causes, and may need the help of a trained counsellor in order to resolve them; see *A therapist's notes* opposite, and *Resources* on page 242 for further help.)

If you find yourself turning to food at times of crisis or unhappiness, try to think of other ways you could give yourself a lift. Treat yourself by going to see a film or a play, booking an appointment at the hairdresser or having a massage or spa treatment – anything that you enjoy. These seemingly simple things can lift your mood and boost your self-esteem much more effectively than eating foods you don't need. By taking the action to give yourself a positive treat or an outing that lifts your spirits, you are telling yourself that you are valuable and deserve to have nice things to do.

Boredom can be another cause of overeating, so resolve to do something active or productive. Going for a walk instead, when you feel bored or upset, can buoy your emotions. Or plan a trip with a friend to an art gallery or somewhere else you'll both enjoy, or go shopping. These will do more to lift your mood than snacking on unhealthy foods.

TRY THIS!

DEALING WITH MID-AFTERNOON HUNGER

If you feel hungry or your energy level dips mid-afternoon, resist the impulse to snack on biscuits, cakes or other calorific foods that supply few healthy nutrients. Instead take a pack of mixed nuts, or nuts and raisins, to work with you, or nibble on some fruit (fresh or dried) or raw vegetable sticks, or even some hard cheese, if you haven't eaten cheese at lunchtime. At first you may not feel satisfied without the 'sugar fix', but gradually your taste buds will adjust, and the energy boost you'll receive from these health-giving foods will last much longer.

If you're at home during the day, prepare some raw vegetables and keep them in a food-bag in the fridge, so they're the first thing you see when looking for something to munch.

Food as fuel

If you had a high-performance car you wouldn't fuel it on low-grade petrol and expect it to function at its best – so why do that to your body?

Paying little attention to your diet and regularly eating junk foods that supply few useful nutrients will eventually result in a deterioration in health and performance. In order to stay as healthy as possible, it's essential to support yourself with good, balanced nutrition at all times. And, when you're under pressure and feeling the strain, eating the correct foods will give you the extra boost needed to cope.

mood-enhancing foods

Feeling depressed, or below par, can often be traced back to deficiencies in diet. Foods that contain tryptophan – an amino acid often referred to as 'Nature's Prozac' – have positive benefits on mood. It is an essential amino acid, which means the body cannot produce it – we must get it from our diet.

The body uses tryptophan to help make vitamin B_3 (niacin) and serotonin. Serotonin is thought to encourage healthy sleep and a stable mood (see also chapter 2). A diet low in tryptophan can lead to low levels of serotonin, which, in turn, can result in depression, bad sleep, poor concentration and weight gain. A study carried out at McGill University in Canada found that healthy males showed a greater reduction in mood after tryptophan depletion, while a recent NIDA (National Institute on Drug Abuse)-funded study in the USA suggests that depleted tryptophan is related to depression and impulsivity.

Serotonin deficiency has also been implicated in cases of obesity and overeating because it is associated with the brain's perception of hunger and satiety; the brain can't tell when you have eaten enough.

When you consume foods high in tryptophan the serotonin levels in the body rise; hence tryptophan is used

EXPERT VIEW

SWEET DREAMS

Tryptophan has been used successfully as a sleep aid. Serotonin does play a role in sleep regulation, but, more importantly, it is the precursor to melatonin, a hormone crucial to the sleep cycle. On its own, melatonin supplementation has been shown to be an effective treatment for insomnia; however, combining melatonin with tryptophan may prove even more beneficial. (See chapter 2 for more information on sleep.)

Where to find **tryptophan**

Try to include a small amount of two or three of the following foods in your diet every day. (Check the healthy-meal suggestions on pages 113–114 and 132–133 for ideas of how to incorporate these foods in your daily meal plans. Bananas, nuts and seeds can be eaten between meals, when you feel like a snack.)

- **Bananas**
- **Cheese** (a wide variety of cheeses, including cottage cheese; Gruyère is especially rich in tryptophan)
- **Eggs**
- **Fish**
- **Meat** (both red and lean meat are rich sources of tryptophan, such as beef, lamb, chicken, turkey and pork)
- **Milk** (including soya milk; drinking milk before going to bed at night is recommended for helping you sleep well)
- **Nuts** (all kinds, including hazelnuts, peanuts, walnuts, cashews and brazil nuts; brazil nuts are also a good source of selenium)
- **Peas**
- **Potatoes**
- **Pumpkin seeds**
- **Rice** (both white and brown)
- **Sesame seeds**
- **Soya beans**
- **Spinach**
- **Spirulina** (a microscopic blue-green alga found in fresh and salt water, available from health-food shops)
- **Sunflower seeds**
- **Tofu**
- **Wheat flour**
- **Yoghurt**

SUPERFOOD SUSTENANCE

Spirulina contains a remarkable concentration of helpful nutrients and is sometimes referred to as a 'superfood'. It is extremely rich in protein and also has a high concentration of beta carotene, vitamin B_{12}, iron and trace minerals, as well as the rare essential fatty acid GLA (also contained in evening primrose oil). It can be taken in tablet form, or as a powder mixed with a fruit-juice smoothie or sprinkled on cereal for an instant breakfast, or in a vegetable-juice smoothie in the afternoon. This easy-to-digest, nutrient-rich food may be particularly beneficial for boosting energy in older people.

in the treatment of depression, anxiety and insomnia, and can function as an appetite suppressant, resulting in weight loss. However, in infants and children a deficiency of tryptophan can lead to weight loss, not gain.

In order for tryptophan to be changed into niacin (which helps keep the digestive and nervous systems healthy), the body needs to have enough:
- Iron
- Riboflavin (vitamin B_2): contained in spinach and other green leafy vegetables, fruits, liver, kidneys and milk
- Vitamin B_6: contained in liver, fish, brown rice, most vegetables, bananas, grapes, lean meat, butter, eggs, cheese and milk

Feed your brain and fight disease

You may have been told when you were growing up that eating fish improves your brain's capacity – and there is now some proof that this old wives' tale is true. The reason for this is fish oils, which contain omega-3 and omega-6. These essential fatty acids (EFAs) are critical for health, normal growth and the development and function of our brains. In a study carried out by neuroscientist and senior research fellow at Oxford University Dr Alex Richardson and colleague Dr Madeleine Portwood, 120 primary-school children with coordination difficulties who were given a mix of omega-3 and omega-6 EFAs over three months showed significant improvements in school performance. Fish oils have also long been shown to protect against coronary heart disease, as well as Alzheimer's disease and rheumatoid arthritis; they have anti-inflammatory properties which protect blood vessels and are also considered helpful in reducing stiffness and tenderness in joints.

DID YOU KNOW? ?

THE WONDERS OF TOFU

First produced in China over 2,000 years ago, tofu has been called 'the wonder food of the East'. Made from the soya bean, it is richer in protein than any other food of equivalent weight, making it an ideal meat substitute for vegetarians. In addition to containing tryptophan, it is low in fat, high in calcium and a good source of iron, potassium, phosphorous, essential B vitamins, choline and fat-soluble vitamin E – so it not only boosts your mood but it's extremely good for you, too. An added bonus is that it is cholesterol-free.

getting enough EFAs

Our bodies can't manufacture omega-3 and omega-6, so we have to get them from our food. But it's important to get the balance right: most people consume sufficient (and often too much) omega-6, present in vegetable oils, but far too little omega-3, whereas ideally we should be consuming them in roughly equal quantities.

Oily fish, such as mackerel, herring, salmon, sardines and tuna, are an excellent direct source of the omega-3s our brains need. Current UK government guidelines recommend eating four portions of oily fish every week. The omega-3 fatty acid ALA (alpha-linolenic acid) can also be obtained from vegetable/plant sources such as green leafy vegetables, flax seeds (which produce linseed oil) and walnuts in particular. Our bodies then convert the ALA into EPA (eicosapentaenoic acid) and DHA (docosahexaenoic acid) – the two critical omega-3 fatty acids the body needs.

Alternatively, you can take supplements, including cod liver oil tablets. Vegetarians can use an algae-source DHA supplement such as Spirulina (see page 119), in addition to many of the sources mentioned above. Some foods, such as milk and eggs, are enriched with omega-3 by feeding the animals a diet that is rich in omega-3 fatty acids.

Oily fish, such as mackerel or sardines, are an excellent source of omega-3.

INUIT SENSE

The heart-health benefits of omega-3 fatty acids were discovered in the 1970s by researchers studying the Greenland Inuits. The Inuits consumed large amounts of fat from seafood, but displayed virtually no cardiovascular disease. The scientists concluded that the high level of omega-3 fatty acids in the Inuit fish diet reduced triglycerides, heart rate, blood pressure and atherosclerosis (hardening of the arteries caused by build-up of fatty deposits in the artery walls).

FISH FACTS

Some fish swim in polluted waters, so may carry the risk of being contaminated with mercury, PCBs (polychlorinated biphenyls – industrial compounds), bacteria or other contaminants. Always check the food label (or ask your fishmonger) if you can, to find out where the fish has been caught. If possible, opt for fish from arctic waters or far off-shore, in the deepest parts of the ocean, where the sea is most likely to be pollution-free. Oils generally go through a purification process (which will be stated on the label of your supplement) and do not usually contain contaminants.

GIVE YOUR OMEGA-3 A HELPING HAND

There are a number of factors that can contribute to low levels of omega-3. A high intake of hydrogenated and trans fats, found in highly processed junk food, along with too much omega-6 (from vegetable oils and processed foods that contain them), can actually block the conversion of omega-3s in the body. Excessive alcohol intake and smoking also help destroy these crucial omega-3 fatty acids. When you increase the amount of omega-3 you consume, therefore, you also need to ensure that junk food is kept to a minimum.

Antioxidants: why we need them

One of the most important things you can do for your body is to protect it from free radicals. Free radicals are unstable oxygen molecules that naturally accumulate in the body and damage healthy tissues by causing changes in cells that can lead to cancer, heart disease and other serious conditions. They are also responsible for ageing. To counteract these predators we need to eat plenty of foods

The most powerful antioxidants are vitamins C and E and beta carotene, found in orange vegetables such as carrots.

rich in antioxidants. These are protective compounds that either stop the formation of free radicals, or disable them before they are able to cause harm.

Research suggests that the more antioxidants we get in our diets, the less likely we are to suffer from cancer. The most powerful antioxidants are vitamins C and E and beta carotene, which is contained in the many fruits and vegetables ranging from yellow to rich orange and red hues, such as carrots, tomatoes, red peppers, apricots and cantaloupe melons (especially rich in both beta carotene and vitamin C), as well as carotenoids found in dark green, leafy vegetables like broccoli, cabbage, kale, kelp, Brussels sprouts, winter greens, watercress and spinach. Antioxidants are also found in green tea and black tea, best consumed without milk to benefit fully from their protective effects.

EXPERT VIEW

GREEN TEA

A study at the Tohoku University Graduate School of Medicine in Japan found that drinking 5 cups of green tea daily, compared with only 1 cup, significantly reduced psychological stress. Drinking green tea also boosts cardiovascular health, according to clinical studies carried out in the USA: catechins, the major compounds in green tea (also found in black tea, in lesser quantities), exert a variety of vascular protective effects and prevent vascular inflammation, crucial in preventing the build-up of arterial 'plaque'. The antioxidant activity in green-tea catechins is also effective in scavenging free radicals, and in reducing intestinal absorption of lipids (oily organic compounds).

Eating for
health and energy

Here are some essential guidelines for eating a healthy, balanced diet and making sure you're getting the most out of your food.

what to do about fats

Contrary to what many people think, fat should not be cut out of your diet altogether. It is necessary for the absorption of the fat-soluble vitamins A, D, E and K, for maintaining healthy cell membranes and for building a strong immune system. It's only harmful when eaten to excess, and should make up no more than 30 per cent of your daily calorie intake, of which no more than a third should be saturated fat (animal fat).

Use olive oil instead of butter or lard, especially for cooking.

OPT FOR OLIVE OIL

Olive oil is a mono-unsaturated fat and has beneficial properties for health, as proven in Mediterranean countries where consumption is high but heart disease is surprisingly low. Use olive oil instead of butter or lard, especially for cooking, as it doesn't oxidise when heated (which other vegetable oils do, producing harmful free radicals). It is, however, very fattening, so consume in moderation; fats contain approximately twice as many calories as carbohydrates and proteins.

Oils should be kept in a cool, dark place or, alternatively, refrigerated for long-term storage to prevent them from turning rancid, as this contributes to the formation of free radicals. It's a good idea to keep a small amount of olive oil out for daily use, however, as it solidifies in the fridge (returning it to room temperature restores its liquidity and colour).

Olive oil contains flavonoids – beneficial antioxidants – which are also found in oregano.

Make it Mediterranean

The Mediterranean diet has long been considered one of the healthiest ways to eat, as it includes large amounts of fresh vegetables and fruits, and is low in processed and packaged food and red meat.

Food is prepared from local, fresh produce, and fish consumption tends to be higher in countries bordering the sea, due to the abundant supplies. Additionally, the extensive use of olive oil in cooking and salad dressings is thought to have health-enhancing properties. Olive oil contains flavonoids – beneficial antioxidants – as do red wine, tea, coffee, fruit, vegetables, cinnamon, oregano (and other herbs) and chocolate.

Scientific research has shown that the Mediterranean diet, in combination with moderate exercise and stopping smoking, can greatly reduce the chance of developing heart disease, cancer and other serious diseases. In addition, a four-year study of over 10,000 healthy adults in Spain found that people were 30 per cent less likely to develop depression if they ate a diet high in vegetables, fruit, legumes and whole-grain cereals, with more fish and white meat than red meat, and mono-unsaturated oils (found in olive oil, rapeseed oil, avocados and nuts) used in place of saturated animal fats.

BEWARE OF SATURATED FATS

Foods high in saturated fats, such as red meat and dairy produce, can exacerbate certain harmful physical effects experienced during the stress response, increasing blood pressure, heart rate and cholesterol (for more on what happens to the body during the stress response, see chapter 3, pages 73–78). Avoid products containing hydrogenated fats, or trans-fats, in particular. Grill or bake foods if possible, rather than frying in fat, and be aware of the 'hidden' fats in food such as pork, breast of lamb, sausages, bacon, egg yolks, gravy, cheese, puddings, biscuits and pastries – and chocolate (although chocolate does have mood-enhancing properties, which makes it an acceptable treat from time to time in small amounts).

cut down on sugar

In the stress response, the body releases extra glucose (blood sugar) from the liver (see chapter 3), so it needs to take less in. But sugar-laden foods are often exactly what we crave when under pressure. Sugar provides 'empty' calories; it gives you energy for physical exertion, but no essential raw materials for replenishing the cells of the body. You may get an immediate 'high' from a sugary food or drink, but this quickly wears off and is followed by a sudden drop in energy and a 'low' feeling. So, while your taste buds may enjoy sugar, overindulging in sugary snacks can cause depressed moods.

In addition, if the energy isn't used in some form of exercise the extra calories will simply cause weight gain, which in itself becomes depressing. A high sugar intake can starve the body of vital nutrients, which is of particular concern in children's diets. Children who are given sweets when they say they are hungry are not getting the nutrients they need – but merely empty calories which will make them gain weight. People who reduce their sugar intake (and their fat intake as well, as many snacks contain excessive fat and sugar) are more likely to eat healthily, reduce their risk of being overweight and, in turn, their susceptibility to diabetes and coronary heart disease.

Children are often given sweets when they are hungry, but these sweets are not really 'feeding' them ...

ALWAYS CHECK THE LABEL

Make sure you read food labels carefully; it's not always obvious that you are consuming sugar, as it's added to so many of our main staple foods, such as cereals, tinned fruit and vegetables, baked beans, bread, sauces and many packaged, instant meals, as well as jams and other spreads and most fizzy drinks and colas. Many so-called fruit drinks are just water, sugar and colouring, containing minimal amounts of fruit, if any.

Eat natural sugar found in fresh and dried fruit, raisins, dates, blackstrap molasses, maple syrup and pure honey. If buying sugar, buy unrefined, raw cane sugar, as this contains trace minerals and nutrients which are stripped out during the refining process, and consume it minimally. Alternatively, agave nectar or syrup – now widely available from supermarkets and health-food shops – can be used instead of sugar.

ALLEVIATING PANIC ATTACKS AND PMS

If you go without food for many hours your blood sugar drops, and this is thought to contribute to panic attacks; the body releases adrenaline to keep its systems functioning, and this excess can cause shakiness and panic-attack symptoms. If you suffer from panic attacks, eat something (preferably starchy) every 3 to 4 hours to keep your blood sugar steady (see also chapter 3, page 79).

Eating carbohydrates at frequent intervals also helps with PMS, reducing weepiness, aggression and general mood swings by keeping blood sugar stable. It may also help to avoid salt (unless you're taking medication, such as lithium, where this is contra-indicated) or salty foods when menstruation is due, as sodium causes fluid retention in body tissues.

say no to salt

Most of us consume far too much salt. Strenuous exercise and excessive sweating in hot weather can increase the body's need for salt, as large amounts are lost through sweat. But generally people eat more than is necessary for the body's healthy function; the recommended amount per day is no more than 6g (2.4g sodium). Excessive sodium can damage your kidneys and cause high blood pressure, strokes and heart failure. Fluid retention can also result from a diet high in salt, contributing to pre-menstrual tension and causing serious problems during pregnancy.

Avoid eating too many salty snacks, such as salted nuts and crisps, and savoury or cheese biscuits. Hard cheeses have a high salt content, as do tinned and processed foods, especially processed meats; people often don't realise how much salt is contained in the foods they consume, so, again, always check nutrition labels carefully. Both salt and sodium content may be listed, but the two should not be confused: 6g salt (the maximum daily allowance) is equivalent to 2.4g sodium. Foods with a high salt content contain more than 1.5g (0.6g sodium) per 100g. Try not to add extra salt to food on your plate, and use small amounts when cooking; enhance flavours instead with herbs, lemon juice or spices. If you find a low-salt diet unpalatable, you could try potassium chloride (stocked at most health-food shops) instead. But if you have a medical condition, check with your doctor first, as taking extra potassium may not be advisable.

TRAIN YOUR TASTE BUDS

You can train your taste buds to need very little salt, and it's best to start young with children so that they never develop the high-salt habit. Many baby foods have been found to contain more salt than is healthy for an infant. Check the labels. Babies up to 12 months need less than 1g (0.4g sodium) daily and the recommended maximum rises very gradually through childhood. By discouraging a taste for salt at an early age, you can encourage children to eat better and avoid future health risks.

If you can't get fresh vegetables, buy frozen: they are usually flash-frozen, preserving most of their nutrients.

nature's best foods

While many of us should be trying to reduce our fat, sugar and salt consumption, there are some foods that most people should eat more of:

FRESH VEGETABLES

Fresh vegetables are one of the best ways to combat harmful free radicals, as they are bursting with vitamins and other vital nutrients which are powerful antioxidants (see page 122). For maximum nutritional value, eat vegetables raw as often as possible – most vegetables taste delicious in their uncooked state. When cooking, steam or use very little water to avoid losing too many vitamins, or use the vegetable water for soups, sauces, stews or simply as a broth to drink. If fresh vegetables aren't available, buy frozen: they are usually harvested at their peak and flash-frozen, preserving most of their nutrients. Tinned vegetables often have a high salt content and never taste quite as good as fresh.

Salad foods are brimming with vitamins and minerals and also have a high water content, which makes them easy to digest.

To avoid a build-up of toxins from chemical pesticides and fertilisers, wash fruit and vegetables thoroughly before consuming. Although the body naturally processes most toxins through the liver, kidneys, colon, skin and lungs, either converting them to harmless by-products or eliminating them from the body, it is best to minimise intake. If possible, choose organically grown produce.

Although the recommended advice is to eat at least three to five portions of vegetables (both raw and cooked) each day, as the minimum for good health, if you can manage more than that your health will be even better fortified.

SALAD FOODS

All the foods normally associated with salad, such as lettuce, cucumber, tomatoes, peppers, celery, celeriac (celery root), radishes, avocados, endive, fennel, parsley, watercress and so on, are also brimming with vitamins and minerals. As cooking destroys many of these nutrients it is vital to obtain maximum nutritional value by eating raw salad foods regularly (although keep raw mushrooms to a minimum as, uncooked, mushrooms contain hydrazines – toxins that can be poisonous in large amounts).

These foodstuffs also have a high water content, which makes them easy to digest. It is more difficult for the body to digest and absorb concentrated foods such as protein, which should therefore be eaten in smaller amounts.

FRESH FRUIT

This is another vital high-water-content food (80–90 per cent water content). Fruit should preferably be eaten uncooked, as cooking destroys most, if not all, of its health-giving nutrients (in addition, sugar is often added to fruit when cooked, making it even less nutritious). Fruit is considered to be one of the most beneficial foods of all, supplying every

Getting your 5-a-day

Juice them, drink them, mash them, combine them, or even disguise them. The easiest way to achieve the recommended 5-a-day of fruit and vegetables is to purchase a liquidiser and make delicious smoothies. Experiment to see what flavours you enjoy: for instance, try carrot, apple and pear, or celery, parsnip, apple and cranberry. Or mix a variety of fruits, such as strawberries, blueberries, banana, kiwi fruit or apples with pineapple and oranges or grapefruit, add a little milk or plain yoghurt, and you have a high-vitamin drink bursting with goodness.

FRUIT ON THE GO

Alternatively, chop up one or two different fruits each morning – bananas are quick and non-messy – and add to the family's breakfast cereal; eat an apple, a pear or a banana as you walk to the bus or tube in the morning; or give your children a piece of fruit to eat in the car on the way to school, or when you meet them from school in the afternoon. Make fruit salad and put it in a jar, topped with yoghurt, for your children to take with their packed lunch, or for you to take to work. Pure fruit juice counts as one of your 5-a-day no matter how many glasses you drink, because the fibre has been removed.

KEEPING CHILDREN HAPPY

If youngsters aren't keen on vegetables, liquidise them into a nourishing soup or, if you don't have a liquidiser, simply mash them up for a more textured soup. If the taste needs a boost, try adding a good-quality can of tomato, mushroom or asparagus soup, or any other flavour you enjoy. You can also 'disguise' vegetables in a cheese sauce: instead of plain cauliflower cheese, add broccoli, carrots, mushrooms and peas.

Or why not try making your own avocado dip: remove the skins and mash ripe avocados with some very finely chopped onion and garlic, add a small amount of plain yoghurt and a little salt and pepper to taste. Eat with warm pitta bread, or strips of raw vegetables such as carrots, peppers, cucumber, celery and cauliflower – great with hummous (a dip made of nutritious chick peas and sesame paste) too. Children will love dipping the vegetable sticks with their fingers.

It may seem like a chore to scrape, peel and chop vegetables or fruit, but once you get into the habit you'll find it actually doesn't take much time at all. Encourage your children, or grandchildren, to get involved with helping to prepare the foods; they will enjoy being included, and it will teach them how to eat healthily.

Children will love dipping vegetable sticks with their fingers.

nutrient needed for optimum health: glucose, amino and fatty acids, minerals and vitamins. Ideally it should be eaten on an empty stomach, as it is digested very quickly, only remaining in the stomach for about 30 minutes before passing into the intestines. If you eat fruit at the end of a large meal, it gets held up in the stomach behind the other food and begins to ferment, often causing flatulence and discomfort. Eating fruit first thing in the morning as part of your breakfast will supply you with plenty of energy to face the day, as well as assisting in the body's elimination processes.

Whenever you crave a snack between meals, eat fruit. It will be more easily digested at this time and will give you all of its nutritional value, when your stomach isn't full of other foods to hold up its digestion.

HELPING HAND

ROUGHAGE ROUND-UP

Foods containing fibre, or roughage, include: fresh fruit, vegetables (especially raw vegetables), whole grains such as brown rice, oats (rich in soluble fibre that binds with 'bad' LDL cholesterol and transports it out of the body), wheat germ, millet, rye, barley, maize, muesli (check for added sugar), wholewheat pasta, wholemeal bread and crispbreads, high-fibre biscuits, oatcakes, high-fibre cereals, porridge, baked potatoes, baked beans, seeds, sweetcorn, unsalted nuts, pulses such as lentils, peas, mung beans, kidney beans and aduki beans. Include a variety of these in your diet to ensure you are obtaining sufficient fibre.

FIBRE

Fibre is another of the most essential components of a healthy diet, especially when you are stressed. Fibre assists the efficient elimination of toxins and waste, one of the main keys to maintaining good health. It acts like a sponge by absorbing undigested food, toxins and excess cholesterol – including the cholesterol produced internally as a response to stress – and ushers them out of the body.

Baked beans are a good source of fibre – an essential component of a healthy diet, especially when you are stressed.

Continued on p134 ➤

Make the right choice

Here are some examples of foods to choose – **and avoid** – for a healthy, balanced diet. Try to choose most of your foods from the 'good' selection, and you will boost your defences against stress and revitalise your energy. 'Bad choice' foods can, of course, be consumed occasionally in moderation, but make sure that they don't form the bulk of your diet.

breakfast

✓ GOOD CHOICE

- Banana and/or yoghurt
- Fresh mixed-fruit salad
- Grapefruit/melon
- Muesli or high-fibre cereal, with skimmed or semi-skimmed milk, porridge, organic unrefined sugar or honey
- Wholewheat or rye toast or crispbread with honey, sugar-free jam, or low-salt, savoury spread (such as Marmite or Vegemite)
- Boiled/poached/scrambled egg (no more than three or four times a week)
- Fruit juice, tea/herb tea, decaffeinated coffee or dandelion coffee

✗ BAD CHOICE

- No breakfast (especially for children)
- Tinned fruit with sugary syrup
- Low-fibre, sugar-enriched cereal
- Fried foods such as egg, bacon, sausages, fried bread
- White, refined-flour bread with high-sugar jam/syrup
- Sugary biscuits
- Sweets/chocolate bars/crisps
- Strong coffee with lots of sugar

lunch

✓ GOOD CHOICE

- Melon/fresh fruit cocktail
- Large salad with plenty of raw vegetables and/or cooked fresh vegetables
- Jacket potato, including skin (avoid high-calorie toppings – try tuna or cottage cheese)
- Rice (preferably brown)
- Small amount of protein (lean meat/fish)
- Cauliflower cheese
- Small vegetable pasta dish
- Soup/wholemeal bread/salad
- Baked beans (reduced sugar/salt variety, if possible)/scrambled egg
- Omelette or veggieburger
- Mineral water/fruit juice

✗ BAD CHOICE

- Fried potatoes (have occasionally as a treat)
- Fried fish, sausages, hamburgers, pork/lamb chops (grill them instead)
- No salad or fresh vegetables
- Tinned vegetables (high salt content)
- Rich, creamy sauces (hard to digest and will make you sleepy)
- Large pasta dish (have a small portion with salad and/or vegetables)
- Rich, creamy dessert/doughnuts/cakes
- White-bread sandwiches/baps/buns
- Sugary soft drinks
- More than 1 unit of alcohol

dinner

✓ GOOD CHOICE

- Melon/avocado/grapefruit
- Prawn/seafood cocktail
- Soup (homemade, if possible)
- Grilled/roast meat
- Baked/grilled fish
- Casserole of meat or fish or vegetable stir-fry
- Vegetables au gratin
- Rice/lentils
- Plenty of fresh vegetables
- Pasta or curry (meat, vegetable or fish)
- Low-fat yoghurt
- Herb/camomile tea

✗ BAD CHOICE

- Processed/high-salt meats
- Smoked fish/meat too often
- Fatty meats – pork, lamb, chicken skin, fatty mince, hamburgers, sausages – more than once a week
- High-cholesterol-forming dishes such as sauces with high butter/cream content
- High sugar/cream-content desserts (such as ice cream, sorbets, gateaux) more than once a week
- Tinned fruit (high sugar)
- Sugary soft drinks
- Strong coffee and/or large quantities of alcohol

ALCOHOL

Alcohol should be consumed in moderation, if at all, with at least two alcohol-free days per week. Drinking too much alcohol can lead to a wide range of health problems, including cancer, liver disease, stroke and high blood pressure, and can also affect mental health. In addition, alcohol is high in calories, so can cause weight gain.

NHS recommended guidelines are up to 2–3 units a day for women and 3–4 units a day for men. If you are worried that you may be drinking too much, visit your GP for advice (see also chapter 10 and *Resources* on page 242, where you will find further guidance on seeking help).

vitamin and mineral
supplements

If you eat a properly balanced diet, your health should be good and your body well buffered against everyday stresses. But if you're under increased strain – for example, due to excessive sleep loss, chronic fatigue, illness, emotional upset, noise pollution or too much change – your body may require a higher level of helpful nutrients to cope with the extra demand. Supplements, however, should be seen as just that – to be taken in conjunction with a healthy diet, not as substitutes for nutritious food. Never take vitamin pills on an empty stomach; they are too concentrated, and need to be mixed with food. It's also advisable to check with your doctor before taking regular supplements.

MULTIVITAMINS AND VITAMIN C

When the demands on you are extreme, it's a good idea to take a daily multivitamin and mineral supplement, as well as extra vitamin C (up to 1,000mg per day). Stress greatly increases the need for vitamin C and also pantothenic acid, or vitamin B_5 (see below), which can be taken in a tablet form or by eating plenty of green leafy vegetables, eggs, wheat bran and peanuts (preferably unsalted). Smoking – already a considerable stress on the body, as it is an external source of free radicals as well as toxic chemicals – also increases your vitamin C requirement: it takes 20mg of vitamin C to neutralise the effect of just one cigarette.

ZINC AND B-COMPLEX VITAMINS

Zinc tends to be depleted at times of stress, although beware of taking it in excess, as this can cause copper deficiency and lead to anaemia. Zinc is found in eggs, meat and seafood (especially oysters). A deficiency can lead to a reduction of sex hormones, which is why oysters have long been considered an aphrodisiac. If you are under a lot of emotional or mental stress, a supplement of the B-complex vitamins could supply extra support, but don't exceed the recommended daily allowance.

Drink plenty of water

Many people don't drink enough water. Accepted guidelines recommend drinking about eight glasses, or at least 1.5 litres, throughout the course of a day, although this may increase in periods of hot weather, or for people who are especially active. Drink a glass of water when you get up in the morning, and keep a bottle in your bedroom so that you can take a drink if you wake during the night.

Getting enough water, doctors say, will help to prevent kidney stones. If you don't drink enough, the body's wastes become concentrated, forming crystals that can bond together and create the stones. One way to tell if you are drinking enough water is by the colour of your urine. It should be very pale yellow or even clear, except in the morning, when you haven't had any fluids all night. If the colour is dark at other times, you should be drinking more.

ON THE MOVE

If you spend much time driving, keep a bottle of mineral water in your car and take frequent drinks. During air travel, it's especially vital to drink plenty of water, as the air pressure inside the plane causes dehydration. You will feel less jet-lagged at the end of your journey if you drink approximately half a litre of water per flying hour on short-haul flights (use your judgment on long-haul flights,

DID YOU KNOW? **?**

BOOST YOUR ENERGY

Drinking plenty of water relieves fatigue and thins the blood – especially beneficial when in the stress response, which produces extra blood-thickening factors (see chapter 3). When you don't drink enough, the cells in your body become too dry, and to counteract this problem they draw water from the most convenient place – your bloodstream. The extra work involved in pumping the blood can cause energy levels to decline, making you feel fatigued, and can also cause raised blood pressure and a racing heart. Drinking sufficient water also benefits your skin and helps prevent wrinkles – an added bonus.

as that amount may be excessive). Try not to consume alcohol or coffee during the flight, as both dehydrate the body, exacerbating the dehydration already caused by the pressurised cabin.

DEHYDRATION FROM ALCOHOL

Alcohol, whether flying or not, is a major cause of dehydration. If you consume large amounts, the hangover you experience next day is due to the cells of the brain being severely dehydrated. The best remedy is water, so if you have overindulged make sure you consume at least two or three glasses of water before going to sleep, and then about half a litre when you wake up. Better still, ensure you drink plenty of water when you consume the alcohol in the first place.

Healthy diet, healthy life

Food is more than just an essential requirement for survival. The foods we choose to eat, and the way we eat them, can make us feel full of energy, ready to face any challenges that may come our way, or, conversely, depressed and fatigued, as we turn to comfort foods to make ourselves feel 'better' – which only results in us ending up feeling more anxious and stressed.

It doesn't take much to achieve a healthier, more balanced diet. By making a few sensible adjustments to your eating habits, following the guidelines in this chapter, your body and health will benefit. As a result you'll have more energy, you'll feel more alert and you'll combat mental challenges more effectively.

6 know your rights

You expect the major traumas of life, such as divorce, bereavement or redundancy, to take their toll. What's often not appreciated is just how much the steady drip-drip of day-to-day 'admin' problems – financial, consumer and legal issues – can destroy your sense of calm and dampen your enjoyment of life. This chapter outlines advice and tactics for dealing with everything from faulty goods to faceless bureaucrats, explaining how to assert your rights if necessary. Armed with this knowledge, you'll be able to stop worrying and start taking practical steps to resolve your everyday concerns.

Your finances

Money issues affect nearly everyone at some time. Perhaps bills always seem to arrive faster than pay cheques, or you find you can manage everyday expenses but worry about the inevitable extras, from household repairs to buying a best friend a wedding present. Or maybe you reach the end of the month struggling to afford necessities, or feel that the latest round of price rises could push you over the financial edge. Worst of all, you may already be facing mounting debts.

And all too often, money worries can lead to mental health problems, such as stress, anxiety and depression. In fact, it's estimated that nearly half of the UK population worried about money and debt in 2009, while a quarter of people who have mental health issues experience debt in some form or another. This has been exacerbated by the so-called 'credit crunch'. Calling the NHS Stressline (see *Resources* on page 242) will put you in touch with professional advisers who can offer practical financial and mental health support.

Read on to find the advice you need about managing your money, rather than letting it manage you, as well as how to find help if your finances are in a mess. It'll also help you to take stock of your current financial situation and assess just how well you're managing your money right now (see the *Spender or saver?* quiz overleaf).

balancing the books

Manage your money well and you'll feel in control – and that's crucial for your mental health. Financial problems are the most frequently cited cause of depression. According to guidelines from the mental health charity Mind, keeping on top of personal finances and good mental health go hand in hand: the stress and worry associated with trying to maintain control over expenditure and keep a household running on an even keel can result in feelings of inadequacy and despair, additional worries about the consequences of getting into debt, pessimism about the future and conflict within the family.

Ideally, you need to know exactly how much is coming into and going out of your household, as well as how to balance the books and put a little aside to prepare for unexpected expenses. Being organised is half the battle. You may have to start by looking at your attitude to paperwork and resolving to make time to sort out money matters,

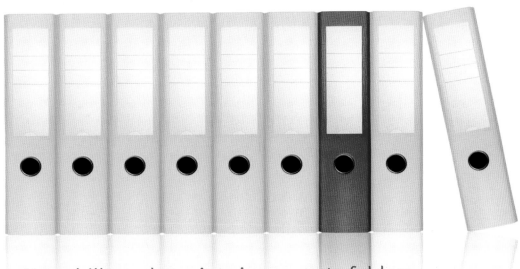

Keep bills and receipts in separate folders and deal with them once a month.

however hectic your daily life. If you're not methodical on a day-to-day basis, for instance, perhaps you'd be better off gathering all your bills in one folder and your receipts in another. You can then make a commitment to deal with them once a month. Or, if you work online, set up the appropriate electronic folders to make sure you never mislay anything that needs attention.

Sensible finance starts with budgeting. Sit down with all your payslips, statements and bills and decide whether you're going to use weekly, monthly or annual figures (stick to the same basis for all figures). Then work out:

● **YOUR TOTAL HOUSEHOLD INCOME** – include regular basic salary after tax, National Insurance, pension contributions and other deductions, but not additional variable items such as overtime payments and tips. Also include any benefits, tax credits, pension, maintenance or child-support payments you receive, as well as any regular contributions from other household members, such as partners, adult children or older relatives.

● **YOUR TOTAL OUTGOINGS ON FIXED ITEMS:** rent (including any ground rent or service charges) or mortgage payments, insurance payments, pension contributions, council tax, utility bills (gas, electricity, water), telephone rental (landline and mobile), car and hire-purchase payments (including road tax and MOT), television licence and any other TV-related bills, as well as school fees, child-care costs, any maintenance payments you make, loan payments and any other regular outgoings. For energy bills, take the total amount paid over the past year and average this out per week or month, as the cost will vary between summer and winter.

Continued on p142 ➤

Spender or saver?

Do you really know how healthy your personal financial situation is? To find out, answer the following questions truthfully, then check the summary to find out what your score means.

1 Do you (tick all that apply):

☐ **A** Have a weekly housekeeping budget – and stick to it?

☐ **B** Keep enough money set aside to support yourself for three months if you were made redundant tomorrow?

☐ **C** Shop around or look for bargains on the internet whenever you face big purchases or insurance renewals?

☐ **D** Check your bank and credit card statements at least monthly?

2 Money is tight and you have friends visiting overnight. Would you be more likely to:

☐ **A** Treat them to a meal at your favourite restaurant?

☐ **B** Take them out for a curry or pizza?

☐ **C** Buy everyone a takeaway?

☐ **D** Cook a meal at home?

3 How do you handle credit and store cards?

☐ **A** You use them regularly but pay off the amount in full every month.

☐ **B** You don't have one – you can't trust yourself to avoid temptation.

☐ **C** You owe more money on cards than you could pay off in one go.

☐ **D** You have several cards, so that you can spread the load.

4 How much do you owe right now (not counting credit cards if you pay the balance in full every month)?

☐ **A** Nothing at all.

☐ **B** You just have a mortgage, and can afford the regular payments.

☐ **C** You have debts at reasonable interest rates (for example, a mortgage, bank loans) that you can handle in your monthly budget.

☐ **D** You have a large mortgage, overdraft and/ or credit card debt that is proving difficult to finance.

5 How much of your income do you save?

☐ **A** None – I often spend more than I earn.

☐ **B** None – I just about break even at the end of the month.

☐ **C** I put a bit of money aside when I can – but not much.

☐ **D** I have a regular high-interest savings account, which I pay into every month.

6 You're shopping for one specific item and spot something else that you really want – but it's a bit of an extravagance. Do you:

☐ **A** Buy it without worrying – you have enough money in reserve for times like this?

☐ **B** Get it anyway – the credit card bill won't come in for ages?

☐ **C** Ask a friend or relative to buy it for you as a birthday or Christmas present?

☐ **D** Walk away – you really can't afford a luxury item right now?

7 You have no choice but to borrow money to pay for an essential major item, such as a car or a new boiler when your old one has broken down. Do you:

☐ **A** Put it on a credit card?

☐ **B** Talk to your bank manager about a loan?

☐ **C** Agree to the finance arrangement proposed by the seller?

☐ **D** Search for the best loan rates on the internet?

8 You have a clutch of unexpected bills that all need paying. Do you:

☐ **A** Pay them all – you have enough to cover it?

☐ **B** Ignore them until the red bills start arriving?

☐ **C** Sit down and work out which are the most important to pay first?

☐ **D** That wouldn't happen – I know when all my bills are due or they're all paid by direct debit.

Score

1 A–1 B–1 C–1 D–1
(award yourself 1 point for each 'yes' answer)

2 A–0 B–1 C–2 D–3

3 A–5 B–3 C–0 D–0

4 A–5 B–4 C–2 D–0

5 A–0 B–1 C–2 D–5

6 A–3 B–0 C–1 D–3

7 A–0 B–3 C–0 D–4

8 A–4 B–0 C–2 D–5

SUMMARY

Score 0–14
Your approach to finances may already have landed you in difficulties. The good news is that it's not too late to take stock, get out of debt (see page 143) and develop better habits for managing your money (see page 142).

Score 15–25
Although you often manage to juggle your outgoings, you sometimes have problems and may worry about money issues to the detriment of your health. Making a few small changes to the way you manage your money could get you back on track. Try the money-management tips on page 142, and start putting something away, no matter how little, to cover unexpected extra expenses.

Score 26 and above
Congratulations! You understand how to deal with money issues and generally manage your finances well. Read the rest of this section to pick up any tips you may have missed.

● **YOUR AVERAGE SPENDING ON NECESSITIES** – such as food, household cleaning items and toiletries, children's clothing and shoes, telephone calls and transport costs (including travel passes and petrol costs).
● **HOW MUCH IS LEFT OVER** each month after fixed outgoings and necessities.

The next step is to work out which bills need paying first – especially your mortgage or rent payments, utilities and council tax. Then devise a budget and arrange each month to pay the important outgoings first. Once you've paid the priority payments, set yourself a spending limit for everything else – and don't overstep it.

If money is tight, think about ways you could increase your income or reduce your outgoings. For example, could you take on an extra shift at work? Do you really need cable TV or a daily newspaper? Could you take a Thermos of coffee to the office, instead of nipping out to the local coffee shop several times a day? You'll be surprised how quickly it all adds up.

HELPING HAND

TOP TIPS FOR KEEPING YOUR FINANCES HEALTHY

If you heed the following tips, you'll find it easier to keep on top of your spending. Get into good habits now, and they will soon become second nature.

● Monitor your outgoings regularly – in one survey, 40 per cent of people admitted they checked their finances less than once a month, even though 70 per cent believed that keeping up to date with financial affairs is important.
● Pay off as much of your credit card bill as you can every month – if you make only the minimum payment, you'll end up paying a fortune in interest.
● Pay important bills by standing order or direct debit – budget for these in advance when working out how much you'll have left at the end of the month. They include: mortgage or rent; gas, electricity and water bills; insurance payments, council tax and telephone rental charges.

● Try to save something every month, preferably by standing order, even if it seems a trivial amount. For predictable major expenses, such as holidays or Christmas, work out what you spend each year on average and divide by twelve; aim to save that much every month into a separate account.
● If you need to buy a major item, don't take out a loan for it unless you really must, and then seek out the best interest rate.
● If you can't pay a bill on time, talk to the company involved – they will often be able to help you stagger payments and perhaps reduce future outgoings. Make sure that suggested monthly payments are within your budget; if not, go back and re-negotiate.

avoiding debt

Britons have one of the highest levels of personal debt in Europe. According to the Bank of England, in 2009 we jointly owed a monster £233 billion on credit cards, overdrafts and other loans.

Many people are finding it more and more difficult to meet credit payments, or are running up new debts that they cannot service just to meet existing commitments. Getting into debt often starts with a major change of circumstances such as a pregnancy, relationship breakdown, ill health or redundancy. That's why it's so important when times are relatively good to start a savings habit.

IF DEBT GETS OUT OF HAND

If debts are mounting and you don't know how to cope, it's essential to get a clear-headed idea of the scope of the problem and formulate a

Pay off as much of your credit card bill as you can every month.

concrete plan to deal with it. By the time it gets to this stage, the chances are you won't feel able to solve all your problems on your own or work out a plan to get back on track. Fortunately, there are many sources of free help and advice, such as Credit Action, Citizens Advice Bureaux and the National Debtline (see *Resources* on page 242). A debt adviser can help you to:

● Work out your household budget.
● Make sure you're claiming all the benefits and tax credits to which you're entitled.
● Look for other ways to increase your income or reduce your outgoings.
● Decide how much you can afford to offer your creditors.
● Summarise your budget plan to discuss with creditors.
● Make arrangements with your creditors for future payments.

In addition, a debt adviser may be able to talk to creditors on your behalf and make offers for paying your debts in manageable instalments.

Finally – but perhaps most important of all – once you have sorted out the problems this time, devise a plan to take control of your spending in future.

A THERAPIST'S NOTES

Mother of two **Anna** *explained to me how she and her husband John, a computer engineer, tackled their debt problems when the stress of it all began to affect her health.*

At the end of the 1990s, Anna and John were a typical double-income-no-kids-yet couple living in London. They worked hard, had a mortgage of just over £100,000, ate out regularly, had holidays abroad twice a year and rarely worried about money.

Over time Anna became anxious that their credit card bills were piling up, however. On top of that, John had a negative-equity loan from a previous property that charged an extortionate amount of interest. John's approach had always been to pay the minimum each month, probably boosted by the belief that he had a steady income for the foreseeable future.

Facing facts

Anna had started to suffer from insomnia because of the level of debt they were accumulating. One day she insisted that she and John tackle the problem head on, so they sat down and prepared to go through all their bills, jotting down the amounts owed on each of the credit and store cards, as well as an outstanding loan on a car.

The amount was shocking – between them they owed over £25,000. But seeing the total on paper for the first time made the couple realise that they had to take action while they had the means to do so. The first step was to consolidate their debts, so they researched the interest levels on credit cards and switched as much of the debt as possible from the cards with the highest rates to those with the lowest. Just reducing the number of bills coming through the door made it all seem more manageable. They then cancelled the credit and store cards they would no longer be using.

John also arranged a remortgage on their current property so that the outstanding balance owed to the negative-equity loan company could be paid off in a lump sum, and the new debt transferred to a lower-rate arrangement.

Making a plan

The next step was to make a long-term plan of how much they could pay off each month, and to try wherever possible to stick to it. It meant giving up most of the treats they'd been used to, but before long it wasn't an issue. They couldn't always stick to the plan, but just having a plan to come back to kept up their momentum and was the way out of debt.

Within three years the couple had paid off all of their debts, apart from the mortgage. Crucially, they were able to do this before they started a family and money became much tighter. Today the couple no longer use credit cards, they have an old car and they often buy quirky second-hand furniture. When Anna talks about it now, she advises that the only way to break down a mountain of debt is to chip away at it, a little bit at a time. It isn't easy, but it does work.

Don't ignore those bills ...

keeping a **clear** head

It's natural to feel anxious when you realise you're losing control of your finances, but whatever you do:

- Don't ignore bills.
- Don't borrow more to fund existing debt payments.
- Don't spend any money on non-essentials until you have dealt with your debts.
- Don't borrow any more on credit cards – these are usually the most expensive form of credit.
- Don't stop payments without talking to your creditors.
- Don't be tempted by offers from private 'debt consolidation' agencies to clear all your debts so that you owe them just a single monthly payment – they charge such high fees that you may be left worse off.
- Don't pay for debt advice.

Consumer rights

Being on the wrong end of a commercial transaction that's gone sour can turn an apparently trivial problem into a major source of anger and frustration – and hence stress. Perhaps you bought an appliance that stopped working after a few weeks, or gave in to an aggressive doorstep salesperson, then regretted signing on for double glazing that you neither needed nor could afford. Or maybe you're experiencing problems with cowboy builders who won't rectify a poor job, or a utility company that provides substandard service – but still demands payment.

Even being pestered by junk mailers or cold-call telephone canvassers can create considerable tension if you're not sure how to put a stop to them. You may be fuming about poor local services, problems with healthcare or education, or just the sheer irritation of facing a wall of bureaucracy when trying to sort anything out. The good news is that, rather than feeling bullied, you can adopt simple, effective tactics to stand up for yourself and assert your rights, putting you back in control.

problems with goods

You may not be aware of it, but you have a number of legal rights when it comes to buying goods from a commercial trader in the UK. Under the Sale of Goods Act 1979 (as amended), anything you buy in the UK must be:

- **AS DESCRIBED** – matching any description given either by the seller or stated on the packaging, label or advert, including any pictures of the item.
- **FIT FOR THE PURPOSE INTENDED** – either its general purpose or any specific use that you explained you needed when you bought it.
- **OF SATISFACTORY QUALITY** – this means that, unless specified at the time of sale, the item should be in good condition, of reasonable appearance and finish, safe to use, free from faults or defects, and should last for a reasonable time.

In addition, if you were given a sample – for example, of a fabric or carpet – the goods supplied must match this.

If you buy something that doesn't fulfil these conditions, you have the right to reject the item and demand your money back – you don't have to accept a repair or replacement. You must, however, act within a reasonable time.

What is considered 'reasonable' will depend on the circumstances. If a pair of shoes leaks the first time you wear them in the rain, for instance, this suggests they're not fit for their purpose; if you wore them when you got caught in a flood, on the other hand, it may not be reasonable to complain. Neither can the seller be held responsible for normal wear and tear or for misuse, such as wearing a pair of loafers for hiking.

CHANGING YOUR MIND

You do not have the right to return an item just because you've made a mistake – for example, if it's the wrong size or colour – or because you've changed your mind or found the same item on sale cheaper

Companies are obliged to collect any heavy delivered items you need to return.

Taking effective action on faulty goods

t's upsetting and frustrating when new products break or go wrong – but you don't just have to accept that you've made a bad purchase. Read through the advice below to find out what you can do to ensure a satisfactory outcome.

● It's up to you to take small items back to the shop.

● For bulky or heavy items that had to be delivered, call the company and explain the problem. If you have the right to return it, the company is obliged to collect it.

● If a problem develops in the first six months and the item should have lasted that long, ask for a refund, or a replacement if you prefer.

● You can't ask for a refund if you have altered or modified the goods in any way, or if you have used them in a manner for which they were not intended.

● After six months and for up to six years, if goods develop a fault or don't last as long as you think they should, request a repair, replacement or partial refund.

● You can't ask for compensation to cover expected wear and tear (such as scuffing on a pair of shoes).

● You have the same rights with sale goods as with any others. However, you can't complain about faults that were, or should have been, apparent when you bought the item – such as a scratch on a display model offered at a reduced price.

● A shop cannot insist that you provide a receipt, but it is entitled to ask for proof that you bought the item from them. Any documentary evidence such as a credit card slip or statement should be acceptable.

● Your contract is with the person who sold you the goods, not with the manufacturer, so you don't have to claim under a guarantee or warranty – although it may be quicker and easier to do so. Your rights against the seller remain even after a guarantee or warranty has expired.

● Most sellers are reasonable, but if you have problems, write to the company head office or talk to the trading standards office of your local council.

somewhere else. Shops that agree to a refund or exchange in these circumstances are doing so as a courtesy. However, many major chains have a returns policy under which you can return unused goods within a specified time for a refund or replacement. Be sure to check the small print on your receipt or, even better, on the shop's literature or website before you buy. It's also a good idea to keep the original packaging for a while after you buy an item, in case you do decide to return it – this is a condition of some stores' returns policy.

Even if the time during which you can reject the goods outright and request a refund has passed, you may be able to claim compensation if an item does not live up to expectations. This usually means you can expect a repair or replacement, or a partial refund to reflect the use that you have had from it. In addition, under European legislation, for six months after you buy an item, it's up to the seller to prove that the item was not faulty when purchased or could not be expected to last that long. After this, the buyer must show that this was the case – but you still have rights for up to six years after purchase.

HAZARDOUS GOODS

What should you do if something you've bought has injured you or someone in your family, or caused damage to your property? You may be able to claim compensation or damages under the Consumer Protection Act. For example, if a new toaster bursts into flames and

If you buy something that injures someone in your family, you may be able to claim compensation.

sets fire to your kitchen, you can claim for the costs of repairing the damage (as well as a refund or replacement for the toaster). Alternatively, if you or a family member is hurt by a faulty item, you could potentially sue the seller or the manufacturer for compensation for the injury.

In these cases, you have up to ten years after the item was purchased, and up to three years from the date of an injury, in which to start the claim. You will need to be able to show that the product was inherently faulty and was therefore not as safe as might reasonably be expected, and that this directly caused any damage or injury. You must also be able to demonstrate that you didn't contribute to the problem by misusing the item (for example, by adding a homemade funnel to a hairdryer to direct the heat or overriding a safety cut-out feature).

An independent report by, say, an electrician can often help to prove a claim for damage due to faulty goods, and this may persuade the company responsible to pay compensation without the need for further action. In addition, it's often possible – and may be simpler – to claim under your household insurance policy instead.

Claims for injury tend to be more complicated, and you will probably need to take legal advice. Many solicitors offer a free consultation to discuss personal injury cases. Alternatively, household insurance policies often include legal protection insurance (if yours doesn't, this is something worth looking into). If so, this will usually mean you can discuss your claim with an expert and, if there's a good chance of you winning, the insurance company will cover the cost of a solicitor to handle the whole thing. You should also report dangerous products to your local trading standards office.

DID YOU KNOW? ?

USE A CREDIT CARD FOR MAJOR PURCHASES

If you buy goods or services costing more than £100 on a credit card, under the Consumer Credit Act 1974 the card company is jointly liable if there are any problems. This means that you can still get your money back even if the company concerned stops trading. But be sure to pay off the credit card at the end of the month to avoid paying interest.

UNSOLICITED GOODS

If someone sends you goods that you haven't ordered, you don't have to return them or pay for them. It's illegal for a company to try to charge for unsolicited goods. If this happens, contact the trading standards office of your local council.

DISTANCE SELLING

When you buy goods over the internet, by telephone, through a TV shopping channel or from a mail-order catalogue – often called distance selling – you have extra rights, on top of your ordinary rights as a buyer, as long as the goods originated in Europe. These include a seven-day 'cooling-off' period, during which you can cancel the order. This extends to three months if you're not given information about your right to cancel.

Goods need to be returned in the same condition in which you received them, and you should get a refund within 30 days. These rules do not apply to internet auctions, perishable goods, newspapers or magazines, however, or to computer software, DVDs or audio recordings if the product has been opened or the seal broken.

get what you pay for

Shoddy workmanship can be particularly upsetting, as it tends to be costly to put right as well as harder to undo. Although you still have legal protection in the same way that you do against faulty goods, it can be much more difficult to enforce your rights. That's why there are so many horror stories about cowboy builders, responsible for an estimated 100,000 complaints to trading standards offices each year.

Your rights, though, are clear. Under the Supply of Goods and Services Act 1982, tradespersons must carry out a service:
● With reasonable care and skill.
● Within a reasonable time (unless otherwise agreed).
● At a reasonable cost (unless a fee has been agreed in advance).

Of course, one person's idea of what's 'reasonable' may differ from another's, so you may have to argue your case. In general, it comes down to whether the service is what you expected. Examples of unreasonable service might include newly fitted windows that don't close properly or a plumbing job that cost five times what your neighbour paid for a similar piece of work.

If the service isn't satisfactory, you're entitled either to claim compensation, which may include putting right the work or rectifying any damage, or to cancel the contract. Not only that; any goods supplied in the course of the service must be (as with the Sale of Goods Act) as described, of satisfactory quality and fit for their purpose. Otherwise, you're entitled to a repair, replacement or compensation. (See opposite for advice on what to do if you need to make a claim against a supplier.)

Making light work
of poor services

There are clear steps you can take when you feel a supplier hasn't fulfilled a contract. Knowing your rights will help you to stand your ground if a dispute does arise, and save you undue worry.

● If work isn't completed satisfactorily, explain to the supplier why you're unhappy and ask that the work be completed in a specified time or the defects put right. Alternatively, request that the price be adjusted to what is reasonable for what has been done.

● If a problem comes to light later on, contact the supplier and ask for the defect to be remedied or repaired, or request that any faulty goods or materials be replaced.

● If the supplier isn't helpful and you need to have repair work done, ask the repairer to give a statement of what was wrong and what was needed to put it right. Keep copies of all estimates, invoices and receipts.

● If necessary, you can claim against the supplier for the cost of putting right defective work, replacing substandard goods and materials, and perhaps any consequential loss that has directly resulted.

● Send the estimates or bills to the supplier with a letter explaining what you want done or how much you expect in compensation.

● If you're not satisfied with the response, contact your local trading standards office or Citizens Advice Bureau for advice (see *Resources* on page 242).

● If you get nowhere pursuing the supplier, you can take action against them for compensation of up to £5,000, as a small claim through the county court. This is relatively inexpensive and you don't need a solicitor – your local Citizens Advice Bureau can advise you on how to make a claim. If the claim is worth more than this, you may need legal advice.

● If you pursue a claim, you may have to get an independent report to prove that the problem was due to faulty workmanship.

● You can claim against a supplier of services for a period of up to six years after the work was carried out.

Don't do
business with
doorstep sellers

DOORSTEP SELLING – DON'T FALL FOR IT

In general, it's best not to enter into any negotiations with strangers who call unannounced, whether they're trying to sell you something, conduct a 'survey' or persuade you to change service providers. They could be offering substandard, unsafe or stolen goods. They may – rarely – even be 'casing' your house for a burglary, or distracting you while an accomplice gains access elsewhere.

It's not unknown for unsolicited salespeople to use tactics such as heavy persuasion or even aggression to coerce you into signing up for expensive goods and services (such as double glazing) that you may not need. If you have given in to pressurising tactics just to get rid of an unwanted doorstep seller, don't panic. Legally, you have an automatic seven-day 'cooling-off' period – as with distance selling – to change your mind about contracts signed at home following an unsolicited visit. During this time, you can cancel the contract

TRY THIS! ✔

SEND LETTERS BY RECORDED DELIVERY

In any negotiation or dispute, it's important to keep copies of all invoices, bills, letters and other paperwork. When you need to write or send anything to a trader, supplier or public official, send it by recorded delivery, so that the person or organisation cannot deny having received it and you can prove when it arrived.

and ask for any deposit to be returned. If you also signed a finance agreement to pay for the service, the company must send you a letter setting out its terms, and you have a further five days from receipt of the letter in which to cancel it.

A door-to-door salesperson is supposed to inform you of your right to cancel. If you weren't informed in a written or durable form such as fax, letter, contract, catalogue, advertisement or email, the contract is automatically invalid, and the company is in breach of the law and could be fined. Report the company to your local trading standards department.

You also have the right to cancel even if you asked a salesperson to return at an agreed time later, following an unsolicited visit, letter or telephone call. However, you don't have these rights if you initiated the first contact – for example, if you asked a firm to visit to quote for new carpets.

DON'T

DEFEATING DODGY DOORSTEPPERS

The best way to defeat dodgy doorsteppers is to avoid them in the first place. Here are some tips to help you to banish them from your life:

● Make it a general rule never to do business at the door.

● Don't open the door to strangers without the chain on (if you don't have a chain, get one).

● Get a door sticker that states something like 'No unsolicited callers, please' (available from many councils and police forces) and display it prominently.

● Don't forget to check the ID of any unknown callers, especially if you need to let them into your house (for example, meter-readers).

COLD CALLERS AND JUNK MAIL

Another irritation of modern life is having mountains of unwanted 'junk' mail pushed through your letterbox – an estimated 17.5 billion pieces of junk mail are produced in the UK every year. Then there's being disturbed by the telephone in the middle of a meal or a television programme only to find it's someone trying to sell you something. There are remedies:

● Tell all organisations you deal with that you do not wish to be contacted for marketing purposes.

● When filling in forms, look for information about being sent further 'offers' from that company or third parties. If the latter, this may mean that your details will be sold on. Responsible companies will ask you to opt in before passing on your details; usually you can at least tick a box to opt out – read the small print carefully.

● Make your telephone number ex-directory.

- If someone 'cold-calls' you, don't allow any conversation; just insist that they remove your details from their database.
- Register with the Mailing Preference Service (see *Resources* on page 242) to remove your details from direct mailing lists. The service is free and should abolish 95 per cent of marketing junk.
- Register with the Telephone Preference Service (see *Resources*). This is also free and should reduce cold calls by around 85 per cent.
- If you're responsible for the estate of someone who has died, register with the Bereavement Register (see *Resources*) to stop the flow of commercial mail to the deceased person.

DON'T

BE WISE TO FRAUDSTERS

To avoid falling prey to dubious traders, whether doorstep salesmen, telephone cold callers, unknown internet sellers, leaflet advertisers or just a bloke down the pub:
- Don't feel pressured into signing or buying anything because you want to be 'polite'.
- Don't do business with anyone who does not provide a proper address (not a PO box number) and a landline telephone number.
- Don't pay for services in advance or in cash.
- Don't give out bank account or credit card details unless you are absolutely sure that the company is reputable.
- Don't send credit card details by email or via websites that aren't secure (look for 'https' at the start of the address and a padlock symbol in the top or bottom right-hand corner).
- Don't feel pressured into agreeing to a deal that's only available 'today' or similar.
- Don't be intimidated into agreeing to additional items or work on top of what was originally agreed.
- Don't fall into the trap of calling premium-rate telephone numbers (starting 09) – they can cost 50p per minute or more.

UTILITY COMPANIES

Did you know that if you have a power cut, you may also be able to claim for unwanted effects, such as food in your fridge and freezer going off? Or that you can also claim if you took time off work to wait in for an engineer who failed to turn up at the appointed time?

All utility companies must meet certain standards and should pay compensation if your supply is lost for more than a certain time. How long that is depends on which service is involved, whether you were given advance notice, and what the cause is. Companies are not responsible for events beyond their control, such as lightning strikes. For example, while you shouldn't be without water for more than 4 hours for a planned interruption, this extends to between 12 and 48 hours for an unforeseen problem, such as a burst water main.

You may have an additional claim against a utility company if you can show that a problem was due to lack of reasonable care or skill. If you have raised a complaint with a utility company and are not satisfied with their response, contact Consumer Direct (see *Resources* on page 242), which may refer your complaint to the energy regulator OFGEM. Be aware, however, that you will have to call a higher-rate phone number.

public services

As with any other service, you have specific rights when it comes to healthcare and education provisions.

HEALTHCARE: YOUR RIGHTS AS A PATIENT

Many people hesitate to question or challenge their doctor, even if they aren't happy with the quality of care they're receiving. Feeling that your healthcare needs aren't being met can be a cause of stress in itself, so it's vital to know what you can and cannot expect. You have the right to:

● Register with an NHS GP, or change your GP when you wish. A GP does not have to accept you, however, and can remove you from the practice list without giving a reason. If necessary, your local health authority will allocate you a GP.

EXPERT VIEW

WHAT TO DO IF YOU HAVE A PROBLEM WITH HEALTHCARE

If you're not happy with certain aspects of healthcare you've received, you don't have to grin and bear it. Instead, take the following steps to put it right.

1 Explain what's wrong to the GP, practice manager or hospital practitioner involved. An informal approach often resolves the problem.

2 If you're not satisfied, make a formal complaint, either direct to the responsible organisation or to the local Primary Care Trust (PCT). Every NHS organisation must have a formal complaints procedure. After an investigation, you should receive an explanation and, if appropriate, an apology.

3 If you're still not happy, refer your complaint to the independent Parliamentary and Health Service Ombudsman (see *Resources*, page 242).

You can get help and support with a complaint from the Patient Advice and Liaison Service (PALS; see *Resources* on page 242). Report a doctor to the General Medical Council (see *Resources*) if his or her actions represent professional misconduct or suggest that the doctor's fitness to practise may be impaired in any way.

In addition, you can sue for an injury resulting from a health professional's negligence; for this you will need professional legal advice. You may receive compensation.

- Be assessed and treated according to accepted standards of care.
- Be informed of significant risks of any proposed treatment, and of other options.
- Be referred to a specialist if your GP thinks that your condition warrants it.
- Have all of your consultations kept confidential and the details disclosed only to those directly involved in your care, except in exceptional circumstances.
- Ask for a second opinion. This request does not have to be granted, but a refusal must be reasonable.
- See or have a copy of your medical records, in most circumstances. (There may be a fee for this.)
- Give birth at home if you choose.
- Refuse any medical treatment or intervention, at the time or in advance, provided you are legally competent to do so. You cannot, however, insist on receiving a particular treatment.

HELPING HAND

10 WAYS TO ASSERT YOURSELF WHEN FACED WITH BUREAUCRACY

Few people enjoy confrontation, but you're far more likely to handle it well if you know what your rights are. Follow these tips and give it a try:

1 Stay calm and polite at all times, both verbally and in writing.

2 As soon as you're aware of a problem, start a log. Note what has happened, dates, times, names of people you speak to and outcomes of conversations. Keep all documentary evidence.

3 Know your rights – if possible, research where you stand first.

4 Decide what outcome you want – for example, an apology, a change to the system, a problem rectified, compensation.

5 If possible, start by explaining your problem directly to the person involved. Often matters can be resolved informally.

6 If you don't succeed with the person you first speak to, ask to talk to a manager or supervisor.

7 Ask about a formal complaints procedure – most large organisations have one.

8 If initial approaches don't work, write a formal letter to the person or organisation involved. Keep copies of all correspondence.

9 Make sure you send all correspondence by recorded post.

10 Ask for help when necessary. Citizens Advice Bureaus (see *Resources* on page 242) can help with most issues, or will be able to suggest other sources of advice.

EDUCATION: YOUR RIGHTS AS A PARENT

All parents want the best for their children, and making sure they get the best education available is often a top priority. You have the right to free education for your children, suitable for their age, ability, aptitude and any special needs they may have, from the start of the term after their fifth birthday until June of the school year in which they turn 16.

But your child's education can also be a major source of worry. Will they get a place at your choice of school? How do you keep track of their progress? What if you're not happy with the method of teaching – can you intervene? You have the right to state which school you'd like your child to attend, and – if you don't get your choice – you can appeal. In addition, you are entitled to a written annual report on their progress, as well as a copy of their school record within 15 school days of a written request. You can also vote for parent governors, or stand as one yourself; that way, you can help ensure the school is being run in the pupils' best interests.

Other rights include being given 24 hours' notice in writing of a detention out of hours. You can also remove your child from certain lessons, such as religious and sex education. If you're not happy, make a complaint – to the child's teacher, headteacher, board of governors or, in extreme situations, the Local Government Ombudsman. You also have the right to educate your child at home, but must ensure that they receive a full-time education from the age of five.

Make sure your children get the best education possible.

Legal problems

Your home is your territory, the place where you most expect to feel safe. Anything that threatens that environment feels like a personal attack and upsets your sense of security. Whether you're faced with noisy neighbours, encroaching tree roots or an attempted burglary, knowing your legal rights will help put you back in control.

neighbours who drive you nuts

Getting on well with neighbours can greatly enhance your sense of belonging to a community and thus increase your overall satisfaction with life. Neighbour disputes, on the other hand, can make life a misery. The biggest stress factor is noise. Almost one in three people claim to be bothered by it at some stage, and one in twelve describe noisy neighbours as a serious problem. Selfish neighbours who play loud music into the small hours can drive you crazy. Other common sources of nuisance noise include shouting and arguments, banging and machinery, children, dogs barking, motor vehicles, and car and house alarms.

Perhaps your problems concern overhanging trees, arguments about shared amenities (such as who's responsible for a blocked drain), access to a neighbour's property in order to carry out repairs, boundary disputes or conflicts about parking? All are common sources of contention.

If you have a problem with your neighbours, the best initial course of action is simply to talk to them. Most people are reasonable, so stay calm and explain what the problem is, and see if you can reach a solution that satisfies both of you. Your neighbour may not even be aware that there is an issue, so a friendly approach could put things right quickly. If not, don't become hostile or aggressive; if you need to take things further, it could count against you if you've resorted to insults and expletives, especially in writing. If polite requests don't work, other options include:

● If your neighbours are in rented accommodation, contact the landlord – they may be in breach of their tenancy agreement.

● In local authority accommodation, talk to the council, which has powers to act against antisocial tenants.

● Contact your local Citizens Advice Bureau for help and advice on any type of neighbour dispute (see *Resources* on page 242). Advice is free.

- Use a mediation service (see right).
- Contact your local authority about noise complaints, intrusive trees and hedges (see overleaf) and breaches of planning rules.
- Talk to your house insurers if a neighbour's building work affects your property – they may cover the damage and claim the costs back from your neighbour's insurers.
- Apply to the court for an order to entitle you to enter your neighbour's property to carry out repair work to your own. Talk to a solicitor or Citizens Advice Bureau for help on how to do this.
- Take legal advice about boundary disputes or damage to property.
- Contact the police if your neighbour's behaviour is violent, aggressive or causes damage to property. Graffiti 'artists', for instance, may be liable for criminal damage, and your local council may clean up any markings that are judged to be racially, sexually or otherwise offensive.

TRY THIS!

MEDIATION

This involves a third party who listens to both sides of a story and tries to help parties to reach agreement. Although mediation costs money, it's usually far cheaper – and quicker – than going to court. Mediation may be provided free for those on state benefits.

Some local councils offer mediation services, or you can contact UK Mediation or the National Mediation Helpline (see *Resources* on page 242). Note that you will have to call a higher-rate phone number.

NOISE

Research increasingly links chronic noise exposure to a range of health problems, including heart disease, stroke, high blood pressure, headaches, fatigue and peptic ulcers. This is thought to be at least partly because

Health problems have now been linked to chronic noise exposure.

If your neighbour won't cut overhanging branches, you have the right to do it yourself.

intrusive noise increases our levels of stress hormones, even while we're asleep. So even if you manage to drop off during your neighbour's late-night party or while their TV or stereo is blaring until the small hours, your health is still at risk.

Your local council's environmental health department can investigate whether noise constitutes a nuisance. If so, and your neighbour does not respond to requests to tone it down, they can serve an abatement notice. Failure to comply with its terms can lead to a hefty fine. You are especially entitled to peace and quiet at night. Under the Noise Act 1996, it is an offence to make excessive noise between 11pm and 7am, and if the person responsible does not respond to a warning notice, the local authority can not only fine the offender but also confiscate any music or other noise-making equipment.

TREES AND HEDGES

It's easy to understand why tall trees and hedges are a common source of neighbour disputes. For one thing, encroaching trees may block out some of your precious sunlight, and we all need sunlight for good health. Trees and hedges may also physically encroach onto your property, or their roots may spread onto your land, both of which can be upsetting – not least because of our natural desire to protect our own territory.

If a neighbour won't act on a polite request to trim any branches that overhang your property, you have the right to do so yourself, but only up to the boundary line. You must also give the cut branches – and any fruit – back to the neighbour. You are also entitled to remove tree roots, provided you use the least damaging method available and there isn't a tree preservation order in force.

If an evergreen or semi-evergreen hedge over 2m (6½ft) tall is blocking light to your property, you may be able to submit an official complaint to the local council, under the 'high hedges' law (Part 8 of the Anti-Social Behaviour Act 2003). You must have made every reasonable effort to settle the matter with your neighbour first, and the council may charge a non-refundable fee. If your complaint is upheld, the council can order your neighbour to reduce the height of the hedge. For more advice, visit the website of the campaigning site Hedgeline (see *Resources* on page 242).

In addition, if you think a neighbour's tree poses a danger, you can ask your local authority to inspect it and intervene if necessary.

keeping your home safe

Protecting your home so that it's less likely you'll experience a break-in is the best way to ensure peace of mind. If your home is clearly well defended, a burglar will usually opt for an easier target elsewhere. What's more, it doesn't need to cost the earth. Here are some tips on keeping your home secure:

- Make sure your front door is secured by a five-lever mortise deadlock, and that all your downstairs windows, or any that are easily accessible, have security locks.
- Lock all the doors and windows whenever you go out and when you go to bed at night. Don't leave doors or ground-floor windows open, even if you're at home or in the garden.
- Don't leave keys in obvious places, such as under an outside doormat or plant pot, or hanging inside the letterbox.
- Join your Neighbourhood Watch scheme. If there isn't one, think about starting one.
- Install movement-activated security lights on your front drive and in any side or rear areas that can be accessed from the road.
- Don't be a target for a distraction burglary – see the advice on page 152 on how to avoid bogus doorstep callers.
- Install a security peephole viewer in your front door so you can see who's calling.
- Fit a chain to your front door and never open the door to unannounced callers unless the chain is connected.
- Get a dog, or put up a 'Beware of the dog' sign even if you haven't got one – barking dogs are a burglar's worst enemy.

Intruders – how much force can you use to defend yourself?

In a few recent highly publicised court cases householders were prosecuted for using force against intruders. As a result many people are confused and worried about the degree of force they can legally use to defend themselves. The Crown Prosecution Service has issued a joint statement with the police to explain what you should do if faced with an intruder in your own home.

● Whenever possible, call the police.

● You may use 'reasonable force' to protect yourself or other people from attack or to prevent crime.

● You may use force only in self-defence.

● The force used must not be gratuitous or excessive.

● You do not have to wait to be attacked.

● The same rules apply if you use something to hand as a weapon.

● If the intruder runs away and you give chase, you can still use reasonable force to recover property or make an arrest, but you must not inflict deliberate injury as revenge or punishment.

● You are not expected to make fine judgments in the heat of the moment about what level of force is reasonable, as long as the force applied is only what you honestly and instinctively believe is necessary. In general, the more extreme the circumstances and the greater your fear, the more force you can lawfully use in self-defence.

● Don't leave items that are attractive to burglars or easy to snatch (such as TVs, stereos, CD players, cameras, mobile phones, car keys or jewellery cases) in clear view through the windows.

● Never leave ladders where an intruder could access them to break in – lock them away in a garage or shed.

● If you're going away, cancel milk and paper deliveries, and set lights on timers in several rooms.

● Consider installing a burglar alarm.

forewarned is forearmed

As in so many areas of life, there's much you can do to equip yourself against the multitude of issues that can threaten to destroy your peace of mind. As you've seen in this chapter, taking the time to find out about your rights and planning ahead for unforeseen eventualities are just two ways of restoring your equilibrium. Most importantly, if you make sure you tackle your concerns directly rather than burying your head in the sand, this will help to protect your mental health and increase your confidence in yourself.

7 nearest and dearest

Loving relationships with friends and family can be a powerful antidote to everyday stresses and strains. Conversely, falling out with your nearest and dearest can be a source of great tension. This chapter looks at the inevitable ups and downs of family life, and offers strategies for coping and creating harmony at home, as well as advice on how to communicate better with those around you. It also addresses issues faced by people living alone and includes tips on recovering from break-ups, building new relationships and forming new interests.

Successful relationships matter

Never underestimate the importance of building friendships and close relationships with your family. Both can provide invaluable emotional support and happiness throughout your life, as well as numerous health benefits – including fewer colds and lower blood pressure. Researchers have also found that those of us who have close bonds with other people or good personal support systems succumb less often to stress and stress-related illnesses than people who feel isolated and unsupported. What matters is not necessarily how many people we have in our lives – rather, it's the quality of our connections. Studies also show that the emotional support we get from friends and loved ones has a positive effect on our cardiovascular, hormonal and immune systems, as well as lowering blood pressure and cholesterol, and ultimately helping us to live longer.

Although we all need some periods alone to be ourselves, it's important to recognise the benefits of making time to nurture our relationships. Here's why.

give and take

When you feel particularly stressed, it's a common reaction to cut yourself off from other people, often because you feel unable to respond to others. This can become a vicious circle: the more you cut yourself off, the more isolated you feel, and even less forthcoming. But in doing so you also deprive yourself of what others could offer you. In fact, when you ask for support you make the people in your life feel valuable and useful, and they'll also feel able to turn to you when they are troubled.

Many of us take our relationships for granted, especially those with the people closest to us. We often expect them to flourish without much

EXPERT VIEW

FRIENDS YOU CAN RELY ON

Creating supportive networks of people around you is sensible life-management, as well as being a wise investment in your future. In today's uncertain world, many things you rely on for your sense of identity and wellbeing (job, home, lifestyle) could suddenly be lost, but strong relationships usually hold firm and, in times of crisis, can provide the most reliable source of comfort and security.

thought or creative input, whereas in reality they need attention, to prevent them from wilting and dying.

A FRIEND IN NEED

Research indicates that many men under pressure withdraw, become uncommunicative and bottle things up, whereas women in stressful situations are more likely to expand and take on more and more responsibility, channelling their stress into displacement activities that can exhaust them unnecessarily. Both responses are extreme and add to the problem rather than resolving it.

This is where friends and relations can be helpful. They may be able to offer a clearer insight into your situation and persuade you to take it a bit easier, or help you talk through what's worrying you. When you feel things getting on top of you, try to see your relationships as resources on which to draw. Don't try to stand alone.

DID YOU KNOW? ?

FRIENDS KEEP YOU HEALTHY

One research study of 2,300 men with heart disease showed that those with a highly stressful lifestyle and few friends were six times more likely to die prematurely than those with less stress in their lives and many friends. This study was documented in the book *The Doctor's Heart Attack Recovery Plan* by David Lewis and John Storey. Many similar studies have found that friends and supportive relationships are significant contributing factors in recovery from illness. One recent ten-year study, conducted for a BBC programme and overseen by professor of science and politician Lord Winston, found that, for men, having no friends poses more of a serious health risk even than smoking.

GOOD RELATIONSHIPS GIVE

- A sense of belonging
- Confidence
- Support
- Increased resistance to stress
- Emotional security
- Encouragement
- Feelings of self-worth
- Stimulation
- Joy and contentment
- A place to express emotions
- Fun
- Recreation and relaxation

BAD RELATIONSHIPS CAUSE

- Depression
- Anxiety
- Social isolation
- Erosion of confidence
- Decreased resistance to stress
- Emotional deprivation
- Feelings of discouragement
- Diminished self-esteem
- Negative introspection
- Tension and unhappiness
- Loneliness
- Envy of others

Continued on p168 ➤

Family time

How often have you put off having fun with your family because you don't have time? Have you ever complained you were too tired to get together or attend a social event, but found, having made the effort, that it boosted your energy and sense of happiness? Here are some suggestions for creating more 'relationship time' with your partner and your family:

● **Book 'couple time'.** It may seem unnecessarily formal, but if you put a date in your diary to be together, it means you can't book that time for anything else. If another demand crops up, you'll have a genuine reason for saying, 'I'm sorry, but I already have an engagement for that date.' Don't cancel for anything except a true emergency.

● **Make sure you arrange 'talking time'** with friends and family. Don't simply go to the cinema together, or dance and drink in crowded, noisy places, or just collapse in front of the TV, enjoyable as those activities may be.

● **Be proactive and arrange frequent get-togethers** over a plate of good food and, if you like, some wine. One of the best times to talk is when you're having a meal together round a table, whether you cook a simple supper, order a takeaway or go out to a local restaurant. This creates and strengthens bonds of friendship and community, but it has to be seen as a priority.

● **Insist that your family eat together** at the table instead of on their laps in front of TV. This may not be possible every day or evening, but aim for at least one day, or evening, a week.

● **Try to persuade your partner or children to join you** for some activities or classes that you enjoy, if your time is limited.

● **Acknowledge that the situation is temporary** and the pressure won't always be so intense during those periods when there are great demands on your time – such as caring for a baby or an elderly relative – and this will make it easier to accept. And don't try to do everything you did before your circumstances changed (see also chapter 8 for further advice).

● **Don't be a perfectionist.** When you're very busy, it's better to let your standards slip rather than your relationships. If you haven't had time to do the dusting, light some candles and the dust won't be noticeable. Don't spend time ironing underwear or sheets, or anything that will never be seen by the rest of the world.

● **Save time by having your groceries delivered.** Many companies offer free delivery on certain days. If you can't make use of the free service, paying a small delivery charge is a justifiable expense if it contributes to your quality of life, and frees up time for your relationships.

● **Let others help to free up your time.** If you have small children, ask a relative to babysit so that you can get out to meet friends for a few hours. Or ask your neighbours if any of their children want to earn extra pocket money by helping out with washing your car, mowing the lawn, weeding the garden or carrying out other chores.

● **Investigate how much it would cost to have a cleaner** for a few hours a week. Again the extra expense will be worth it if it allows you to spend more time with loved ones.

● **Enlist your children's help with household chores,** especially to work alongside you – cleaning the windows, for instance, or helping to prepare food. Older children, particularly teenagers, need their parents' time and attention, even though they may not admit it, and doing chores together can enable you to chat in a relaxed atmosphere where confidences might be shared, as well as making them feel more useful. In fact, doing work together with any family member or friend is a great way to draw closer in a natural way.

Book some 'couple time' and don't cancel for anything except a true emergency.

Communication

Good communication is central to good relationships, but it's usually the first thing to suffer when problems arise. Keeping the channels of communication open and clear is difficult if you feel upset by the actions or words of a family member, partner or friend. Honest communication can usually resolve differences or hurt feelings.

But it's during times of conflict that communication tends to break down; intense emotions affect our thought processes, so when we're upset it's very difficult to get through to other people calmly or rationally. If you find yourself getting caught up in the same old arguments with your partner, parents or children, going round in circles but getting nowhere, you might like to try a technique called 'mirroring' (see overleaf), which is now being widely used by family therapists to help couples and families learn how to communicate better.

the power of touch

Communication is not only about words. Touch is a powerful means of interaction: it can uplift, calm down or reassure someone, depending on how it's imparted. Just a light hand on someone's arm or back can give a sense of support. New scientific findings back this up. The Touch Research Institute at the University of Miami School of Medicine, for example, has carried out over 100 studies into the benefits of touch and reports many significant effects, including pain reduction.

Here are some easy ways to use touch as a stress-reliever:
● Take hold of your partner's, or child's, hand to convey reassurance and affection. Stroking his or her back is a soothing gesture, without the need for words.
● Hug your partner – it can be the best antidote to a stressful day. Physical contact relaxes you and

Hug your partner –
it can be the best
antidote to a stressful day.

brings you closer emotionally. It may even reduce your blood pressure, according to researchers at the University of North Carolina, who studied 69 premenopausal women and found that those who received the most hugs had a lower, healthier heart rate.

● If your child is finding it hard to get to sleep, gently stroke his or her forehead, then the top of the head, in a rhythmical movement. This is calming and will impart a feeling of security.

● Learn the basic techniques of massage (see *Resources* on page 242). Massaging and stroking any part of the body is a loving gesture; it relieves tension and reduces blood pressure far more effectively than words. This may be appreciated especially by elderly relatives, particularly if they live alone or are in hospital, and miss physical contact with loved ones.

● When you can't find the words, just reach out with a gentle touch: it demonstrates that you care.

think before you speak

Various sociological studies have found that the words we use when we talk to other people are the least important part of any message. These studies have reached a consensus that words carry only 7 per cent of a message, tone of voice carries 38 per cent and body language conveys 55 per cent of the sense. What's important, whether in an argument or a loving exchange, is not so much what you say as how you say it. Consider how your tone of voice can change the meaning of words: try saying the same thing gently, aggressively, loudly, angrily, softly, then humorously.

Learn to listen and talk just one at a time.

Mirroring

True listening needs to take place if difficulties in a relationship are to be resolved. Usually, the people arguing are so keen to put forward their own point of view and have their own opinions heard that they block out what the other person is saying, instead focusing on thinking up their next argument, so that they can shoot down the other person and win.

In order to have good relationships, winning is not the point. You need to make an effort to give others, including children, enough listening time to state their viewpoint and feelings – and take them seriously. For the 'mirroring' exercise to work effectively, each person has to be committed to having a good relationship, rather than having their own way. You have to be willing sometimes to see things from the other's point of view and be prepared to compromise.

If you're having trouble communicating and are unable to resolve an ongoing problem, you may benefit from trying the 'mirroring' technique:

● If you have something important to say, ask your partner to listen for an agreed amount of time, which can be 5–15 minutes, without interrupting.

● When you've finished speaking, your partner – the listener – should repeat what you said and ask for confirmation that he or she has understood correctly; this includes grasping your feelings about the problem. (The listener should not respond by justifying himself or herself, as often happens in ordinary exchanges, nor become defensive or make any reactive response to what you've just said. The only comments allowed at this point are mirroring comments.)

● The listener then speaks for the agreed amount of time without being interrupted, while you listen. You then repeat their message – again acknowledging your partner's feelings about the issue under discussion.

You don't have to find immediate solutions for what you've heard, and in fact it's usually best not to discuss what has been mirrored for at least 24 hours. Just respect what's been said, think about it, and accept that how the other person feels is real for them, even if you consider it to be nonsense, unimportant or untrue. When you do talk the issue through again, it should be easier to resolve your difficulties.

WHY MIRRORING WORKS

Fights often escalate and end up with people saying things they don't mean, veering away from the original problem. The mirroring technique turns the exchange into an information-finding situation rather than a fight about who's right or wrong, paving the way for further discussion. Even if it doesn't solve the issue in question, it kickstarts a different kind of communication which brings you closer together, whether husband and wife, parent and child, or just good friends.

If you have something important to tell someone, practise saying it in different ways beforehand, so that your tone of voice adds to the meaning of your words, rather than confusing the message. Also become aware of what your body language may be saying. You could look threatening without realising it if you're clenching your fists, hunching your shoulders, frowning or screwing up your facial muscles, or leaning forward in an overbearing manner. Check whether your body language is open and relaxed, and try not to appear defensive and inaccessible by crossing your arms across your chest, or by turning away from the other person when you're speaking.

respect

Respect is another essential component of any successful relationship. When you listen to and understand what someone else is saying you show respect for both their thoughts and their feelings – something that's often lost in personal conflicts.

It's especially important in relationships between people of different generations; everyone has a right to their point of view, even though you may not agree with it, and showing due regard for someone's opinions communicates that you value and appreciate that person. Parents usually demand that their children show them respect, but often don't return the compliment, forgetting that it has to be mutual for strong ties to flourish.

what are you really arguing about?

Arguments are not always as they appear on the surface; a seemingly trivial dispute may be masking a more important issue. Fighting over money, sex or who does most housework, for example, can often be about the fact that deeper needs are not being met. For instance, an argument about who pays for what may really be about who takes responsibility, or who has the power in a situation. Rows about housework are often about unfulfilled needs for respect and self-worth. Arguing about how often to have sex is nearly always an issue about feeling loved and cared for and the need for affection. So when the same old subject comes up again and again, ask yourself what lies behind it. Then try to address the real problem.

UNDERLYING ISSUES

Many arguments are rooted in old hurts from childhood. If a parent left when you were young, for example, you may find yourself overreacting if your partner arrives home later than expected, or suddenly announces that he or she has to go away on a business trip. The feeling behind this reaction may be a fear of being abandoned again – the real issue that needs to be addressed (see chapter 1 for more on past influences).

There is usually more going on in every relationship than meets the eye, which is why it's vital to take time to unravel the 'hot spots'. You may discover that you're fighting battles relating to the past, not the present.

Sex is one of the things we argue about most.

Money matters

Money is often a cause of conflict. You and your partner may have very different views about how to handle money and its purpose. You may be a spender, while your partner may be a saver, or vice versa. According to the UK charity Relate, more than 70 per cent of relationship breakdowns are caused by debt and money worries.

Discuss how to deal with any money issues. There's no right or wrong, but you must each feel equal in the discussion, and you need to be honest. Make financial planning an ongoing part of your relationship and be open with each other about income, and also about debts. Try these suggestions to make the financial side of life run more smoothly (see chapter 6 for further advice):

● Consider having a joint account for household bills and joint treats, such as eating out or visits to the cinema, and so on (if one of you has a smaller income, the contribution should reflect that).

● If viable, maintain individual accounts, too, which gives you some freedom and privacy. Agree that you each have the scope to spend or save your own money without needing to disclose the details, as long as you're living within your means.

● Discuss what money means for each of you – what it symbolises – and what expectations you have. Your relationship to money will probably depend on how your family regarded the subject.

● Decide who's better suited to take responsibility for paying bills, and who's prepared to shop around for the best deals.

● Plan together how you'll pay for holidays, house renovations, new furniture, car repairs and other larger expenses, so that they don't cause unnecessary rows when they arise.

Family fun

It's easy to lose the playful element in a relationship when you're struggling to keep up with the many mundane demands of daily life. But stepping back from the day-to-day stresses and allowing yourself some enjoyment can work wonders for your personal connections, and for your own sense of wellbeing.

Couples in successful relationships report that they laugh a lot. Laughter has been proven to be good for your health, and a research study carried out by psychiatrists in California reported that laughter mimics the effects of exercise; it provides a circulation boost, lowers cholesterol, reduces the levels of stress hormones, boosts the immune system and releases the feel-good chemical endorphin. Laughter and fun relax you, and put problems into perspective (see also chapter 4).

Go out after dark and gaze at the night sky.

10 ways to make your relationships happier

You'll find lots more tips on enjoying life to the full in chapter 8, but here are ten suggestions to ensure you spend special and memorable moments with your loved ones.

1 Learn to play again: this means letting go of your serious, grown-up persona and becoming childlike. There's a difference between being 'childish' and being 'childlike', and it's the latter you're aiming for. Being childlike means looking at the world through the eyes of a child – in other words, with wonder and enthusiasm.

2 Other forms of play, such as card and board games, can put you in a more lighthearted mood – providing you don't become too competitive – and are great for bonding between generations.

3 Go to the seaside and eat ice cream while walking barefoot on the beach.

4 Take regular time out from your daily routine and go for long, uplifting nature walks with your partner, children or friends, instead of sitting in a café, or at home in front of the TV. Visit local parks or gardens, or drive into the countryside to discover somewhere that can become your special place. It may even extend your life: a study conducted in Tokyo found that older people living near a green space live longer than people boxed in by concrete.

5 Hire a boat and go out on the river, or on the lake in a local park.

6 When you're outdoors, take the time to stand and stare at the natural world – at the trees, flowers, rivers, birds, butterflies, sunsets and so on. Dismiss everyday thoughts from your mind and concentrate on what your senses are experiencing. Sharing simple pleasures such as these with someone important can be as uplifting as more costly pursuits.

7 Read to each other, possibly revisiting your favourite childhood stories, or sharing thought-provoking or humorous books.

8 If you ferry children around a lot, try singing with them in the car. This keeps their spirits up and distracts them from fighting with each other. Singing is also very good for preventing car-sickness in children, as it makes them breathe deeply.

9 Get friends and family together and encourage them to gather round the piano (or play instruments) for a sing-song instead of endless talking.

10 When you're in the country, go out after dark with your partner or children and gaze at the night sky, at the stars and the moon. Instead of taking these phenomena for granted, really look and marvel at the vastness of space. Learning the different star constellations could also be fun.

happiness is catching

Researchers from Harvard Medical School and the University of California, San Diego, have found that happiness is not necessarily an innate attitude you're lucky enough to be born with – it's more to do with the social group around you. They maintain that happiness is a collective phenomenon that spreads through social networks like an emotional virus.

The study, which looked at the happiness of nearly 5,000 individuals over a period of 20 years, found that when a person becomes happy, the network effect can be measured up to three degrees. This means that one person's happiness triggers a chain reaction that benefits not only their friends, but their friends' friends, and their friends' friends' friends. The effect is not fleeting, but lasts for up to a year.

However, our ability to influence others appears to stretch to three degrees only, and the closer people are to us in geographical terms, the stronger the effect. So your influence is greatest among those living in the same house, but also affects your closest neighbours as well as family members or friends living nearby.

It's not surprising that children brought up in happy households tend to have a sunny disposition and a positive outlook on life. The more you can surround yourself with happy people, therefore, the better you feel and – according to this study – the better your health will be. So making yourself happy is not self-centred indulgence; rather, if you're happy, you'll actually exert an important influence on those around you.

Interestingly, the converse does not seem to be the case: sadness was not found to spread through social networks as robustly as happiness, giving lie to the old adage 'misery loves company'.

HELPING HAND

HOW TO KEEP FRIENDSHIPS STRONG

You'll reap the benefits if you work on strengthening your friendships. Don't forget that each time you put yourself out for your friends, or show them affection, you're adding to, and deepening, the relationship. Here are some key things to aim for:

● Remember your friends' birthdays – send cards or flowers on special anniversaries.

● Write or call to say 'thank you'. This shows you don't take your friends for granted.

● Arrange regular celebrations. Getting together for a happy event reinforces the positive aspects of your relationship.

● Listen to their troubles – a true gesture of friendship. Limit the amount of time you spend on negative issues, though.

● Try to remember your friends' good points when you feel irritated or frustrated with them, and if you fall out be the first to say 'sorry'.

When relationships are strained

Outside influences often place stress on otherwise healthy relationships. Interference from extended family members, for example, is a well-known cause of emotional strain. In response, it's common to take out our frustrations or anxieties on our nearest and dearest, when we should instead be turning to them for comfort and support. If this sounds familiar, take steps to avoid reacting in ways that might damage your core relationships. The tips that follow can also be applied to dealing with unwanted interference in general.

coping with interfering in-laws

You may be among the lucky people who get on well with their in-laws, but this is often a difficult relationship for all concerned. You can choose a partner but you can't be sure you'll like his or her parents or other family members. Here's how to make the best of the situation:

● **Respect others' values.** Many conflicts are rooted in differences between your own and your partner's upbringing. Your in-laws will have had their own particular rules, routines and attitudes, which they assume to be right, and which could be very different from those of your family. If you accept from the outset that your in-laws may think that their values are being disregarded or undervalued, causing them to feel threatened, you'll be less distressed than if you interpret their attitudes or criticisms as an attack on you personally.

● **Unite.** Certain sensitive areas, such as how to bring up your children, how to share the household chores, how to spend your income, where you take your holidays or who pays for what, can lead to family disagreements. It will take patience to stick to your guns and slowly demonstrate that you and your partner have your own thoughts and opinions about these subjects. It's important to present a united front. If you are gently firm about how you choose to conduct your own family life, eventually your in-laws on either side will have to accept your approach.

● **Make your own way.** Many parents think their children's lives should be a replay of their own, and they're often reluctant to relinquish their influence or relevance. Try to explain gently that they did things their way, but now you're doing things your way.

● **Have clear boundaries.** In-laws may unconsciously feel rejected, as their once-loving child turns to someone else for comfort and even advice. If you can, try to make them feel loved and needed, but be firm about your own boundaries.

● **Be flexible.** You and your partner need to agree about what you can shrug off, or laugh about together, and which interferences or criticisms you won't accept. Discuss how best to deal tactfully, but firmly, with sensitive areas. And be prepared to compromise from time to time.

● **Communicate.** You might need to work on your communication skills to avoid inadvertently offending or hurting your parents or in-laws. The advice on pages 168–172 should help.

Family celebrations needn't be stressful if they are planned well.

how to enjoy
family celebrations

Christmas and other family occasions – weddings, anniversaries, birthdays, bar mitzvahs, graduation celebrations, to name a few – can be very stressful and sometimes end with everyone longing to get away from each other. We often have such huge expectations of these events that we're bound to be disappointed. But it needn't be like that if you follow a few simple guidelines.

MAKE A PLAN

One of the most important ingredients for a successful occasion is good planning. Make sure everyone knows exactly what's expected: what to wear, who else is being invited, how long the celebrations will continue and what kind of day or evening is planned – for example, a sit-down lunch, a buffet supper or a formal dinner followed by dancing or a karaoke session. Will there be speeches? Who will make them? And so on.

Plan the timings for each part of the day. A structure makes people feel more comfortable than leaving things open and vague. The more you organise people at a large family gathering, the less likely it is that feuds and arguments will break out.

CRACKING CHRISTMAS

Christmas attracts the highest expectations, and can therefore lead to the greatest let-down. People are often together for a long time on Christmas Day, so there's always the risk that some may drink and eat too much, and become tired and quarrelsome. That's why it's a good idea to plan an activity for after the main meal. It could be playing charades or some other team game, listening to music and dancing, or you could lay out a number of board games so that people can drift off into separate groups to play against each other.

Your family tradition will dictate when you have the present-giving ceremony. If you're having your main Christmas meal at lunchtime, it's advisable to save most of the presents until afterwards, so there's another exciting event to look forward to when things might begin to fall flat. The children could be allowed to open one or two presents before lunch,

Christmas attracts the highest expectations, but can also lead to the greatest let-down.

and the rest afterwards. This helps stop them becoming overwhelmed all at once, and ensures they have plenty to occupy them until bedtime. They will also be more likely to drop easily into an exhausted sleep. And, if things don't turn out as you'd hoped, remind yourself that it will all be over tomorrow, and that you have to sustain your goodwill for only a few hours.

Holiday hell

Holidays are another potential cause of strained relationships. We have high expectations of what we'll get out of a holiday – a chance to relax, have fun and perhaps reawaken our romantic passions – and it sometimes feels like a catastrophe if it fails to deliver. Here are some tips on avoiding holiday hell.

● **Research your trip thoroughly.** Look it up on the internet or search through holiday brochures first – don't just accept a friend's recommendation. If you book by phone, it'll give you the opportunity to ask questions. The website TripAdvisor includes travellers' reviews of many holiday destinations.

● **Discuss what each of you expects.** If you want to lie on a beach all day but your partner wants activity, choose a destination that can fulfil both your needs. Try to accommodate each other.

● **Be realistic.** Finding yourselves together for 24 hours a day may be stressful if you're not used to it (Relate reports increased business every September after couples return from holiday). If you fear this, don't stay in an isolated villa; make sure there are other people to interact with. Arrange periods away from each other, so that you look forward to meeting up for the evening.

● **Go prepared.** Camping, for example, may seem like an exciting adventure, but it can turn into a nightmare of damp clothes and even damper spirits. Make sure you have the right equipment in case the weather turns bad, and check out your campsite carefully; facilities vary widely.

● **Consider children's needs.** Small children are usually happy with a bucket and spade on a beach, but older children are likely to want more action, especially at night. If age groups vary, opt for an all-inclusive holiday village that offers varied activities.

● **Take a trip to the coast.** Seaside locations provide sporting opportunities as well as reading and sunbathing for the less active. An added bonus is the healthy sea air, which is highly charged with negative ions that boost energy and have been found to stimulate the body's healing processes (see chapter 9 for more information).

● **Avoid getting worked up.** Make a pact with your family that there will be no arguments. Try to sink into a laid-back holiday mood as quickly as possible. If you see conflict brewing, suggest an activity to dispel the tension.

● **Leave work at home.** Don't endlessly check emails – just enjoy the present moment and your current surroundings. Refresh your *joie de vivre*.

● **Keep your sense of humour.** If things go wrong, it might feel catastrophic at the time, but disastrous holidays often end up becoming amusing anecdotes years later.

Small children are usually happy at the beach.

little angels or
little monsters?

The key to creating harmony in all relationships, but especially those involving children, is patience. Children learn how to behave from the people around them, so adults need to demonstrate tolerance and understanding. As a parent, the way you cope with everyday problems inevitably sets an example, affecting your children's reactions, and not just in later life – it starts with the pressures of school, exams, peer pressure, popularity issues and, sometimes, bullying (see opposite).

● **Don't react.** If your children are being disruptive or unmanageable, don't react too quickly to their behaviour. Try instead to understand what's causing it. Sometimes, it's when children are at their worst that they most need loving care and attention – even though you may feel it's the point when they least deserve it.

● **Ignore bad behaviour.** Experts recommend that you reward good behaviour in very young children with praise and encouragement and a hug or kiss, if appropriate, and that bad behaviour is mostly ignored. Focusing on what the child has done wrong tends to reinforce it and give it too much importance. Providing the behaviour is not too alarming, take no notice, as this indicates your lack of interest; because it doesn't provoke a reaction, the child will probably abandon it. Rewarding good behaviour, on the other hand, means you're likely to get more of it.

● **Practise the art of distraction.** With small children, one of the best ways to change a type of behaviour is to distract them with something else. If a child won't share a particular toy with a friend, for example, pick up another toy and talk about it with enthusiasm – make it do a dance or sing a song. He or she will soon lose interest in the first toy.

- **Walk away.** If your child has a temper tantrum, walk away as if you hadn't noticed. Don't go too far, as you may alarm your child, but then casually turn round and ask a question, or make a remark, about something totally unrelated, as if the tantrum wasn't happening. Children usually come out of a tantrum quite

quickly if you don't inflame the situation by getting angry. If your child is screaming, don't respond by shouting – this simply escalates the emotion. Of course, it's difficult to keep control if you're very tired or feeling particularly pressured, but try to avoid taking your feelings out on your child. If it all gets too much, you can call the UK family-support charity Parentline Plus for advice (see *Resources* on page 242).

- **Take time out.** A simple technique, if you're tired and stressed, is to sit down with your child and watch a TV programme together. This gives you a rest but still maintains the closeness between you. Alternatively, lie on a bed or sofa with the child and read a story together, or lie on the floor and draw with lots of coloured crayons and large sheets of paper (lining paper for walls is ideal, and inexpensive).

beating the bullies

Although bullying has received much attention in recent years, many children – and adults – still find it hard to admit they're being bullied. Carrying this burden can cause personality and behavioural changes, especially in children; key signs are the child becoming more subdued, seeming less confident, withdrawing into themselves or spending more time alone. (For advice on bullying in the workplace, see chapter 10.)

Here are some steps to enable you to help a child who's being bullied:

- If you find it difficult to broach the subject, try to open a conversation about bullying in a general way. Emphasise that bullying is totally unacceptable, and should never be tolerated. Try to diminish the power of the bully by pointing out that people who indulge in this kind of behaviour are generally cowards, particularly if the bully is hiding behind technology and sending text messages or emails.
- Encourage the child to find someone they can trust to talk through the problem. It may be a family member or a teacher at school.

Talk to the school about its anti-bullying policies.

- Talk to the school about its anti-bullying policies. The Government has made tackling bullying in schools a key priority, and the Department for Education has emphasised that no form of bullying is to be tolerated. It's compulsory for schools to have measures in place to encourage good behaviour and respect for others, and to prevent all forms of bullying. Companies and organisations have a similar responsibility to protect their employees.
- Get a copy of the Anti-bullying Alliance's leaflet, 'Keep an eye on it', produced to help parents support a child who's being bullied. Search online to arm yourself with information, or contact organisations in the telephone directory to request material (see also *Resources* on page 242.)
- Explain the meaning of the saying 'Sticks and stones may break my bones, but words can never hurt me'. Empowering a child with the thought that these are just words and should not be accepted as true will help them treat the bully with contempt, which will show the bully that any intimidation is not working.
- Above all, bullying must never go untackled; bring in the relevant authorities to deal with the problem as soon as it comes to light – this may be a head teacher, a manager, or the police, if the bullying involves physical abuse. It's never a good idea to retaliate with the same type of abuse, but it is imperative to stand up to the bullying and report it.

Living alone

If you've recently lost an important relationship through divorce or bereavement or because your children have left home, this is a huge life change and, understandably, you need plenty of time for grieving and/or readjustment. The stress of loss is very depleting, so it's entirely natural if you want to withdraw for a while. It can be tempting to cling to the past, as all your happiest memories are there.

But it's vital that you take steps to get back into the swing of life as soon as you feel stronger. Living alone doesn't have to mean *being* alone. You have many years of fulfilment ahead, and there's no reason why you shouldn't create more happy times and strong new bonds of friendship in your new capacity as a single person. It's common to feel that you're not needed any more, but you can ease this by finding different ways to help others. Becoming involved in your religious community, helping out at a charity or joining a class or museum group are all good ways to make sure you move forward with your life. Take small steps at first, and see how you get on (see chapter 8 for information about volunteering and many more activities).

be liberated, not lonely

Going through a divorce or bereavement can leave you feeling alone or abandoned, and it's not unusual to feel that no one will ever love you again. When we grieve, the world often takes on a strange perspective. This is quite natural, and we need time, reassurance, protection and help to recover and plan for the future. It's important to look at the parts of your life that you haven't lost, and especially important to recognise the people in your life who still love and care for you.

If you can embrace change (once you feel ready) as an opportunity for developing a new stage in your life, you might find yourself becoming excited at all the possibilities waiting to be grasped. Here are four simple ways to get started:

● If your confidence has taken a knock, rethink your image. A new hairstyle, for men or women, can take years off your age and make you look at yourself anew. Or consider a new exercise regime – keeping active, working out or visiting a health spa are all good ways to lift your mood.

● Redecorating, or rearranging your furniture, can stop you feeling that you're blocked from moving forward.

● Taking the holiday you've always dreamed of, perhaps an active break or a luxury cruise, may help you to see the benefits of pleasing yourself.

HELPING HAND

FURTHER HELP

If the relationships in your family life, or with close friends, are causing you distress, and you don't know how to deal with them, consider talking to a family therapist or a relationship counsellor. If you're experiencing violence at home, or emotional abuse, it's important to seek the help of a third party. See chapter 10, *Helping Hands*, and also consult the Resources section on page 242 for details of agencies that can help. Don't be afraid to ask for help and support.

● Getting a dog or a cat can be a great comfort if you're living alone. It's well documented that stroking a pet has a calming effect on the body, mind and emotions. Having to care for an animal will take your mind off yourself, and walking a dog will get you out into the fresh air and give you exercise, which lifts your mood.

SUIT YOURSELF

Many people who live alone discover that it has great advantages, once you get used to it. It can be very liberating to organise your timetable to suit yourself: going to bed when you like, eating meals at times that suit you, watching the TV programmes that you choose, or reading into the early hours. It may take time to adjust, but once you've tasted the freedom, you may never want to cohabit again.

If you do feel pangs of loneliness, you might try renting out a spare room to a lodger. This could augment your income and provide a degree of companionship. There are agencies that specialise in Monday-to-Friday lets if you prefer, so that your home is all yours again at weekends, when you might want to entertain or have grandchildren to stay.

Don't forget ...

Good relationships are good for you. Connections with other people are the spice and seasoning of our lives; without them, life would be dull. Try to work positively and creatively at your relationships, and they will reward you in so many ways. Here's your checklist for happiness:

● Appreciate the people in your life – don't ever take them for granted.

● Learn to communicate your feelings and desires, and to listen to what other people want to convey to you.

● Make time for your friends and family; think about all the things you can do together – then do them.

● Build up a solid support network. Let others help you as you help them.

● Be open to the idea of making new friends.

enjoy life

Enjoying life should be a priority, but everyday worries often get in the way. Don't let them. Making time for yourself and your interests is important for your wellbeing and helps to buffer the effects of stress. Think about reviving a past hobby, enjoying a new social activity or perhaps taking up local voluntary work. The key is to reawaken your enthusiasms and discover how seizing opportunities with both hands increases energy and motivation, while reducing any feelings of tension.

A question of balance

There may be times when you look back nostalgically to a younger, more carefree self. Growing up and taking on new responsibilities can sometimes squeeze the fun out of life. But it doesn't have to.

Simple adjustments could make a huge difference. By analysing what you do every day, and why you do it, you'll be able to identify the elements of your life that have been restricting your enjoyment. Learning to relax could be part of the solution, but your relationship with friends and family may also need a health check (see *The 'wheel of life' test*, page 188). A 2010 study in the *Journal of Hypertension* discovered that participants who were socially isolated tended to have higher blood pressure levels (a risk factor for cardiovascular disease) than those who saw friends more frequently, while an intriguing experiment at the University of Toronto suggested that people who are socially excluded actually feel colder – the chilling effect of being frozen out by a group.

Is work taking over?

Spending too much time at work or worrying about work is a major cause of imbalance in many people's lives. A 2010 survey for Mind, the mental health charity, found that 9 per cent of those interviewed had seen their GP as a direct result of increased work pressure related to the recession, while 20 per cent said stress at work had made them physically ill, with 25 per cent having been reduced to tears. Britons work some of the longest hours in Europe. Just over a fifth of us – around 6 million people – work more than 45 hours a week, according to a government survey. Those working the longest hours tend to be fathers aged 30–49, employed in the private sector.

Difficult economic conditions and a heavy workload may necessitate long hours, but some people work longer than required through habit. This can have a negative effect on health, because we all need time to rest and relax. Relationships can suffer too if time with friends and families is constantly restricted by work commitments. If work has been steadily encroaching on your personal life, you need to take steps to redress the balance. Here's how to do it:

Take a lunch break but avoid eating junk food.

● **MANAGE YOUR TIME MORE EFFECTIVELY**

- Monitor how you spend the day.
- Stop doing things you don't have to.
- Do the most important tasks first.
- Get help from others and ask them to do tasks that are not strictly your responsibility.
- Say 'no' sometimes when asked to do extra work: don't give reasons, just say that you're not able to do it.
- Take a lunch break, and leave on time at the end of the day.

● **SET GOALS**

- Plan what you will do during each day or week.
- Accept that you can switch from one task to another as long as you undertake to spend a set amount of time on each during the day.
- Be clear about what you want to achieve and how you'll know when you've achieved it.

● **TAKE ACTION**

- Having set yourself goals, take steps to make them happen.
- Do something each day towards reaching your bigger goals.
- If you feel stuck, break the goals down into small steps that are more manageable.

● **LOOK AFTER YOURSELF**

- Exercise each day, even if it's walking further from the bus stop or car park, or using the stairs rather than the lift.
- Eat more fruit and vegetables, and stop eating junk food.
- Take a healthy packed lunch or choose a healthy meal if you eat at your workplace.

the 'wheel of life' test

People are generally happier when all the aspects of their lives are well balanced. But what exactly does a well-balanced life entail? Some people find it helpful to take the 'wheel of life' test (see also *Resources* on page 242). This is an eight-segment pie chart, often used by professional life coaches, that symbolises the various elements of everyday experience, such as: home/physical environment, relationships, health/fitness, personal growth/learning, career/work, money/finances, family/friends, fun/recreation. The centre of the pie chart represents zero fulfilment, while a line drawn at the outer circumference scores 10 out of 10.

HOW TO FILL IN THE WHEEL

Draw a line across each segment to represent how you assess your current fulfilment in that area of your life. For example, if you feel unhappy about your career, place this line near the centre of the wheel, perhaps at the level of a 1 or 2, but if your relationship with your partner is happy and stable, draw the line near the circumference, at about an 8 or more. Try to assess each life area as accurately as you can.

Once completed you should have a graphic representation of the balance of your life. A relatively smooth inner circle indicates a good balance; an uneven inner circle, with both low and high-scoring segments, suggests you need to reconsider certain aspects. For those parts of your life where you feel unhappy or unfulfilled and have a low score, ask yourself what you could do to improve things. And read on.

Photocopy the blank wheel (right) or draw your own, then fill it in (see example below).

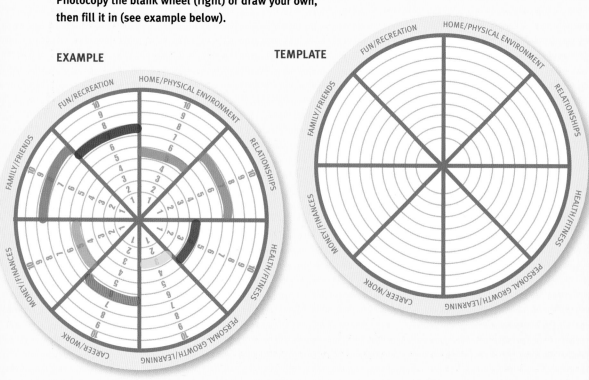

EXAMPLE

TEMPLATE

squeezing in me-time

We all need some time to relax and be ourselves. Without it, the pressures that affect most people – whether full-time parents spending the day running around after young children (see also chapter 7), overworked employees, or full-time carers (see panel on page 191) – can be overwhelming. Looking after yourself is far from self-indulgent; it's essential for your health and wellbeing.

MANAGING YOUR TIME

If you're someone who neglects your own needs because you're always doing things for other people, you may need to coach those around you into giving you some space. Here are a few tips:

● Make a careful note of how long you spend doing tasks in the course of the day. Other members of your household may be surprised when you show them the results, and it may be the motivation you need to cut your chore time.

● Tell your family that the household routine needs to change so that some tasks are shared, and that they'll be involved in deciding who does what (they're more likely to do tasks if they pick them themselves).

● If you tend to overload yourself at work, delegate some of your tasks to members of your team.

● If it's essential that you do certain tasks (for example, because you're the only driver), find a more efficient way to do them. Could you share some with a friend, taking turns each week, for instance?

● Discuss your need for personal space and decide where it will be. The important thing is that it's somewhere where you can shut the door and spend time undisturbed when you need to.

● Make a diary appointment with yourself to do the things that you never have time to do. Be realistic and

DID YOU KNOW?

TAKING WORK STRESS HOME

Work worries can be as damaging to health and relationships as long hours. But men and women appear to respond to stress in different ways. After analysing thousands of studies, researchers at the University of California, Los Angeles (UCLA) have found that although men often react to anxious situations with a 'fight-or-flight' response, women are more likely to display a 'tend-and-befriend' approach, reaching out to care for their young, say, or talking to a friend on the phone.

The researchers suggest that the hormone oxytocin, which has been shown to calm people and make them more sociable, may hold the key. Male hormones seem to dampen its effect, while the female hormone oestrogen amplifies it. (For more on work-related stress, including advice on bullying, see chapter 10.)

TOP **5** REASONS TO TAKE TIME OUT FOR YOURSELF

Making time for yourself – if only a few minutes a day – pays dividends. This is why:

- It's a vital part of maintaining a healthy body and mind.
- It helps you to remember what you enjoy (it's easy to forget who you are when you're busy in the role of worker, parent or carer).
- It's a way to 'be', a time when you can switch off from the pressures of work or home life, to do something completely different.
- It'll help you get some perspective back into your life and think about what matters. This in turn will help you to connect with others, whether colleagues, friends, family or partner.
- Quite simply, you've earned it.

start small on big tasks. It's better to do something for half an hour each day than to wait for that illusive 'free' day.

- Stop doing what doesn't need to be done. You don't have to iron everything. Ask yourself if it's essential to wash the car as often as you do.

Too often, the excuse for not doing something is, 'I'll do that when I have enough time.' The reality, however, is that you'll never find the time unless you make a specific commitment to do what you want to do (see chapter 4 and *Resources* on page 242 for more advice on time management).

HOW TO START MAKING TIME

One of the easiest ways to make time is to create order. If you can organise your life more efficiently, so that you know where everything you need is and what's happening when, you'll save time and cut down on the stress that results from a chaotic environment. Make 'a place for everything and everything in its place' your mantra. Take time and effort to put your affairs into order, to clear out cupboards and file away valuable documents; the rewards will always repay the effort.

Stop doing what doesn't need to be done …
You don't have to iron everything.

Help for **carers**

In the UK, 6 million people are 'carers', responsible for looking after a parent, partner or disabled child. If you're one of them, you know that this is a long-term commitment, which makes it all the more vital to build in time for yourself. No matter how devoted you are, stress can make you less able to care and less effective. Here's how to look after yourself as well:

● Learn how to relax completely (see chapter 3 for details of various relaxation methods) and make whatever technique you use part of your daily routine. Take 5 or 10 minutes to relax while the person you care for is resting or asleep, and you will quickly feel the benefits.

● Exercise to balance your stress. Being constantly alert to the needs of the person you care for is similar to being in the fight-or-flight response, and will cause stress over time without physical activity to balance it. Do some aerobic exercise – dance, or go for long walks or bike rides – when you can.

● Keep in touch with friends and family and talk to them on the phone or face to face regularly.

● Contact a local care home or another carer to find out about longer periods of respite care, which will enable you to have a few days alone or away. If necessary, pay a professional to come and stay occasionally so that you can visit friends and get some proper rest.

● Get in touch with other carers through local support groups or forums on the internet. Sharing experiences can help and you may also pick up some useful information.

If your task seems overwhelming, take it in stages and introduce small steps one at a time. You might find, for example, that you're more focused if you deal with incoming post and emails at a set time each day. Or you may decide to rethink your kitchen and perhaps introduce more work surfaces or create that efficient 'magic triangle' of sink, cooker, fridge that kitchen specialists recommend. Freeing up extra minutes can make all the difference in busy lives.

Think about better ways of streamlining your chores. Could you make and freeze meals, for example, or have a week's worth of shirts, work outfits or school uniforms washed, ironed and hanging up in advance? Where could you squeeze in time for yourself? Perhaps you could set your alarm to wake you an hour earlier on set days, to give you some time before the children wake up. Or designate one night a week where you have a ready meal or takeaway and ignore other chores.

Whether you're male or female, if you work full-time but long to spend more time with your children, you could ask to work more flexible hours (see chapter 6 for more information about your legal rights) or to work at home on certain days. That way, you should be able to take the children to school and pick them up sometimes. And make sure you plan time to do things together as a family at the weekends.

Inspiring new activities

People who aren't used to pleasing themselves may find it difficult to take up a new interest or allow themselves to devote time to it. It takes confidence to go out and join a new club, meet new people and leap into the unknown. But if, like most people, you have some latent interests – in sport, gardening, films or literature, perhaps – you should be able to develop those green shoots, expanding horizons and finding like-minded people. That way, they will become stimulating pastimes that bring real pleasure, and keep you feeling truly alive.

Spending time on yourself in this way can benefit your general health, especially if other people are involved. Numerous medical studies suggest that having strong social ties reduces the risk of heart disease and certain cancers, and may even help to extend life.

finding the right activity

There are so many activities out there, from evening classes at schools and colleges and daytime sessions at community and sports centres through to weekend and residential courses that may even be held in a different country. Your choice will obviously depend on your interests, your talents and, to some extent, what you can afford.

To find out more about anything that appeals, try checking local newspapers or 'What's On' magazines. Your nearest library or sports or community centre may have notices or leaflets about events or courses. For general information or details of activity holidays, look at national newspapers or search the internet (see also *Resources* on page 242).

Whatever you decide to do, don't limit yourself. By trying several different activities, you'll benefit from those that stretch you mentally and spiritually as well as those that build a skill or provide exercise. Meeting new people can also open your mind to fresh ideas and exciting opportunities you may not have previously considered.

MUSICAL MEDICINE

Listening to music brings many positive health benefits. Musical rhythms resonate with brainwaves and help to calm the mind, according to a study at Stanford University's Center for Computer Research. Music inspires as well as soothes, triggering a relaxation response, lowering blood pressure and bringing about a positive feeling of wellbeing. It's also easier to

Self-starter or team player?

Take this quick quiz to help you discover more about your preferred approach to new interests. Tick one answer for each question, then total up how many of each letter you've scored before checking the summary at the end.

1 Your doctor has told you to take more exercise. Would you:

- [ ] **A** Attend an aerobics class?
- [ ] **B** Employ a personal trainer?
- [ ] **C** Jog around your local area?
- [ ] **D** Join a ramblers group and walk with them regularly?

2 You have always wanted to paint and draw. Would you:

- [ ] **A** Join a local adult-education class?
- [ ] **B** Have private tuition from an art teacher?
- [ ] **C** Buy some paints and an easel so you can paint at home?
- [ ] **D** Go away for a painting holiday?

3 You love music and want it to play a bigger part in your life. Would you:

- [ ] **A** Join a local choir or music group?
- [ ] **B** Have private singing lessons or tuition in a musical instrument?
- [ ] **C** Buy a book to teach yourself how to improve your musical abilities?
- [ ] **D** Find an intensive course where you can learn an instrument or improve your singing?

4 You're looking for a new indoor hobby to take up. Would you:

- [ ] **A** Go along to your local community centre to see what's going on there?
- [ ] **B** Take up coin or stamp collecting?
- [ ] **C** Buy a craft-making kit with full instructions?
- [ ] **D** Invest in a specialised weekend to learn a new computer program or other skill you can practise on your own once you know the basics?

Summary

There are no right or wrong answers. The goal is for you to discover what will help you get the most enjoyment out of life.

Mostly As: you are a sociable sort of person who wants to enjoy not only your new hobby but also meeting others with similar interests.

Mostly Bs: you prefer your own company and enjoy getting absorbed in a new activity once you have the basic information.

Mostly Cs: you are self-sufficient and internally motivated. Go for what you want to do.

Mostly Ds: you are a combination of all of the above. You enjoy some company while you learn intensively with like-minded people and then take pleasure in getting on with your new interest by yourself.

QUICK QUIZ

exercise to music and, as exercise also raises endorphin levels, the two in tandem are likely to boost your mood.

If you love to sing, consider taking lessons or joining a choir. According to Professor Graham Welch at London University's Institute of Education, singing offers both physical and psychological health benefits. 'Singing ... is an aerobic activity that increases oxygenation in the bloodstream and exercises major muscle groups in the upper body, even when sitting,' he says. The psychological benefits result from its generally positive effect in reducing stress levels, through the action of the endocrine system, which is linked to our sense of emotional wellbeing.

These benefits are also evident when people sing together, because of the increased sense of community, belonging and shared endeavour, he adds.

Alternatively, you could take up an instrument you once played or learn a new one. It might be worth seeking out a local teacher or joining a music group as you gain confidence (see *Resources* on page 242).

If you simply enjoy listening to music, perhaps now's the time to start researching a particular composer, singer or group you've always found appealing. The key here, as with everything, is to do something that will capture your imagination and make you want to pursue it.

DRAMA: ON STAGE AND BEHIND THE SCENES

Many people enjoy amateur dramatics, or drama workshops. Acting is a useful tool for increasing your confidence and your problem-solving abilities, as well as improving your capacity to understand others. When you play a role, you often gain from seeing what the world is like from another perspective, from the character's point of view.

If you don't enjoy performing but would like to write, produce, build theatre sets, design costumes or become a make-up artist, find out about drama activities in your area, then have a go. Your local theatre or church may have an amateur dramatics group, and schools and colleges often have drama groups. Otherwise, check your local library for information.

THE WRITING PROCESS

If you enjoy writing, why not keep a journal to write down your hopes and plans for the future. Author Julia Cameron, in her book *The Artist's Way*, describes the benefits of using 'Morning Pages' to record thoughts as they occur – often called 'stream of consciousness' writing.

Every morning, she says, just as you wake up, pick up your journal and write down anything that comes to mind. Don't edit yourself and don't reread it. Cover about three pages each day. Even if you don't know what to write, put 'I don't know what to write' over and over until something springs to mind or you've filled your pages. The idea behind the exercise is that you'll start to find new ideas coming to you, and as a result you'll discover what you would really like to be doing.

Writing about emotional upheavals in our lives can improve physical and mental wellbeing, says Dr James W. Pennebaker of the University of Texas at Austin, who has designed several studies showing the links between writing and health. Describing traumatic experiences boosted mood and strengthened the immune system response of healthy students in one study, while another found that, among students vulnerable to depression, those who expressed their feelings had fewer depressive symptoms after six months than those who wrote about everyday events.

When you wake up, pick up your journal
and write down anything that comes to mind.

Try a class in cake decoration –
a skill guaranteed to please
family and friends.

Whatever you write about, this could be the beginnings of the book that you've always felt you had inside you, or the short stories that take shape when you read certain headlines or overhear a conversation. You could join a local writing or book group, whether your interest is prose or poetry, or you may simply decide to put aside some time to catch up on your reading, if that's what you enjoy most.

ARTISTIC ENDEAVOURS

Art therapy has long been used in hospitals, schools and even prisons to aid healing and to help people express their innermost feelings. The creation of art is thought to boost mood, self-awareness and self-esteem.

So, if sketching or painting is something you once enjoyed and would like to try again, finding a way to express yourself through art is likely to bring you a great deal of pleasure. It may be less daunting to start out on your own, drawing or painting at home, or if you enjoy nature or architecture, you might want to sketch or paint outdoors. You could also try recycling bits and pieces to turn them into interesting collages or artworks.

Joining a class at a local adult-education centre would enable you to try something new, such as oil or watercolour painting, landscape or life drawing, photography, pottery, sculpture or wood carving. Or, perhaps try a class in cake decoration – a skill guaranteed to please family and friends.

EXERCISE YOUR WAY TO HAPPINESS

Because our bodies are designed for movement, too little exercise can affect both physical and mental wellbeing. Researchers in San Francisco who uncovered links between depression and heart disease probed further and discovered that a key trigger in the process was lack of physical exercise.

Whether you choose to cycle to work or to the shops, become involved in team sports, take up gardening and grow your own vegetables or go to a dance class, you'll soon reap the benefits, as exercise you enjoy will help you to relax. And the more you relax, the more you'll take pleasure in it, so it's vital to pick something you can do regularly. (For more advice on staying active, see chapter 3.)

EXPERT VIEW

BOOST THOSE ENDORPHINS

Group exercise has some distinct advantages, according to a recent study. Not only will friends spur you on if you're flagging, but the shared effort may give your endorphin levels an extra boost. Researchers in 2009 found that college crews who rowed in synchronisation had an increased rush of these feel-good hormones compared with those who rowed alone. But all exercise is good, whether solitary or with others. Try walking, dancing, aerobics and running to transport yourself into a trance-like state. The rhythm of continuous exercise releases endorphins and encourages reflective thought.

DEVELOP YOUR SPIRITUALITY

Both formal religious practice and other forms of spiritual comfort have been found to be beneficial for health and wellbeing. For instance:

● Stephen and Rachel Kaplan, professors of psychology at the University of Michigan, have shown that connecting with nature helps to counteract stress and put worries into perspective, which in turn helps people relax. Those who enjoy nature are also less likely to drink or smoke excessively.

● Similarly, creating green spaces around housing estates seems to reduce levels of aggression and violence. Just taking a walk in the park has been found to improve both attention and memory, as well as sociability.

● Church attendance may increase life expectancy, according to a study published in the *International Journal for Psychiatry and Medicine*. It can help counter stress and emotional problems and appears to protect against heart, respiratory and digestive diseases, possibly due to the support and moral guidance received from belonging to a like-minded community.

● Meditation slows the heart rate, lowers blood pressure, reduces anxiety, and, as a result, relieves stress. Studies have found that athletes who meditate improve their performance. (For more on meditation and relaxation techniques, see chapters 3 and 4 and *Resources* on page 242.)

Volunteer work can be highly rewarding.

Become a **volunteer**

If there is a local project that interests you, you may want to volunteer your help. It's an excellent way to become involved in your local community and also gives you the opportunity to meet new people and learn new skills. This is turn increases your confidence.

Before you approach an organisation, think about what role might suit you best. What skills can you offer? How much time do you have available? Do you want to work a few hours a week or could you make a greater commitment? Do you prefer working indoors or outside? You'll benefit most if you're prepared to accept new experiences.

There are plenty of ways to find opportunities: search on the internet, visit your library or check local newspapers. If you enjoy nature and outdoor activities, why not help a wildlife organisation or join a rambling group, or volunteer to be a guide or help renovation with the National Trust. There are also opportunities to get involved in conservation work through the charity BTCV, an organisation that arranges for volunteers to work on practical environmental conservation projects, from drystone-walling to creating sensory gardens. The BTCV website has information on ongoing projects throughout the UK.

Many people take up volunteer work when they retire. In one study by the Institute for Volunteering Research, 90 per cent of volunteers aged 50 plus said they enjoyed the work. As well as the social aspects, volunteers appreciated the opportunity to use their skills.

HELPING OTHERS

Helping people can be highly rewarding. You'll be supporting others and the work can boost your self-confidence and sense of self-worth. Becoming a mentor can be especially fulfilling, as it's a way to share your skills. If your background is in writing or science, for example, you could offer a few hours a week to help young people who may be struggling in these subjects. Even if you don't have specific training, just by listening and being available to help you could transform someone's life.

Many people volunteer for work abroad. If you have a useful skill, which could be anything from optometry to town planning, the Voluntary Service Overseas (VSO) is a good option. The VSO offers people aged 18–75 placements lasting anything from one month to two years, depending on level and area of expertise; 18–25 year olds can also opt for a 10 week placement in a developing country through a scheme called Platform 2.

Reach Online is a British charity that helps to place skilled volunteers with organisations that need them. Community Service Volunteers (CSV) also places volunteers, and provides training. (See *Resources* on page 242 for details of all of the organisations mentioned.)

learn something new

Lifelong learning is not only enjoyable and rewarding; it also keeps your brain active as it continues to make new neural connections. More and more research is emerging to indicate that this helps to combat many of the natural effects of ageing on mental performance. For instance, the so-called 'Nun Study' has followed a group of 678 elderly nuns from the School Sisters of Notre Dame since 1986. Evidence suggests that the nuns' busy lifestyles and communication skills – they often continue teaching well into old age – may help protect them against Alzheimer's disease.

If you have the time and desire to learn something new, check out your local adult-education programme. Perhaps you could improve your computer skills, or learn how to play chess or bridge? If you enjoy history, you could join a local civic society or become a Friend of a museum (see *Resources* on page 242). Or why not learn a language? In a 2004 study, researchers at York University in Canada found evidence to suggest that people who regularly use two languages perform better at complex mental tasks. Put your new-found language skills into practice and take a trip with family and friends, or go alone with an organised group.

You could also join the Open University (OU). You can work at home in your own time, using the internet, and will be allocated a tutor to advise on written assignments. You may also have the option to spend a week living on campus at an OU summer school (see *Resources*).

Women who want to take part in various activities and campaign on important issues could join the WI (Women's Institute). It's the largest women's voluntary organisation in the UK, and offers a variety of opportunities (see *Resources*).

The quickest and easiest way to keep mentally active is by tackling puzzles. A study in the *New England Journal of Medicine* in 2003 found that elderly people who did crosswords four times a week almost halved their risk of dementia, compared to those who did them only once a week.

HELPING HAND

OVERCOMING SHYNESS

If you find it difficult to introduce yourself and talk to new people because of lack of confidence, the following tips may help:

1 Subtly mirror and match the person's body language and posture.

2 Position yourself on the same level (so, sit or stand, as appropriate).

3 Notice their breathing and try to get yours to follow the same rhythm.

4 Make eye contact but don't stare; look away from time to time.

5 Allow enough personal space (this varies in different cultures, so be sensitive).

6 Be interested, and ask about their life.

A THERAPIST'S NOTES

Jane explained to me how she was finally able to realise a lifelong desire to see the world when she discovered an organisation called Women Welcome Women World Wide.

Jane was devoted to her husband and children. Whenever they took a holiday it would either be to the Lake District or Cornwall, though occasionally they ventured as far as the west of France. The family always camped, partly because it was so much cheaper and partly because her husband thought it was fun.

Although Jane enjoyed these holidays, she often felt constrained by the demands of her family and she dreamed of travelling the world. But she knew deep down that this wouldn't be possible with her husband and three children; cost was an issue but the things she wanted to do didn't interest her family. She regretted not having a gap year before university, as the idea of fulfilling her wish to travel now seemed impossible.

A new opportunity

Jane came across an article in a magazine describing an international women's friendship organisation that had started in the UK but now has members all over the world. Its aim was to help women from different cultures increase their self-confidence by meeting other women. The founder, Frances Alexander, believed that many women would be willing to offer friendship and accommodation for a couple of nights to other female travellers, allowing them to gain some mutual insight into their different ways of life.

Opening a door

Jane joined Women Welcome Women World Wide (see *Resources* on page 242), and decided to take a trip alone without her family. The experience helped her to find out who she was beyond her roles as wife and mother. Being away from her family also allowed her to accept that they could cope without her. And realising that she was capable of making decisions on her own, without having to ask her family what they wanted, was similarly liberating.

Joining the organisation not only increased her enjoyment of life when she was travelling but led to her becoming much happier with her home life in general. She also had the confidence to make constructive changes to her lifestyle. Because she felt more self-assured and assertive in dealing with other people, she was able to stand up for herself and was better able to say no when she didn't want to do something. Although members of her family were initially surprised by the changes they saw in her, they were very supportive when they realised she was living the life she truly wanted.

Jane's life has been enriched, not only by travelling the world, but also by the new friends she has made. Joining Women Welcome Women World Wide was for Jane a door that opened into a richer, more fulfilled life. It has helped her to recognise and address her own needs and realise that she does have choices and the power to live life to the full.

Preparing for retirement

Retirement can be a challenging prospect. After years of knowing exactly where they'll be each day, people suddenly find themselves without a regular routine. Their identity, often linked to their role at work, alters and, while coping with their own change in status, they also have to deal with other people's perception of who they are.

But it's is also a chance to do the things you've always dreamed of doing but were too busy to take on. It's a long-anticipated reward for years of hard work. Many people recognise this and look forward to the opportunities they suddenly have to enjoy life and be re-energised. Parents may also experience that changing identity yet sense of freedom when children leave home and they shed their immediate duties as parents and carers. In both cases, it's a chance to be a bit more selfish and to forge ahead with exciting plans. Both also offer the opportunity to live a healthier, more balanced life.

When people retire, they tend to react in one of two ways: either doing very little initially, enjoying having time to relax, recharge and plan, or leaping into hyperactivity and becoming involved in numerous activities, or doing a lot of travelling. After a while most people find a middle way and begin a different and often very fulfilling stage of life.

taking action

Advance planning is crucial in preparing yourself emotionally for retirement. Start by determining what you want to do once you retire, then decide how you'll manage your time effectively each day so that you can move towards your goals, bit by bit. While allowing yourself time for rest and relaxation, you need to stay focused on what you want to achieve; it's easy to spend too much time doing very little, or trying to please others.

TRY THIS! ✓

AFFIRMING AND ANCHORING

Psychologists suggest using affirmations – positive statements that reinforce your self-esteem – if you need a confidence boost. Tell yourself: 'I am confident and I'm really going to enjoy this', even if you feel apprehensive. The more you repeat the phrase to yourself (ideally, in front of a mirror), the more your unconscious mind begins to accept what you say and the more confident you start to feel.

Alternatively, try 'anchoring'. Think about a time when you felt particularly in control. As you focus on this, close your eyes and feel confidence flow through your body. Then make a small movement, such as squeezing your thumb and forefinger together, to reinforce that sense of confidence. If you practise regularly, repeating the thumb/finger gesture when you're anxious should restore your sense of calm.

Use the internet to contact old friends.

You may want to meet new people or get in touch with old friends, especially if your social circle has revolved around work. The internet can help you to contact old school pals, relations or friends abroad. Do a general search, or try social networking sites such as Friends Reunited or Facebook (see *Resources* on page 242).

It's also important to nurture your relationship with your partner; US researchers found that depression and marital conflict increased among the newly retired. Your plans for the future should be ones that you both agree and discuss. Being considerate, talking over problems and keeping your sense of humour are key to a happy partnership (see also chapter 7).

Whatever you decide, you will need to make it happen. However wonderful your dreams about life post-work, they'll come to nothing unless you are proactive and take the necessary steps to achieve them.

Enjoying life matters

There are so many good reasons to live your life to the full, doing things you enjoy and meeting new people. Here are just five:

● **YOU'LL IMPROVE YOUR MENTAL HEALTH** When you pursue activities you enjoy, your mood improves, you become more positive and you feel happier. You'll also laugh more and deal with setbacks more competently.

● **YOU'LL BECOME FITTER** Even if you enjoy sedentary activities, you can still improve your physical health by walking up stairs instead of taking the lift, or parking the car further away. Little things make a difference.

● **YOU'LL GAIN IN CONFIDENCE** If you're having fun, you'll radiate that sense of wellbeing to others. Their response and your own enjoyment will boost your confidence and your self-esteem.

● **YOU'LL BECOME MORE EFFICIENT** Now that you realise how essential it is to find time for the things you enjoy, you'll be more organised at home and work, by doing only what's necessary, sharing tasks with others, defining your personal boundaries and communicating more effectively.

● **YOU'LL LOOK AFTER YOURSELF** Living life to the full means recognising the importance of good health, which in turn means eating healthier food, getting enough sleep, exercising and connecting with nature. You're learning to care for yourself and do whatever's right for you.

9 home sweet home

Your environment undoubtedly affects your mood, and facing a cluttered desk or returning to a messy, noisy or uncomfortable home is unsettling and can destroy your peace of mind in seconds. This chapter offers numerous suggestions for organising your external space to help you feel more tranquil and in control. It provides strategies for working on your surroundings, bit by bit, to create a home in which you can feel calm and comfortable – a space where you can simply relax and unwind.

Creating a personal haven

Whether you're aware of it or not, your surroundings – at home or at work – can have a marked effect on your emotions, your moods and even the way you view the world. Most people need some peace and calm in their lives – to chase away negative thoughts, counter work or other sorts of external stress, and relax and recharge at the end of the day and at weekends. Your home can be that sanctuary, but there are obstacles and also key ingredients for success.

Obstacles vary from person to person, but generally include clutter, noise, dirt and appliances that don't work – a smooth-running home is much more conducive to calm. It helps to have your finances in control (see chapter 6), and a harmonious relationship with family and friends (see chapter 7). Subtle decor, colour and lighting can also help create a relaxing, welcoming atmosphere. Below are some practical ideas.

Clear out your clutter

One of the greatest obstacles to feeling relaxed and peaceful at home is clutter. It's easy to get so used to your own untidiness that you hardly see it any more, but it can still have a subliminal effect on your mind and emotions. Paperwork, books, newspapers, letters, bills, clothes and shoes scattered about, or randomly balanced in untidy piles, are not conducive to calm.

Newspapers, letters and bills, randomly balanced in piles, are not conducive to calm.

Clutter sends out a constant message that there's work to be done, making you feel guilty every time you focus on any of it, be it a heap of papers that needs sorting through, a mass of clothes you don't wear any more or unwanted gifts you can't quite bring yourself to throw out. All of these lead to overcrowded surfaces and overflowing cupboards, creating a psychological burden you'd be much better off without.

WHEN DOES CLUTTER BECOME A PROBLEM?

Clutter is a problem if it:
- Causes tension with family members or friends.
- Prevents you from inviting people into your home, entertaining your friends or having people to stay.
- Becomes a regular topic of discussion with others.
- Makes you feel stressed in your own home.

WHY CLEAR UP?

You'll benefit from clearing clutter because you'll:
- **Create extra space.** By reorganising your possessions and throwing some items away, you may be able to create space for a home office, a playroom or play area for your children or grandchildren, or simply more space to move around in.
- **Save time.** You'll find things more easily in a clutter-free home. It will also be far easier to maintain, leaving more time to do the things you enjoy.
- **Be calmer.** A clutter-free home makes you feel in control, leading to clearer thinking.
- **Boost your self-esteem.** Your environment is a reflection of yourself. When you clear things up, this gives you the opportunity to create an elegant and stylish environment that you can truly feel proud to call your home.

TRY THIS! ✔

CREATE A PLACE JUST FOR YOU

Pick a single spot in your home to which you can escape to calm down, meditate, read, listen to music or whatever else you do to relax. It could be a bedroom, the bathroom, the attic or a wooden shed at the end of the garden. Then clear it entirely of clutter. If necessary, give it a quick coat of paint in a colour you find soothing (see page 214), introduce a comfortable chair and just one or two favourite objects – perhaps books, poems, candles or pictures. If you have a family (and your children are old enough to be left on their own for a short time), agree to a sign that means 'do not disturb unless in an emergency'. Once you have your haven, it will be easier both to face the stresses of life and to tackle the changes you might want to make elsewhere in your home.

strategies for de-cluttering

It can take time and effort to sort through accumulated clutter. The trick is to do it a bit at a time. Here are some tips on getting started.

- **Be brave.** It can feel 'wrong' to throw out possessions – things you bought or were given. But if you haven't used or worn something for a considerable time, ask yourself why – this may help you let it go.
- **Think quality not quantity.** Liken the process to 'editing' what you own, weeding out everything that is not essential to your wellbeing.
- **Tackle one room at a time.** Set aside a day to deal with each room and make a commitment to finishing it. Anything that doesn't belong in that room can be put into cardboard boxes for you to go through later. Once you've achieved order and style in one area, you will feel more encouraged to tackle other parts of the house.
- **Store like with like.** Have a single place where you store identical or related items, so that you know exactly where to look when you want a new light bulb, fuse or battery, say.
- **Think small.** If you feel overwhelmed by a single room, break the work down into smaller, easy-to-manage tasks. Start by sorting through your wardrobe, for example, and leave the rest of the bedroom for the next day. Or focus on tackling a cluttered desk, until you've sorted

Have a place where you store related items,
so you know exactly where to look.

EXPERT VIEW

CALL IN THE PROFESSIONALS

If you're having serious problems de-cluttering, an option might be to contact a professional who will come and help with the work, or who will give you regular telephone coaching. You could also take a look at the many websites offering help and advice on clutter-clearing. (See *Resources* on page 242 for details.)

out the muddle. Create more order by putting stray papers into a wallet-type folder or a box file, and use stick-on labels to identify the contents. Buy a wicker or wire basket for letters and bills that need to be dealt with, so that they are contained and easy to find. Place pens, pencils, rulers, highlighters and so on in a container.

- **File away.** Buy a small metal or cardboard file, divided into alphabetical sections, for storing household bills and receipts. Keep it somewhere handy and it will be easy to routinely put bills, receipts and guarantees in the appropriate place. And, in future, they'll be easier to find.

- **Find good homes.** If there's no logical place for something, ask yourself if you should be keeping it. Clutter accumulates precisely because things have no specific 'home' and so are left lying around on surfaces or on the floor. Work at finding a 'home' for everything, then try to put things back in their place when you've finished with them. Let the 'homeless' items go.

KEEP WHAT MATTERS – AND DISCARD WHAT DOESN'T

There are bound to be certain things you'll want to keep because of their personal significance. While they might be deemed clutter by someone else, it's important to keep the items that have meaning for you. Clearing some space means the possessions that matter don't get lost and can therefore have more impact. Another great reward of the clearing-out process is that you often find forgotten treasures, such as old letters or your children's first drawings, which can spur you on and more than justify the time spent.

You can take unwanted clothes and items that are still in good condition to a charity shop, or donate them to a national charity or sell them at a car-boot sale. More valuable items can be sold at a local auction house, or on eBay. If you don't want to bother with eBay yourself, some companies will collect and sell things for you on commission. For everything else you can try one of the number of organisations that will come and collect unwanted items. (See *Resources* on page 242 for details.)

Storage solutions

Exploit and use all the storage potential of your home. Whether you live in a medium-sized flat, a one-room studio or a vast, rambling manor house, stylish storage can be an integral part of your interior design. The more built-in cupboards you can install, the more you'll create a feeling of spaciousness and harmony. Also consider free-standing storage options, many of which look good while keeping clutter out of sight. It's still important, though, to have regular 'clearing-out' sessions – don't just stash things away in boxes.

Put toys away in containers at the end of the day.

Here are some top storage tips:

● Gain extra storage by buying wicker or rattan boxes in different sizes that can double as side or coffee tables. Placing a wooden or silver tray on the lid will make the surface more stable, and can add an elegant touch.

● A wooden chest is another stylish storage item that can also serve as a coffee table in the living room. Or use one to hold children's toys; in a child's bedroom it can be painted to match the colour scheme of the room or decorated with transfers or stencil sets. With foam cushions and removable, washable, cotton covers on top, it can also provide seating for children.

● Have specific containers for children's/ grandchildren's toys and possessions and ensure that the children put their things away at the end of the day — this is a good habit to instil for later life.

● In children's bedrooms, use plastic, Perspex or wooden stacking boxes, which take up vertical space rather than valuable room on the floor.

● Similarly, if you don't have much free space, consider the vertical storage potential of your walls. Shelves for books or other objects can be fitted in the most unlikely places, such as the nooks above doors, in the hallway or under the stairs.

● If you have bay windows, use the curved area beneath them for a window seat with storage space inside.

● Hang plastic or fabric containers with compartments for shoes, ties, scarves or underwear on the back of your bedroom door, or inside your wardrobe.

● Fit hooks over the top of doors to hang towels in the bathroom, or clothes and bathrobes in the bedroom.

● Have extra cupboards made if your home has a serious shortage of storage space. It's often worth the expense for the increased sense of calm you'll feel in your more streamlined, tidy home.

keeping up the good work

To maintain your calm and harmonious space once you've cleared the clutter, you'll need to create some simple rules for yourself and, if necessary, other family members. For example, you might allocate 10 minutes at the end of each day for tidying and putting things back in their designated place. If you can't face such a disciplined approach, at least promise yourself that you'll tidy your main living area before you go to bed: straighten cushions, take any glasses, cups or plates into the kitchen, put books back onto the bookshelves, tidy magazines or papers and move items of clothing, shoes or toys to their proper 'home'. It can make such a difference next morning to be greeted by a well-ordered, attractive room, instead of having to deal with yesterday's mess.

HELPING HAND

STAY SAFE

It's important that you feel secure in your home so that you don't spend time worrying about what would happen if you were burgled or if a fire broke out. Make sure your home is secure (see chapter 6), that you have enough working smoke alarms and that everyone knows the best escape route. These simple steps will make your home a safe haven.

allergy minefield

If you need another good reason for cutting clutter, consider this: you'll reduce dust because there will be fewer places for it to accumulate. Dust is one of the most prevalent allergens in the home, so if you suffer from allergies, it makes sense to keep your home as fresh and dust-free as possible. The more dust, the more food there is for dust mites, which are a major source of allergies – 90 per cent of people with asthma have positive skin tests to dust mites. These mites are most rampant in the bedroom, particularly in beds, where they thrive on the many skin cells we shed and the amount we sweat during the night.

Steps you can take to reduce allergens throughout your home include:
● Covering your mattress and pillow with fabric or semi-permeable polyurethane. You should also vacuum your mattress every month.
● Washing your bedding in hot water (60C) at least once a week. Or drying your sheets for an hour in a hot dryer. Researchers have also found that adding eucalyptus to your wash may help kill the mites.
● Treating your carpets every four to six months with a product that targets dust mites. Better still, replace your carpets with hard flooring.

Reduce allergens by keeping pets out of your bedroom.

- Cleaning the tray under your fridge with a bleach solution and sprinkling it with salt – this will cut down on mould and bacteria.
- Minimising food and drink at your workspace; turn your keyboard over and give it a gentle shake – if crumbs fall out, you need to eat elsewhere.
- Keeping pets out of your bedroom – and bathing your pet regularly. Consider trying a product such as PetalCleanse, which removes allergens from dogs, cats and small animals.
- Using natural cleaning products, such as lemon juice, bicarbonate of soda and vinegar, to cut down on VOCs (volatile organic compounds) around the home. VOCs are found in many household cleaners and materials, and can aggravate allergies.
- Keeping your home well ventilated; as well as making everything feel fresher, this helps to remove chemical residues from synthetic cleaning products (see also *Improve your air quality*, below).
- Avoiding air fresheners, because the perfume they contain can exacerbate asthma.

Improve your air quality

Most of us don't give too much thought to the quality of the air in our homes, but research indicates that poor air quality aggravates sinus problems, allergies, headaches and respiratory problems. It can also make us feel tired and lethargic. The good news is that there are plenty of things you can do to purify and enhance the air you breathe inside your home.

open your windows

It may sound obvious, but opening windows and doors to ventilate your home – especially in winter – is one of the best things you can do to improve the air quality. This is particularly vital in modern, energy-efficient homes, which are designed to keep the heat in, often at the expense of fresh circulating air. Good ventilation is crucial to a healthy indoor environment. Research suggests that the rate at which indoor air is exchanged for fresh air is now ten times lower than it was thirty years ago. Even opening windows for as little as 10 minutes a day will help. In addition, if you can (and your home is secure), keep a bedroom window open at night; most new windows have air vents that allow the air to trickle in (these also help to protect the building against damp).

Ventilating your home is doubly important if anyone living in your home is a smoker. In addition to the health risks posed by active smoking, research has shown that long-term exposure to second-hand smoke can dramatically increase the risk of dementia. In a study of more than 5,000 non-smoking adults, Cambridge University researchers found that those with the highest levels of cotinine (a marker for second-hand-smoke exposure) were 44 per cent more likely to have dementia than those with the lowest levels. Make sure you open doors and windows regularly, and insist that smokers refrain from smoking indoors when possible.

HELPING HAND

COMBATING DEHYDRATION

If you use air-conditioning, keep the temperature at about 19–23C, and try to maintain a comfortable level of humidity, as it can make the air too dry unless you drink sufficient fluids. This can also have an adverse effect on your skin and on your eyes, particularly if you wear contact lenses.

Central heating can also cause the atmosphere to dry out. If the air around you feels too dry, buy a humidifier or place bowls of water above your radiators or around your room to increase the humidity. Plants and vases of fresh flowers will also contribute to the humidity, as well as breathing out oxygen, so the more plants, the better your air quality.

nature's air filters

Cultivating plants known to act as natural air filters, such as gerbera, English ivy, lady palm, spider plant and peace lily, is a simple and effective way to improve air quality. Research conducted by NASA and the Associated Landscape Contractors of America in the 1980s,

Air purifiers

There are a number of different air-purifying products on the market. While the extent of their effectiveness is still being investigated, many people claim to experience beneficial results.

Air cleaners are grouped according to how they remove pollutants from the air. Mechanical and electrostatic filters are used to remove dust particles, but have no effect on gas and vapour molecules, which are best removed using carbon filtration (such as in cooker hoods). Air purifiers capture airborne allergens, and may bring some relief from allergies to mould and pet dander. They use different types of replaceable filter, the most effective of which are HEPA (High Efficiency Particulate Air) filters (also used in vacuum cleaners), since they trap allergens such as dust, pollen and smoke particles as small as 0.3 microns.

Ionisers, on the other hand, rather than using filters, create negative ions using electricity. The ions attach to particles such as dust, smoke, bacteria, pollen and other allergens, passing on their static charge. These particles then seek out the nearest 'earthed' surface (such as a shelf or wall), while ions that travel further into the room gradually slow down as they attract more and more pollutants, eventually falling to the ground when they become too heavy. They can then be cleaned or vacuumed from surfaces. A study carried out by the University of Leeds at St James's Hospital found that the rate of airborne infection of the bacteria acinetobacter, a key source of hospital infection, fell to zero during a year-long trial of a negative air ioniser in an intensive care ward.

Negative ions are also thought to be natural mood-boosters, because they increase the oxygen-carrying capacity of the blood, thereby increasing the amount of oxygen reaching the brain. Researchers studying the effects of ionisers at the University of Columbia in New York report that they appear to relieve depression as effectively as antidepressants. Negative ions may also enhance performance: a 16 week trial at Surrey University found that negative air ionisation could improve participants' task performance by as much as 28 per cent. (For more information on ionisers and HEPA filters, see *Resources* on page 242.)

Chrysanthemums are natural air fresheners.

investigating how to keep the air fresh inside space capsules, showed that these plants, among others, may help combat the damaging effects of the three most harmful household pollutants: benzene (found in polystyrene foam, and used in the manufacture of a vast range of products including computers, cooking utensils and household fabrics), formaldehyde (found in shampoos, bubble bath and household cleaners, for example) and trichloroethylene (sources include aerosol products, paints, varnishes and air fresheners).

Other good natural air fresheners include poinsettia, azalea, chrysanthemum and orchid. A few healthy specimens dotted throughout your home will help to keep the air pure, as well as brightening up your living space.

Creating
atmosphere and mood

The power of colour to influence mood has been recognised for many thousands of years; individual colours affect our physical, emotional and spiritual wellbeing in different ways, often at an unconscious level. In colour counselling, a popular modern therapy, practitioners work with people's instinctive response to colour to help them deal with crises. (See *Resources* on page 242 for more information.)

The colours you choose in your home can create a distinctive atmosphere, so it's helpful to know their alleged properties and powers (see overleaf). Practitioners of colour therapy believe that each colour has a different energy, which resonates with the chakras, or energy centres, of the body. But for most of us colour is a personal choice. Some people love bold, bright geometric designs, while others feel more comfortable with paler shades. Although, ultimately, you must decide what pleases you, the following ideas reflect the advice of colour specialists.

in the bedroom

Relaxing colours work well in a bedroom, as they soothe rather than stimulate. Choose pale, gentle tones, such as cream, sand, mint, honey, peach or a pale turquoise-blue that reminds you of the sea. Although brilliant white can be a little stark, consider one of the many off-white paints containing a hint of another tone – for example, jasmine-white or barley-white – to soften the effect.

Pink can have a womblike, soothing effect. Various trials have found that painting police cells pink has a calming influence on potentially aggressive people. Young children (girls and boys) can also be soothed by pink: it's thought to convey the emotion of love, creating a feeling of security. Pale blue is a calming choice for a baby's bedroom and is also good for anyone who suffers nightmares or has trouble sleeping.

TRY THIS! ✓

ARTISTIC LICENCE

Minimise the damage children can cause by scribbling on walls. Hang up an old roller blind in the hall, kitchen or bedroom for them to draw on. You can then roll it up out of sight when you have visitors. Or buy a small blackboard or artist's easel with coloured chalks and crayons and be firm that this is where they demonstrate their artistic talent. Most children aren't destructive if they have some direction.

Choosing the right colours

Before you redecorate your home, consider the following meanings and influences often ascribed to different colours.

Red   for vitality, activity, energy, enthusiasm, interest and passion

Orange   for creativity, playfulness, exploration, change, zest, stimulating the appetite

Blue   for calm, peacefulness, relaxation, enhancing the easy flow of communication

Yellow   for joyfulness, clarity of thought, alleviating confusion, lightening mood, improving memory and decision-making

Green   for calm, harmony, balance, restfulness and fertility

Pink   for universal love, love of self and others, caring, tenderness, beauty, and neutralising disorder, aggression and violence

Purple   for wisdom, spirituality, understanding and tolerance, intuition

Brown   for grounding, stability and convention

White   for purity, clarity, freshness, cleanliness and new beginnings (white contains all the other colours, so is the colour of unity)

Black   for protection, withdrawal, concealment, mystery and feelings of restful emptiness

Grey   for serenity, sorrow and maturity

SLEEP EASY

Creating a calm atmosphere in your bedroom is one of the best aids to peaceful sleep. Here are three easy first steps to help you achieve it:

● Avoid having a perpetual pile of clothes flung on a chair. If you have boxes, suitcases or other clutter stashed under your bed, hide it from view by fitting a valance sheet under your mattress.

● Tidy up your shoes. Having them scattered about the room is not relaxing. Preferably store them in well-labelled shoe boxes; this also keeps them dust-free.

● Research the best mattress for your needs. Your bed and mattress are paramount for restorative sleep. It's worth being prepared to pay a little extra for good quality. A new material called 'TEMPUR' (first used in the

DON'T

AVOID PRIMARY COLOURS

Children's bedrooms are often painted in bright, primary colours, but beware: this could overstimulate and be an obstacle to peaceful sleep.

space industry), which gives all-round support, moulding itself to your body contours and returning to its original shape when you leave the bed, could be an excellent option, especially if you have back problems. (See also chapter 2, *Sleep Tight*.)

Cushions and throws add to the ambience of a room.

in the living room

Peaceful living rooms need predominantly tranquil colours, with perhaps a few bursts of stronger tones in the same range – for example, cream with chocolate and coffee. Or you could try a contrast, for instance, combining pale-blue walls or upholstery with sand and fuchsia for cushions and throws, rugs or lampshades, to add interest and liveliness. As a general rule, pick one main background colour, and have just one or two related coordinating colours – an instant way to harmonise a space.

ADD TEXTURE

Textural elements such as rugs, upholstery, curtains or blinds, bed linen, cushions and throws all add to the ambience of a room. Using wallpaper in your living room or bedroom can add a feeling of texture and depth.

Interesting and creative accessories help to make a home your own, which is key to relaxation. Cushions and throws, for example, can transform a sofa and also create a sense of comfort – important when you want to rest. Soft, squashy cushions will make you feel cosseted. Choose fabrics that are soothing to touch, such as velvet and suede, or add a little luxury with a few silk cushions that shimmer with reflected light. Wool or cashmere throws that you can snuggle into on cold winter evenings will make you feel extra cosy and comfortable.

DON'T

PROTECT YOUR CALM SPACE

Here are two ways to ensure technology doesn't interfere too much in your life:

● Don't keep your computer in the living room. If you don't have a home office or study, put it in the kitchen, so that you don't think of work or end up sending emails when you're supposed to be relaxing.

● Don't position your main telephone in the living room, and turn off the ringer when you really don't want to be disturbed. Don't sacrifice your relaxing-at-home time, or allow unwanted demands to intrude into your calm space; this is key stress management.

If storage is lacking in your kitchen, make it into a positive feature.

in the **kitchen**

Kitchens can be decorated in bolder, more energising colours such as orange, ochre, terracotta, red or cranberry. Interestingly, restaurants are often advised to use orange and pale blue in their colour schemes – because blue is calming, and orange is believed to stimulate the appetite. A relaxed atmosphere and hungry customers are crucial for a restaurant, but these are ideas that can also work well in the home.

While some people opt for a lively kitchen, others prefer a minimalist look, with everything out of sight (for this, of course, plenty of storage is a prerequisite). But don't despair if storage is lacking: make it a positive feature of your kitchen to display everything artistically – for example, by hanging utensils on an easily accessible central hanging unit.

in the **home office**

You may be able to make your study or home office a more stimulating space by painting the walls in a strong colour such as red or mulberry. Alternatively, if that's too much for you, try painting one wall in a bold colour and the remaining walls in a paler, but toning shade; or paper one wall with a particularly vibrant wallpaper.

Bright colours can aid creativity, so consider displaying lively paintings or photographs. Or frame inspiring sayings or snippets of poetry (change them regularly, if you can, for fresh motivation) to hang up around your workspace. Most importantly, be inventive. Surround yourself with whatever inspires you, including the colours that make you feel happy.

in the **bathroom**

The goal here is to create a place that is both functional and relaxing. So, again, clear the clutter – no overflowing dirty linen baskets or towels in untidy piles. Smooth out the towels on display into clean lines (they'll dry better) and have good-sized bathroom cabinets to hide the inevitable mass of bottles, lotions, medicines, make-up and shaving paraphernalia. If possible, fit your basins into a storage unit, or commission a carpenter to box in unsightly pipes and build cabinets to contain cleaning materials and other bits and pieces, to keep your bathroom looking sleek.

Your colour scheme should complement your home. If your bathroom tends to be cold in winter, avoid cold colours such as blues and blue-greens, or white. If you like blue, choose purple, which contains some red, or opt for a blue-tinged wine-red, which would be visually warming – either as a wall colour or for tiling around the bath and basin. Alternatively, combine blue with a bright, sunny yellow – a match often seen in Mediterranean countries. If you favour a neutral look, try adding splashes of strong colour with your towels.

BATHE THE STRESS AWAY

When you have the time for a luxurious long soak, make it extra special by using scented candles – bathing by candlelight is a wonderful way to relax – or just dim the lights if you can, to create a soothing atmosphere. The bathroom is the place to indulge your senses; add scented oils to your bath, or warm aromatic essential oils in an oil burner. If you prefer showers, fitting a power or rainfall shower can bestow a feeling of luxury, although you may need to install a pump if your water pressure is low. An added benefit of taking a shower is that it's thought to supply more health-giving negative ions (see page 212).

TRY THIS! ✓

ADD SOME GREENERY

Plants usually love the damp and steamy tropical atmosphere of the bathroom, and will also enhance your space and your enjoyment of it.

Mood lighting

The way you light different parts of your home can influence the atmosphere of each room. Using a few lamps is a relatively inexpensive way to create a calming atmosphere in a living room or bedroom, as the light they produce is far more relaxing than ceiling lighting. Just changing your lampshades for a more up-to-date look or buying uplighters can feel refreshing.

Here's how to maximise the effects of your lighting around the home:

● **In the living room**, consider installing dimmer switches so that you can alter the mood; during the day you may want brighter light, but in the evening low lighting will help you relax. Eye specialists advise having some lighting on while watching TV, as viewing in total darkness strains the eyes. Table lamps add a gentle and intimate feel to a room, and opaque lampshades in dark colours contain the light so that it illuminates just small areas, creating a peaceful atmosphere.

● **In the kitchen or home office** you need strong, bright lighting to keep you alert and to safeguard your eyes, as poor lighting can cause eye strain. Try installing spotlights to direct the light into specific task-centred areas of the room, or set up anglepoise lamps that can be adjusted. Use opaque shades to reduce glare, and point the light bulb away from your sight line.

● **In the bedroom** it makes sense to have low lighting, so dimmer switches could be helpful if you need stronger lighting for reading in bed, or when applying make-up. If you're a bedtime reader but your partner isn't, and you're concerned about disturbing the other's sleep, consider positioning a dual spotlight above the centre of the bed to direct the light to each side; bedside lamps don't always give a strong enough light to read by.

● **In the bathroom** you need lighting from three sides: from above and on either side of the mirror, to minimise shadows. Or you could install theatre-dressing-room-style lights all around the mirror, to ensure shadow-free light for applying make-up.

Avoid fluorescent lighting if possible, or buy full-spectrum bulbs that simulate daylight. Non full-spectrum fluorescent lights have been associated with drowsiness, lethargy, headaches and eye strain, as well as exacerbating skin problems. If you have to work under standard lights, be sure to take the recommended daily dose of vitamin A or a daily cod liver oil capsule.

DID YOU KNOW?

LIGHT UP YOUR LIFE

Sir Isaac Newton used a prism in 1666 to see the rainbow of colours now known as the electromagnetic spectrum. He discovered that sunlight is not one colour: the spectrum is red, orange, yellow, green, blue, indigo and violet – the seven basic colours. Research has shown that certain aspects of light can be employed in different ways for their healing properties – sufferers of SAD (seasonal affective disorder), for example, find daylight-simulating light boxes particularly effective (see chapter 10 and *Resources* on page 242), while blue light is used for its calming effect in some psychiatric hospitals.

The personal touch

Nourish and uplift your senses by bringing nature into your home in the form of freshly cut flowers. Attractive plants – such as elegant ferns and palms, or the peace lily plant, which produces surprising white, leaflike flowers – can also transform a room. Bowls of scented flower petals or pot-pourri add another relaxing note. The gentle sound of running water is also soothing: a small, indoor water feature can create calm in a living room or a bedroom.

You can also influence the mood in your home using natural scents: lavender, jasmine and rose are calming and soothing, for example. Warm essential oils in ceramic oil burners to perfume your home, or use scented candles to combine beautiful aromas with soft lighting. Incense sticks or cones impart stronger scents such as sandalwood, pine, musk, patchouli or lemongrass; use these for their energising effect during the day.

EXPERT VIEW

SOUND ADVICE

Noise pollution is a source of stress that's often overlooked. Although many of us manage to filter out continuous noise, such as the roar of traffic, there's evidence that too much noise could seriously damage our health, adversely affecting hearing and blood pressure and, in severe cases, leading to heart failure. According to scientists, our bodies respond to noise even when we're asleep. The World Health Organisation found that 3,000 heart disease deaths a year could be attributed to noise.

If noise affects you in your home, consider installing double glazing. Cheaper solutions include hanging heavy curtains, using good-quality earplugs with a high noise-reduction rating (NRR), or noise-cancelling headphones. If it's still noisy at night, petition your local council to install low-noise road surfaces and mend potholes, which increase traffic noise.

pet power

Keeping a pet is good for your health and a known stress reliever, and also helps alleviate loneliness in people who live on their own. Petting and caring for an animal can be a wonderful way to wind down after a hard day. Studies show that pet owners have measurably lower levels of cholesterol and blood

Pet owners have measurably lower levels of cholesterol and blood pressure.

Top 5 tips for creating a garden sanctuary

If you're lucky enough to have a garden, whether it's a small patio or a large expanse, you can create a tranquil and beautiful outdoor haven in which to relax. Gardening itself is a very peaceful and stress-reducing activity, as it takes your mind away from timetables and pressures, and puts you in touch with the slower-moving natural world.

1 Think about installing a water feature or a pond with a small fountain in the centre; moving water produces health-giving negative ions, as well as preventing the build-up of algae.

2 Don't give yourself too much work; plant sweet-smelling, easy-care plants. Honeysuckle and jasmine both give off a heady scent, especially at night, and only need occasional pruning.

3 A small statue or two, half-hidden within a shrubbery bed, or proudly positioned on a plinth, can add an artistic element, and a well-placed mirror can give the illusion of a larger space.

4 Even if your garden space is limited, try to grow some herbs, including parsley, mint, lemongrass, rosemary, basil, thyme or coriander, either in containers or alongside your flowers. As well as scenting your garden, they will enhance your culinary efforts.

5 If your garden is large enough, create a restful, secluded area by screening it off with a trellis – you can use it to train a climbing rose to beautiful effect. Here you can place a wooden bench or arbour seat, creating a special place in which to enjoy moments of tranquillity and rest.

pressure than people who don't own pets, and one American study found that men who own cats or dogs have a lower resting heart rate than those who don't. Follow the tips on pages 209–210 to ensure pet dander doesn't exacerbate any allergies suffered by family members or anyone living in your home.

Relax in your home

Your home environment is not necessarily a reflection of your inner state, but your inner state is undoubtedly influenced by your surroundings. Don't allow your environment to dominate you; instead, recognise that you have the power to organise your home as you wish. By taking a little control of your space you will be able to mould it into somewhere that instantly makes you feel calm and relaxed. Your home can be a peaceful sanctuary, and now you know how you can make it so.

10 helping hands

To overcome stress and focus on the joyful aspects of life, you have to examine your anxieties and address their source. But you can't always do it on your own. Sometimes the way forward is to recognise and accept the need for outside help. Whether you're finding it difficult to cope or you want to advise a friend or relative, this chapter offers practical tips and guidance on the many sources of expert help and the different types of treatment available.

Tackling stress **head-on**

Life offers many happy and exciting opportunities, new beginnings and positive life changes, from the birth of a baby to passing your driving test or embarking on a new relationship. But it can't always be like that and everyone experiences difficult periods when it's hard to bounce back from major setbacks.

As you'll have found throughout this book, there are plenty of good strategies for changing aspects of your life and dealing effectively with stress, but self-help techniques are not always enough. If your anxieties get out of control and seriously disrupt your everyday life and your relationships, you may need outside help.

There may also be times when it's important to make sure there isn't a medical reason for any symptoms that you've been putting down to stress, such as sleeping problems or weight loss. The next section looks at times when it's wise to see your GP – either to rule out other causes for your symptoms or to seek effective help for your anxiety.

Everyone experiences difficult periods when it's hard to bounce back.

Getting **medical help**

There's evidence to link prolonged stress with a variety of illnesses, so it's worth discussing any stress-related problems with your GP, who will help you to address any issues properly and effectively. You need to see a doctor, for example, if you have trouble sleeping (see chapter 2, *Sleep Tight*), feel generally anxious or develop panic attacks, or if you have new indigestion, constipation, diarrhoea or chest pain. It is also sensible to see your GP if you have an existing illness and you experience any further physical or psychological symptoms. Stress can cause symptoms that either mimic or exacerbate specific medical problems, so if you are ill already, you need to treat the stress before it makes your condition worse.

If you have problems related to drugs, alcohol or smoking, or if you suffer from seasonal affective disorder (SAD, see page 227) or anxiety, it's also wise to consult your doctor to find out about sources of help.

When to see your doctor

Many of us hesitate to seek medical help, hoping the problem will go away on its own. But it's wise to see your doctor if you experience one or more of the following symptoms, because these could indicate that you have developed a condition called generalised anxiety disorder (GAD – see page 23) or some other medical or mental health condition that needs further investigation.

These are the top signs which indicate that you may need to see your GP:

PSYCHOLOGICAL SYMPTOMS

- You find it increasingly difficult to concentrate or to make even simple decisions.
- You regularly experience a sense of panic.
- You remain upset for a long time after even minor setbacks.
- You often feel detached from your immediate environment.
- Friends or family say you are unusually irritable or miserable.
- You feel unable to control your actions or worry that you are 'going mad'.
- You frequently experience loss of libido or other sexual difficulties.
- You are smoking or drinking much more than usual, or are drinking alcohol early in the day.
- You have a general sense of dread, or feel constantly on edge.

PHYSICAL SYMPTOMS

- You have put on, or lost, a lot of weight for no apparent reason.
- You suffer from a dry mouth, or have difficulty swallowing.
- Your muscles often feel sore or tense for no obvious reason.
- You get a lot of headaches.
- You feel excessively thirsty, or need to make frequents trips to the toilet.
- You've noticed a change in your bowel habits.
- You sometimes suffer from chest tightness or pain.
- You often feel nauseous or suffer from stomach aches or diarrhoea.
- You have serious sleep problems, or you feel constantly tired.
- You regularly suffer from shortness of breath, or other respiratory problems.
- If you are a woman, you have missed one or more periods.
- You feel dizzy sometimes.
- You sweat more than you used to.
- You sometimes feel your heart beating rapidly (palpitations).
- You have experienced panic attacks or tremors.

what your **doctor can do**

Certain physical and psychological symptoms are associated with stress (see page 223), and also with various other medical conditions such as anaemia or diabetes, or problems with your thyroid gland or your heart or blood pressure. When you see your doctor, he or she may ask you, for example:

- How you're feeling generally.
- How long any symptoms you've been experiencing have lasted.
- Whether your work or home life is causing you stress.
- Whether you have any fears or worries.
- If you know of any triggers that tend to precipitate your symptoms.
- If you feel happy with your personal life.
- Other lifestyle issues, such as smoking, exercise and diet.

It's important that you are open and honest with your GP so that you can get the best help available. You may need further tests or referral to a specialist to determine the root cause of your symptoms. If they are due to an anxiety disorder, your GP may be able to offer you two main forms of treatment:

- Referral to someone who can offer additional psychological support, such as a counsellor or therapist (see pages 236–237).
- Medication.

You may benefit from one form of treatment or a combination of both, depending on your circumstances.

Your GP may also be able to provide you with information on the many organisations and outside sources of support (see page 233) that you can turn to if you are suffering from stress.

MEDICATION FOR ANXIETY DISORDERS

If your doctor feels that you may benefit from medication, he or she will discuss the different options with you, taking into account factors such as:

- Your symptoms.
- The types of medicines available.

- The length of treatment.
- Any possible side effects.
- Possible interactions with other medicines.
- Your lifestyle – some drugs cause drowsiness and must not be taken while driving or operating machinery, for instance.

Your doctor will prescribe you a course of anti-anxiety medication only after assessing all your circumstances. The drugs most often prescribed for anxiety include:

TYPE OF DRUG	DRUG NAMES	NOTES	POSSIBLE SIDE EFFECTS
Benzodiazepines (anxiolytics)	Diazepam, alprazolam, chlordiazepoxide, clobazam	These may be useful in severe anxiety disorders, especially if you also have insomnia. They are taken for short periods only, as they are potentially addictive if taken for longer than four weeks	Confusion, loss of balance, memory loss and drowsiness
Other anxiolytics	Buspirone	Usually taken for short periods only	Vertigo, headache, agitation, nausea, drowsiness, insomnia; may affect your ability to perform skilled tasks (such as driving) and enhance the effects of alcohol
Selective serotonin reuptake inhibitors (SSRIs)	Paroxetine, escitalopram, pregabalin	Some of these antidepressants also have anti-anxiety effects that may help chronic anxiety occurring with clinical depression. They are also sometimes used for generalised anxiety disorder (GAD), panic attacks and phobias. It takes a few weeks for these antidepressants to become effective; your doctor will want to monitor your progress regularly	Nausea, loss of libido, blurred vision, diarrhoea, constipation, insomnia, anorexia, skin reactions
Beta blockers	Propranolol, atenolol, metoprolol, acebutolol	These drugs, used to treat high blood pressure and heart disease, also work to dampen some of the physical symptoms of anxiety, such as palpitations and tremors. They do not affect psychological symptoms such as worry and tension	Slow heart rate, may bring on asthma attacks, fatigue, cold extremities, sleep disturbances
Serotonin and noradrenaline reuptake inhibitors (SNRIs)	Venlafaxine	An antidepressant sometimes taken by people who are not helped by SSRIs. It may occasionally be used to treat GAD. This drug cannot be taken by anyone with uncontrolled high blood pressure or certain heart problems, and if you take it your blood pressure will need to be monitored	Nausea, headache, drowsiness, constipation, indigestion and insomnia

Alcohol and drug problems

Addictions and depression or other mental health problems often go hand in hand. Dealing with stress by turning to alcohol or drugs is counter-productive. Although drinking a moderate amount of alcohol is socially acceptable and can benefit your health, excessive drinking may cause potentially damaging long-term problems (see below). If you can't reduce the amount you consume on your own, speak to your GP or consider seeking help from Alcoholics Anonymous (see page 232 and *Resources* on page 242), where support is offered in a group setting.

KNOW YOUR LIMITS

Did you know that people who regularly drink above the recommended upper limits of alcohol (for men, 3–4 units a day; for women, 2–3 units a day) are more likely to develop medical problems? Men are four times as likely to have high blood pressure; women are three times more likely to suffer a stroke or heart disease. Alcohol is also a risk factor for several cancers, including breast, bowel and liver cancer, as well as for cirrhosis of the liver.

quitting smoking

If you smoke, make it your number one priority to give up. Discover other more productive ways to deal with stress, such as exercise or participating in new activities instead (see chapter 8). There's lots of information online to help you find the impetus to quit, from organisations such as QUIT and NHS Smokefree (see *Resources* on page 242). Your doctor can also help, both by putting you in touch with local support groups and by prescribing:

- Nicotine replacement therapy (NRT), in the form of patches, nasal spray, lozenges or chewing gum.
- A course of drug treatment, such as Zyban.

DID YOU KNOW?

IN A NUTSHELL

Research has shown that smoking reduces life expectancy by about eight years. On average, each cigarette smoked shortens your life by 11 minutes. Doesn't that make you want to quit?

Smoking reduces life expectancy by about eight years.

The evidence suggests that if you take NRT or Zyban and get the support of a local stop-smoking group, you're four times more likely to quit successfully.

Behaviour modification techniques also help many people to stop smoking, either on their own or in conjunction with NRT. Behaviour modification works by helping you find new ways to behave in situations you automatically associate with having a cigarette, such as finishing a meal, facing a deadline at work or simply having a cup of tea. To start, you may find it easiest simply to avoid certain situations, perhaps by changing your daily routine. Then you can substitute new healthier forms of behaviour such as chewing gum or eating fruit or other healthy foods.

Whatever method you use to quit smoking, the most important thing is to keep trying. Accept that it's not going to be easy – it may take a number of attempts to quit successfully – but finding another way to manage your stress will improve your general health.

seasonal affective disorder (SAD)

This syndrome is a form of depression affecting people over the winter months, when days are short and light levels are low. Symptoms include low mood, sleep problems, lethargy and carbohydrate craving, which may lead to weight gain. They may start as early as September and continue through until April, but are generally at their worst from December to February. SAD affects up to an estimated 4 million people in the UK, 75 to 80 per cent of them women, with many more people afflicted by similar milder symptoms, known as 'winter blues'.

SAD is caused by the marked difference in daylight hours between summer and winter in the northern hemisphere. It is thought to have become more common because so few of us now work outside, instead

A THERAPIST'S NOTES

Peter and Ellen *explained to me how they both found relief with the help of others, when the stress of everyday life started to take its toll.*

Peter's story

Peter had a very stressful job, working on confidential government projects. He wasn't allowed to talk about his work, and the stress he experienced led to the break-up of his first marriage. To cope, he smoked heavily and ate too much. He became ill with angina and eventually collapsed, needing a triple heart bypass operation. He felt lucky to have survived, and this forced him to take action.

Working with a hypnotherapist not only helped Peter to stop smoking but also taught him how to relax whenever he felt himself getting stressed. He retired soon afterwards and used the self-hypnosis techniques whenever he felt anxious and also as a regular practice to help him sleep better.

With hindsight, Peter wished he'd sought help at an earlier stage. If he'd had a check-up from his GP, his serious health problems could have been highlighted much sooner. This might have prompted him to change his lifestyle and try to give up smoking. He also regrets not seeking the help of a hypnotherapist earlier, so that he could have learned and used relaxation and self-hypnosis techniques before his stress got out of hand. Nevertheless, even after suffering so much, Peter feels very fortunate that he's had the chance to act on his health issues and turn his life around.

Ellen's story

Ellen had so many things happening at the same time in her life that it was little wonder she became very stressed. She had an unhappy marriage and her husband left her during the same year that both her parents died, her daughter was diagnosed with depression and she moved house. She began suffering from headaches and palpitations, had trouble sleeping and couldn't concentrate, so also became worried about losing her job – and, consequently, about money too. Whatever she tried, she couldn't escape her negative way of thinking. Although she was loth to talk to her GP because she felt she should be able to snap out of it herself, a friend finally persuaded her to make an appointment.

Her GP was very sympathetic and arranged for her to have several tests to check her general health and heart function. She also recommended a creative-writing course at the local adult-education centre. Joining this class and starting to write regularly was therapeutic and helped Ellen to let go of her stress. She learned useful techniques, such as stream-of-consciousness writing, and writing about what was happening to her as if it were fiction, allowing her to distance herself from it, which brought great relief.

Ellen is convinced that without the help of her GP she might never have found the strength to emerge from her downward spiral of negativity. She continues to use writing as a means of dealing with her stress and has since joined other writing groups, where she has found both support for her writing and sympathetic emotional back-up.

spending most of our waking hours under artificial light. Insufficient daylight upsets the body's biological clock and interferes with the circadian (day-to-day) rhythms of hormone production. Secretion of melatonin, the 'sleep hormone' produced by the pineal gland in the brain (see also chapter 2), usually peaks in the middle of the night and is 'turned off' by light in the morning. This rhythm controls numerous other hormone cycles throughout the body and may be disturbed during the winter months. SAD sufferers seem to have high daytime melatonin levels during the winter, disrupting their sleep–wake cycles. At the same time, serotonin, important for mood, is triggered by sunlight, so quantities decrease in winter. The end result is a chemical imbalance that can lead to depression, affecting some people more than others, depending on the extent of the imbalance and their body's ability to react to it.

OVERCOMING SAD

It helps to get out in the sun for 15 minutes a day, without sunscreen (take care if you burn easily), soaking up the rays. Unfortunately, in the winter months, sunlight in the UK is in short supply and generally too weak.

This is where light therapy comes in. Treatment with strong artificial light using fluorescent bulbs that mimic natural daylight has been shown to be effective in about 85 per cent of SAD sufferers. In one Canadian study over three winters, light therapy was as effective as antidepressant drug treatment. Users sit in front of a light box once or twice a day for 15 minutes or up to a few hours as necessary, and the idea is that this resets the body's internal biological clock and brings hormone cycles back to normal.

Light therapy is not available on the NHS. You can hire or purchase a light box for home use from a variety of outlets (see *Resources* on page 242 for details).

Get out in the sun for
15 minutes a day.

Emotional and psychological help

Whether you've experienced a one-off stressful life event, such as an acute illness or bereavement, or you're feeling the pressure from the steady drip-drip of life's inevitable hassles, it's important not to be tempted to turn to crutches that offer a quick fix. Excess alcohol consumption, smoking, resorting to prescribed or illegal drugs or even getting a short-term fix from shopping or gambling will not solve your problems in the long term. It is far better to recognise when things are getting out of hand and to seek other sources of help, which will have a more effective, ongoing effect without hazardous side effects on your health, lifestyle or wallet. Your GP may be able to refer you for specialised counselling, hypnotherapy or cognitive behavioural therapy (CBT), or you may choose to seek help from one of the practitioners mentioned overleaf (see panel on page 232).

If you think things are starting to slip and you feel increasingly unable to cope, it's vital you talk to someone.

Whatever your issues, if you think things are starting to slip and you feel increasingly unable to cope, it's vital not to carry on in isolation. A useful starting point may be one of the many support groups and organisations that have been set up to help people get through difficult periods of their lives. Many people find that making contact with others with similar issues gives them a boost. Ask your GP, check online or in your local library, or look at the *Resources* section on page 242, which lists information for the organisations below, as well as for many other sources of support. Here are seven of the many that can help (if you need assistance with financial or legal problems, see also chapter 6, *Know Your Rights*):

● **CRUSE BEREAVEMENT CARE** Helps people who have suffered bereavement to understand their grief and come to terms with their loss.
● **RELATE** Offers advice, relationship counselling, sex therapy, workshops, mediation and support to anyone experiencing relationship difficulties. Eighty per cent of Relate clients say that counselling has strengthened their relationship, though the organisation will also help to smooth the break-up if couples decide to split up.

Bullying in the workplace

It's been estimated that 13.5 million working days are lost annually through stress in the UK, at a cost of £4 billion per year. Stress often leads to further physical and mental health problems, more days off work because of sickness and less efficiency on the job. And a major cause of stress is bullying in the workplace.

Bullying at work may happen at any time, but it becomes more common when there's a recession. According to the trade union UNISON, in early 2010 more than a third of 7,000 workers reported being bullied over a six-month period – double the number in a similar survey from 1997. This, coupled with general job insecurity, leads to stress. As the workforce is cut back, a smaller number of employees may be coerced into doing the work of several people. Or they may be under increased pressure to do more with fewer resources.

But it's not just workers who suffer; managers may experience bullying too, through increased target-setting and pressure to perform in an ever more competitive market. Other forms of bullying include targeting someone because of their gender, sexuality, ethnicity, disability, age or religious beliefs. It may not necessarily be face to face – often it comes in the form of emails, texts or other written communications – and it may not be one individual, but a group who bully one or more of their colleagues. But the end result is the same, with the person left feeling humiliated, frightened, anxious or angry.

What can you do if you feel you're being bullied?

1 Find out if anyone else is experiencing similar problems and, if you can predict a likely incident, get someone else to witness what's going on.

2 Keep a diary of incidents, along with copies of any bullying memos and emails. Build up a dossier.

3 Raise issues with your human resources department and/or senior managers.

4 Join and get support from your trade union.

5 Inform the person who is bullying you, preferably with another person present, that his or her behaviour is unacceptable.

Employers are required by law to protect the health and safety of all their employees, so failure to take reasonable steps to prevent or deal with bullying could be unlawful. Employers who fail in their 'duty of care' for employees – which includes protecting them from workplace violence, verbal abuse or harassment – may be vulnerable to a legal action for constructive dismissal, if you feel you have no option other than to resign as a result. (See *Resources* on page 242 for more information.)

Help from an expert

Where can you turn if the stress you feel is so overwhelming that you can't get through the day without extreme feelings of agitation? And what can you do if this creates more stress, which in turn increases your anxiety? If this sounds familiar, it may be time to seek help. People often put off seeking help because they don't understand what the different experts do. Here's a brief guide:

- **Counsellors** help you cope with stress and/or chronic problems you are facing, and may look for sources of stress in your past. They listen and reflect, helping you to make your own decisions, rather than offering specific advice.

- **Psychotherapists** vary in their approach: some examine past experiences, and how these may be affecting your life now, while others focus more on what's going on in the present. They offer insights into your problems, and also offer specific coping strategies.

- **Cognitive behavioural therapists** encourage you to look at the way you view yourself, the world and your future prospects, and help you see how your thoughts, feelings and actions are interrelated. They help you to challenge existing patterns of behaviour and devise strategies for dealing with stress.

- **Psychiatrists** are medical doctors who specialise in mental health problems. After diagnosis, they usually treat with medication and often one-to-one or group therapy. You need a referral from your GP.

- **Life coaches** look at what you want to achieve and encourage you to move forward without necessarily examining past issues.

You can approach a counsellor, therapist or life coach direct rather than being referred by your GP, although seeing your doctor first is recommended, in case of an underlying health problem. Your doctor may refer you to a psychiatrist or an NHS counsellor. You can also find a practitioner (who will charge a fee) from one of the organisations listed in the *Resources* section (see page 242), or by searching on the internet.

- **ALCOHOLICS ANONYMOUS** A fellowship of people who meet up to share their experiences of alcohol addiction and hear the experiences of recovered alcoholics, while offering each other mutual support to help them stop drinking. Members follow a 12-step programme with the aim of achieving total abstinence.

- **QUIT** An independent charity that aims to save lives by helping smokers to stop and offers free, individual advice from trained counsellors as well as useful leaflets and brochures.

- **GAMCARE** A charity that offers non-judgmental support to those with gambling problems.

- **STRESS MANAGEMENT SOCIETY** A non-profit-making organisation dedicated to helping people tackle stress, whether as part of a company or as an individual. Offers free, accessible information and the latest news on useful stress-busting services and products.

- **NATIONAL DEBTLINE** Provides free, confidential advice for anyone with debt problems.

stress-reducing therapies

Although the most widely used therapy is cognitive behavioural therapy (CBT), your doctor may recommend other psychological therapies, such as other forms of behaviour therapy, interpersonal therapy, problem-solving therapy and short-term psychodynamic psychotherapy, depending on your circumstances and resources in your area.

USEFUL COURSES

Your GP may suggest that you attend an NHS stress-management course. Sessions are usually free, and aim at helping people give up smoking or deal with alcohol or other stress-related problems. They may take place at your local health centre, GP surgery or hospital. To find out more, talk to your GP or look at the NHS website, NHS Choices, for more information.

Assertiveness training is useful if you find it difficult to say no. You'll be coached in speaking your mind non-aggressively and communicating your wishes effectively. In one study of 60 nurses in Taiwan, just six 2-hour workshops over a fortnight produced significant reductions in their stress scale ratings, along with higher assertiveness scores. Courses are available locally and nationally. Combining assertiveness training with time-management skills is a good way to avoid the stress of taking on too much at once.

If you have a problem controlling your anger, anger-management courses will help you learn how to deal with your own and others' emotional outbursts. These courses may be offered at your workplace or at local adult-education centres. The NHS's own website offers advice on anger-management issues and your GP may direct you to local services. Or check the website of the British Association of Anger Management (see *Resources* on page 242).

EXPERT VIEW

COGNITIVE BEHAVIOURAL THERAPY (CBT)

CBT is based on the belief that you can change the way you react to stressful situations by altering the way you think and behave. Courses are usually between 5 and 20 sessions; it can also be learned from a book or computer program (two computer-based programs are approved for use in the NHS).

CBT therapists encourage their clients to talk about the goals they want to achieve, then help them to deal with undesirable situations in a calm and logical way. One study in Sweden showed that four months of CBT produced significant improvements in self-rated stress, stress-related behaviour, anger, exhaustion and quality of life, accompanied by improved measurements of blood pressure, heart rate and stress hormones. Contact the British Association for Behavioural and Cognitive Psychotherapies (BABCP) for more information (see *Resources* on page 242).

Continued on p236 ➤

10 ways to work with a life coach

Often the first step to reducing your stress is realising that you have some control over whatever is causing it. If you'd like to redress the balance in your life, but you're getting nowhere on your own, a few sessions with a life coach can be useful.

A life coach is similar to, but different from, a counsellor or therapist. You will be encouraged to look forward and discover ways to set and achieve your goals. Many life coaches work with their clients on the telephone rather than face to face, and coaches usually charge fees for their services. (See also *Resources* and chapter 8 for help with finding a life coach, as well as *Finding the Right Counsellor or Therapist* on page 236 – this advice also applies to finding a life coach.)

Working with a life coach on the following may help to reduce the effects of stress in your life:

1 INTRODUCE MORE BALANCE The aim is to find ways to help you reduce the amount of time you spend working, if this is a cause of your stress, or to take time out for yourself from other stressful obligations such as childcare. You will be coached in learning to say 'no' when asked to do extra work, especially if it's outside your normal working hours.

3 STOP DOING WHAT DOESN'T HAVE TO BE DONE A life coach will help you to step back and examine why you're doing some of the things that you do. Maybe there is no longer any reason but they've become habits that need to be stopped. You will also be encouraged to prioritise tasks and not to spend over-long on jobs that could be completed more quickly.

Introduce more balance in your life.

2 DELEGATE Learning to delegate certain everyday tasks is crucial. Perhaps a colleague could take on some work tasks, or family members be asked to help more with domestic chores. You may be able to share or swap some tasks with a friend – join forces to alternate doing the school run, or grocery shopping, for example. If you can afford it, sometimes it's worth paying someone to take on difficult or time-consuming tasks, such as decorating, cleaning or gardening, whether on a one-off or a regular basis. You'll be encouraged to explain clearly what you want and how you want it done and to leave the other person to get on with it while you go off and do something else.

4 GET HELP IN A CRISIS An important lesson is asking for help when you feel a crisis point looming, whether you approach a friend or family member or pay someone to help lighten your load.

5 LOOK AFTER YOUR BODY Many life coaches will also suggest that you pay attention to your diet, perhaps by reducing your intake of comfort or junk foods. You'll often feel much less stressed if you change your habits and start to eat fresh, healthy food without additives or sugar and keep to low-fat foods. Similarly, you may be encouraged to avoid tobacco and excess alcohol and to keep your body flexible and de-stressed by taking regular exercise.

6 **BE MORE ORGANISED** A life coach will help you to notice how much less stressed you feel when you know where everything is. Tidying your workspace, garage, wardrobe or kitchen is a good start.

7 **CLEAR CLUTTER** In addition to being encouraged to tidy up what you need, you'll learn that it's counter-productive to hoard stuff just in case you might need it some day. Throwing stuff away if you haven't needed it for several years or if it's broken or out of date is liberating.

8 **NURTURE YOUR SPIRIT** This is crucial in becoming a well-rounded, balanced person, so you may be encouraged to connect with nature each day, to watch the sunrise or the stars, to make time for your spirituality, however you view it, through formal or informal religion or otherwise.

9 **CARE FOR YOUR MIND** You'll often be urged to keep your mind fresh and lively – by keeping up to date with current events, reading regularly, attending concerts or going to the theatre or cinema, and/or by doing puzzles – both as a way to relax and to keep your brain active. Enjoyable mental stimulation can keep your mind off other problems and reduce your stress, too.

10 **KEEP IN TOUCH WITH SUPPORTIVE FRIENDS AND FAMILY** They say that blood is thicker than water. Love them or hate them, your family matters, and they'll often rally round to help in a crisis if you explain your problems, as will true friends. However, you may need to cut back on seeing anyone who makes excessive demands or saps your spirit. A life coach can help you to find out the level of contact with friends and family that works for you.

A life coach will help you to clear clutter
and throw away stuff you haven't needed for years.

Finding the right counsellor or therapist is vital – someone with whom you feel comfortable.

finding the right
counsellor or therapist

'The most important factor in determining whether your therapy is successful is your relationship with the therapist,' says Phillip Hodson of the British Association of Counselling and Psychotherapy. 'If a counsellor is brilliant at the theory but doesn't have much empathy with people, their results won't be so impressive.' Finding someone with whom you feel comfortable and really able to explore your feelings is vital if the process is to go well. What works for one person won't always work for another.

First, decide if you'd prefer a male or female to help you, or if you'd be more comfortable with someone of a certain age or with a similar life experience. You could be referred by your GP to someone within the NHS; you wouldn't have to pay, but you may not be able to be specify any preferences, as through a private organisation. Always ensure that the person you approach is reputable, trained, qualified and competent.

Some of the best ways to find a counsellor or therapist are:
● By asking your GP, who will have information both about free counselling and various private counsellors and therapists in your area.
● By seeking a recommendation from a friend or colleague, though do bear in mind that everyone has different expectations, so the person recommended may or may not be suitable for you.

- By contacting professional organisations, either by phoning or visiting their websites (see *Resources* on page 242 for suggestions).
- By having a trial consultation (a fee may apply). This is useful in getting a sense of whether you'd be able to work with the person. As you'll be discussing your personal feelings and situation, it's vital that you trust your counsellor and feel able to talk openly. Ask yourself if you feel you're being listened to properly by someone who understands your situation – not talked down to by someone who's judging you.

HELPING HAND

WHY COUNSELLING HELPS

Counselling sessions have a purpose – to help you see your problems more clearly and discover a positive way ahead – so are different from a chat with friends. You will be challenged and may have to think about aspects of your life in a fresh way. You may also be expected to try new methods of doing things between sessions. For example, if you always agree to do overtime at work, you may be encouraged to practise saying no the next time you're asked. It's important to tackle these tasks if you are to overcome your symptoms of stress and move on with your life.

Stress-management techniques

Learning new stress-reduction techniques, especially if they involve meeting other people in a group setting, is often an effective way of keeping yourself active, helping you relax and taking your mind off your problems. Any physical activity reduces stress levels and improves your mood (see also chapter 3 for more about the benefits of exercise, and chapter 8 for more on activities that could enrich your life and reduce your pressures). Here are two tried-and-tested stress-busting techniques:

- **MASSAGE, INCLUDING AROMATHERAPY** It's very soothing to experience a massage, and may be even more relaxing if aromatherapy oils such as lavender or ylang-ylang are incorporated. In a small study of eight hospital patients in Sussex, six reported improvements in anxiety and depression scores following a weekly aromatherapy massage for six weeks. The best thing about massage is that if you and a friend or partner learn the basics, you can both give each other treatments for free. There are plenty of books and DVDs available, or you could attend a workshop or take a course. You can learn more about the different types of massage through Massage Therapy UK (see *Resources* on page 242).

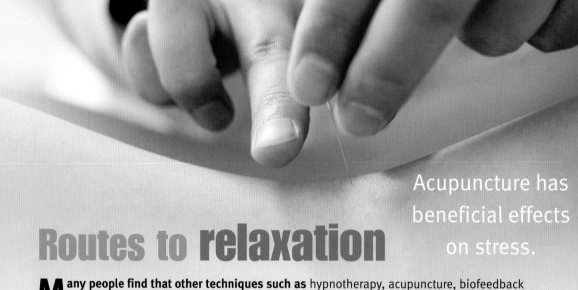

Acupuncture has beneficial effects on stress.

Routes to **relaxation**

Many people find that other techniques such as hypnotherapy, acupuncture, biofeedback and colour therapy help them deal with stress. These are not usually provided by the NHS; although some GPs will provide some therapies in their practices, more often you will be charged a fee. See *Resources* on page 242 for more information on each.

HYPNOTHERAPY A hypnotherapist uses hypnosis to induce a deep state of relaxation, during which time he or she will make beneficial suggestions about how you can change your behaviour. Although you will be aware of your surroundings and can react in case of an emergency, you may not remember all that was said to you afterwards; your subconscious mind, however, *will* remember, so the hypnotherapist's suggestions will remain with you and help to make you feel more relaxed. A group of students at Imperial College Medical School who were taught self-hypnosis to cope with the stress of exams reported increased calmness and higher energy ratings, and were also found to have improved measures of cellular immunity. It's also possible to learn self-hypnosis techniques, either from an expert or using a self-help guide. For more information on hypnotherapy and to find a practitioner, contact the UK Confederation of Hypnotherapy Organisations.

ACUPUNCTURE This ancient Chinese procedure involves having very fine needles inserted just under the skin along so-called acupuncture points. According to Chinese medicine, these points are situated on meridians (channels) along which a life force called *chi* or *qi* flows, and are believed to connect your internal organs. It has been shown that acupuncture has beneficial effects on stress,

causing the release of endorphins, among other things. In one study in Leicester, 94 per cent of volunteers reported reduced stress ratings after four brief acupuncture sessions, with an average 44 per cent fall in stress scores. Several treatments are usually recommended; your acupuncturist may then suggest ongoing treatment to top up the effects of the initial sessions. For more information and to find a practitioner, contact the British Acupuncture Council.

BIOFEEDBACK This is based on the principle that being aware of how your body physiology changes when you are stressed – for example, your heart rate increases – will help you to control it. It is usually best to learn the techniques from an expert, but you can buy biofeedback equipment to use at home. This works non-invasively and displays your body's responses, to help you to monitor these changes and learn how to respond differently. For more information, contact the Association for Applied Psychophysiology and Biofeedback.

COLOUR THERAPY Colour is known to affect our physical, spiritual and emotional wellbeing; certain colours are more stimulating or calming than others, for example. To find out more about colour therapy, see chapter 9.

● **MEDITATION** Learning how to meditate not only lessens feelings of stress but also has a positive effect on your overall health. In one trial, participants on an eight-week stress-reduction programme based on mindfulness meditation experienced significant reductions in reported daily irritations (24 per cent), psychological distress (44 per cent) and medical symptoms (46 per cent), and the benefits were maintained at follow-up three months later. You can practise meditation in a group or by yourself. Find out more through websites such as Meditation Expert (see *Resources* on page 242); see also chapter 4.

(see *Resources* on page 242); see also chapter 4.

TRY THIS! ✔

SPEAK UP

Sometimes, simply talking through your worries with a friend or relative helps to relieve some of your stress. Giving voice to your concerns may help to dispel any hidden fears, the sort that often come out to haunt you in the middle of the night. Some people find that writing down their feelings in a diary or journal is also very helpful.

Moving on

Of course, as you've learned in the course of the book, there's much you can do yourself to help you to feel calm and stay healthy. You can learn to take time out so that you find balance somewhere in among all the demands of a busy job coupled with a hectic home life. You're not a robot, but a human being who needs time to recharge your personal batteries. Even a few minutes between tasks to do some slow breathing, take a brisk walk or concentrate fully on something outside your window can relieve stress and renew your energy for the next task.

But it's important to recognise that, however much you want to deal with life's ups and downs on your own, there are times when you will benefit from some help and encouragement from others, especially experts who have experience of treating people with similar problems.

Don't be afraid to seek help when you need it. You don't have to deal with emotional or physical discomfort on your own. You'll gain tremendously from seeking help and advice from those who know about tried-and-tested techniques for banishing stress and other associated problems, and about additional ways to look at what's happening to you. Then you can move on and enjoy all the best things that life has to offer.

glossary

[*Italicised* words have their own definition]

acupuncture A Chinese medical procedure where fine needles are inserted just under the skin to alleviate pain and treat various physical, mental and emotional conditions by balancing energy flow.

adenosine A chemical in the body associated with carrying energy to cells, and believed to be involved in sleep initiation.

adjustment insomnia A short-term form of insomnia caused by a specific, identifiable reason, such as bereavement or marriage difficulties.

affirmations Positive statements that reinforce your self-esteem.

anchoring The process of associating a particular stimulus with a state of mind for beneficial effect.

antioxidants A nutrient that helps to counteract the damaging effects of *free radicals* within the body. Examples are vitamins A, C and E.

atherosclerosis A disease in which arterial walls become thickened and hardened due to the build-up of *cholesterol* and other deposits (plaque).

beta blocker A type of medication that controls blood pressure, that can affect the release of *melatonin*.

beta carotene An antioxidant and type of *carotenoid*.

biofeedback A technique that uses electronic monitoring equipment to help people become aware of their physiological reactions, so that they can learn how to respond differently.

biological clock The brain mechanism that regulates 24 hour (circadian) rhythms in the body and fosters the daily alternation of sleep and wakefulness.

burn-out Physical or mental collapse caused by overwork or stress.

carotenoid Any of a class of mainly yellow, orange or red fat-soluble pigments, including carotene, which give colour to plant parts such as ripe tomatoes and autumn leaves.

catechin A type of *flavonoid* found in tea which exerts vascular protective effects and scavenges *free radicals*.

central sleep apnoea (CSA) A sleep-related breathing disorder that occurs when the brain's control of breathing weakens.

cholesterol An important constituent of cell membranes, but high concentrations are linked with heart disease and *atherosclerosis* (see also *HDL* and *LDL cholesterol*).

cognitive behavioural therapy (CBT) A therapy based on the belief that a person can change the way they react to stressful situations by altering the way they think and behave.

colour therapy Using the healing powers of colour to bring about balance and restore wellbeing.

conditioned (psychophysiological) insomnia Difficulty sleeping as a result of worrying about sleep, creating a vicious cycle of poor sleep, daytime irritability and poor concentration.

cortisol A hormone secreted by the adrenal gland and produced in increased amounts during the *stress response*.

diabetes A condition in which the body cannot regulate the levels of sugar in the blood.

endorphins Chemicals produced in the body that have pain-killing and mood-enhancing effects.

essential amino acid Amino acids (the building blocks of proteins) that cannot be synthesised in the body and must be obtained through diet.

essential fatty acid (EFA) Fatty acids that cannot be manufactured by the body and must be obtained through diet, essential for health, normal growth and development and function of the brain.

fight-or-flight response see *stress response*

flavonoids A group of naturally occurring chemical compounds, found in foodstuffs such as fruit, vegetables and tea, that act as beneficial *antioxidants*.

free radicals Highly reactive chemical products formed during metabolism that may damage body cells and contribute to ageing and disease.

ganglion cells Part of the retina (the light-sensitive part of the eye) feeding information directly into the *biological clock* via the optic nerve.

generalised anxiety disorder (GAD) A long-term condition in which the person constantly feels anxious without really knowing why.

glucose The type of sugar produced from digestion of foods and used by the body for energy (also referred to as blood sugar).

HDL (high-density lipoprotein) cholesterol The 'good' fat that mops up *LDL cholesterol* from the bloodstream.

hypnotherapy The use of hypnosis as a therapeutic technique.

idiopathic insomnia Insomnia that starts in infancy or childhood and is difficult to overcome.

insulin A hormone produced by the pancreas and important in the regulation of blood sugar (*glucose*).

isoflavones Plant-derived oestrogen (found primarily in soya) that may help to alleviate some symptoms of the menopause.

LDL (low-density lipoprotein) cholesterol The 'bad' fat that may accumulate in the bloodstream to promote plaque formation.

light therapy A treatment for *seasonal affective disorder (SAD)* that uses strong artificial light to mimic daylight.

melatonin A hormone secreted by the pineal gland that has an effect on our *biological clock* and plays a role in the sleep/wake cycle. It is often used for controlling jet lag.

mindfulness training Learning to fully engage with the present moment as a way to release oneself from worry and anxiety and help improve physical and mental wellbeing.

mono-unsaturated fats 'Healthy' fats, such as olive oil, that are usually liquid at room temperature.

narcolepsy A rare chronic sleep disorder characterised by excessive sleepiness and sudden and uncontrollable episodes of deep sleep.

neuro-linguistic programming (NLP) A therapeutic process which focuses on educating people in self-awareness and changing patterns of mental and emotional behaviour for the better.

niacin A type of B vitamin that helps keep the digestive and nervous systems healthy.

obstructive sleep apnoea (OSA) A sleep-related breathing disorder occurring when the muscles of the throat relax and either cause a total blockage (apnoea) or a partial blockage (hypopnoea).

ombudsman An official appointed to investigate individuals' complaints against maladministration.

omega-3 fatty acids *Essential fatty acids* found in oily fish and some plant sources/vegetables.

omega-6 fatty acids *Essential fatty acids* found in natural and processed vegetable oils.

positive visualisation The process of calling to mind an inspiring image or statement to focus the subconscious mind on the positive and boost confidence.

refined carbohydrates Starchy foods that have been heavily processed and are thus nutrient poor, for example white flour, white bread, white rice and pasta.

REM (Rapid Eye Movement) One of the three main states of sleep, and the type of sleep commonly associated with dreaming; REM occurs roughly every 90 minutes, with REM episodes becoming progressively longer as the night progresses.

Restless leg syndrome (Ekbom's disease) Creepy-crawly sensations in the legs (and sometimes arms), usually experienced late at night.

riboflavin Vitamin B_2, essential for metabolic energy production and key in maintaining health.

saturated fat The type of fat found in animal products and processed foods, usually solid at room temperature. High intakes may increase *LDL cholesterol* levels, which can lead to *atherosclerosis*.

seasonal affective disorder (SAD) A form of depression affecting people during winter months, caused by lack of exposure to sunlight.

serotonin A neurotransmitter that regulates a number of functions including sleep, mood, behaviour, body temperature and appetite.

Spirulina A microscopic blue-green alga that contains a high concentration of nutrients and is sometimes dubbed a *superfood*.

stress response An automatic reaction triggered in the body when the brain registers something it perceives as a threat, resulting in a number of physiological changes.

stressor Some form of stimulus from your outer environment or inner thoughts and emotions that upsets the body's normal rhythm and compels it to adapt or adjust in some way.

superfood A natural food that is popularly regarded as especially nutritious or otherwise beneficial to health and wellbeing.

trans fats A type of fat created during the processing of vegetable oils and found in junk food, that acts like *saturated fat* in the body.

triglycerides The main constituents of natural fats and oils. High levels in the blood may lead to heart disease and *atherosclerosis*.

tryptophan An *essential amino acid* sometimes known as 'Nature's Prozac' that has positive benefits on mood, and is also used as a sleep aid.

resources

Note: calls to 0845 numbers may cost more than those to ordinary landlines.

Activities and social organisations

Amateur dramatics Find out more about amateur dramatics and groups near you. www.amdram.co.uk or www.amateurdramatic.co.uk

Ballroom dancing Britains's dance monthly: www.dancing-times.co.uk

Belly-dancing www.mosaicdance.org or www.sevenveils.co.uk

British Association of Friends of Museums www.bafm.org.uk

Contacting old friends www.friendsreunited.com or www.facebook.com

Creative writing www.oca-uk.com, www.lonelyfurrowcompany.com or www.fire-in-the-head.co.uk

Hobby ideas www.ideashelper.com/hobby-ideas-21.htm or hunch.com/hobbies Magazines: www.magazine-group.co.uk/magazine/hobbies-leisure

Keep Fit Association (KFA) Tel: 01403 266000 email: kfa@emdp.org www.keepfit.org.uk

Martial arts www.martialartsclubs.co.uk

Massage Therapy UK For information about different types of massage treatment, finding a practitioner and training. www.massagetherapy.co.uk

National Trust www.nationaltrust.org.uk

Online Wheel of Life assessment For advice on drawing up your own Wheel of Life: www.embody.co.uk/blog/post/test_the_balance_of_your_wheel_of_life

Open College of the Arts An educational charity offering distance-learning courses. www.oca-uk.com

Open University www.open.ac.uk

Painting and drawing www.painters-online.co.uk

Pilates www.pilates.co.uk

RSPB (Royal Society for the Protection of Birds) www.rspb.org.uk

Singing Sing For Fun provides adult singing workshops for people who wish to learn to sing and meet new friends in a stress-free environment. www.uksinging.com

Tai chi

Easy Tai Chi DVDs www.easyTaiChi.com

International directory for tai chi and related exercises/martial arts www.taichifinder.co.uk

Learn tai chi online www.GetTaiChiOnline.com

Tai Chi Union for Great Britain Includes national listings for over 800 tai chi instructors. Contact: Peter Ballam (Secretary), 5 Corunna Drive, Horsham, West Sussex RH13 5HG Tel: 01403 257918 www.taichiunion.com

Topiary International association of topiary growers: www.topiary.org.uk

The University of the Third Age Offers people no longer in full-time employment opportunities to meet and learn about a wide range of subjects. Tel: 020 8466 6139 www.u3a.org.uk

Walking

Nordic walking Tel: 0845 260 9339 email: info@nordicwalking.co.uk www.nordicwalking.co.uk

The Ramblers (formerly The Ramblers' Association) A British registered charity which promotes rambling, protects rights of way, campaigns for access to open country and defends the countryside. 2nd Floor, Camelford House, 87–90 Albert Embankment, London SE1 7TW Tel: 020 7339 8500 email: ramblers@ramblers.org.uk www.ramblers.org.uk

Walking tours abroad Walking tours in mainland Greece, the Greek Islands and the central French and Spanish Pyrenees. Contact: Jonathan and Myriam Peat, Chambres d'hôtes, 58 av. Noël Peyrevidal, 09800 Castillon en Couserans, France. Tel: 00 33 561 046 447 email: myriam.peat@wanadoo.fr www.jonathanstours.com

The Wildlife Trusts www.wildlifetrusts.org

Women's Institute www.thewi.org.uk

Women Welcome Women World Wide
Women's international friendship organisation.
www.womenwelcomewomen.org.uk

Woodworking
www.popularwoodworking.com

Yoga

The British Wheel of Yoga The UK's national governing body for yoga. Contact BWY Central Office, British Wheel of Yoga, 25 Jermyn Street, Sleaford, Lincolnshire NG34 7RU
Tel: 01529 306851 email: office@bwy.org.uk
www.bwy.org.uk

Iyengar Yoga Association
www.iyengaryoga.org.uk

Laughter Yoga International #22, Sri Balaji Pride, Flat No.F-2 5th Cross, Bendre Nagar Bangalore – 560 070 India
Tel: + 91-80-26660284
email: info@laughteryoga.org
www.laughteryoga.org

The Sivananda Yoga Vedanta Centre
51 Felsham Road, Putney, London SW15 1AZ
Tel: 020 8780 0160
email: London@sivananda.net
www.sivananda.co.uk
(also www.sivananda.eu)

Allergy information and air purifiers

Allergymatters The UK's number-one resource for allergies, offering expert, unbiased advice.
Tel: 020 8339 0029
www.AllergyMatters.com

Allergy UK Helpline and advice for sufferers of allergy, asthma, hayfever, food intolerances and chemical sensitivity. www.allergyuk.org/

Amazing Health For ionisers and ionising light bulbs. Tel: 0845 838 6263
www.amazinghealth.co.uk

The Ionizer Site For Astrid negative air ionisers, which don't emit ozone.
www.djclarke.co.uk

Anger management

British Association of Anger Management
Offers support, programmes and training.
Tel: 0845 1300 286 email: info@angermanage.co.uk
www.angermanage.co.uk

NHS Choices: anger management
www.nhs.uk/livewell/angermanagement

Bullying

Anti-bullying Alliance A network of over 70 organisations, dedicated to preventing bullying and influencing policy. National Children's Bureau, 8 Wakley Street, London EC1V 7QE
Tel: 020 7843 1901 email: aba@ncb.org.uk
www.anti-bullyingalliance.org.uk

Bullying UK email: help@bullying.co.uk
www.bullying.co.uk

Childline Confidential helpline for children, provided by the NSPCC. Tel: 0800 1111
www.childline.org.uk

The Equality and Human Rights Commission
Information and guidance on discrimination and human rights issues. Helpline: 0845 604 6610
(/5510 Scotland; /8810 Wales)
email: englandhelpline@equalityhumanrights.com
(scotlandhelpline@; waleshelpline@)
www.equalityhumanrights.com

NSPCC Helpline If you are concerned about a child, tel: 0808 800 5000 email: help@nspcc.org.uk

Preventing workplace harrassment and violence
Download a free guidance pack at
www.workplaceharassment.org.uk

UK National Work-Stress Network Dedicated to eradicating bullying, harrassment and the causes of work-related stress. www.workstress.net

Carers

Goldsborough Home Care Professional care workers providing individual care of the elderly, within their own homes, also hospital discharge care, and care for people with other health problems. Branches across England and Wales.
www.goldsborough-home-care.co.uk

The Princess Royal Trust for Carers Help and support for carers. Tel: 0844 800 4361
www.carers.org

Support for carers
www.direct.gov.uk/en/CaringForSomeone
or www.carersinformation.org.uk

Cognitive behavioural therapy & NLP

Association for Neuro Linguistic Programming (ANLP) For information on NLP and Rapport, the magazine of the ANLP. Tel: 0845 053 1162 or 020 3051 6740 www.anlp.org

Beating the Blues An eight-session programme to help overcome depression and anxiety using CBT. www.beatingtheblues.co.uk

British Association for Behavioural and Cognitive Psychotherapies (BABCP) Tel: 0161 705 4304 www.babcp.com

The Mood Gym Free interactive online training programme that teaches the principles of CBT to help prevent depression. moodgym.anu.edu.au

PsychNet-UK Mental health and psychology directory. www.psychnet-uk.com/ psychotherapy/psychotherapy_cognitive_ behavioural_therapy.htm

The Royal College of Psychiatrists 17 Belgrave Square, London SW1X 8PG Tel: 020 7235 2351 www.rcpsych.ac.uk/mentalhealthinformation/ therapies/cognitivebehaviouraltherapy.aspx

Cold callers and junk mail

Bereavement Register Tel: 01732 467940 or 0800 082 1230 (24-hour automated registration service) www.the-bereavement-register.org.uk

Mailing Preference Service Registration line: 0845 703 4599 www.mpsonline.org.uk

Telephone Preference Service Registration line: 0845 070 0707 www.mpsonline.org.uk/tps

Colour therapy and advice

Colour Affects For advice on colour for your home, your business and personal use. 3rd Floor, 50 Great Portland Street, London W1W 7ND Tel: 020 7637 3965 www.colour-affects.co.uk

Colours of the Soul For advice, information, workshops and courses. www.coloursofthesoul.com

Colour Therapy Healing www.colourtherapyhealing.com

Embody For You Colour therapy for health and healing. www.embodyforyou.com/Treatments/?t=136

Iris International School of Colour Therapy Offers distance-learning courses. www.iriscolour.co.uk

Counselling and psychotherapy

Assist Trauma Care Help and support for individuals and families in surviving trauma. 11 Albert Street, Rugby CV21 2RX Helpline: 01788 560800 www.assisttraumacare.org.uk

British Association for Counselling and Psychotherapy (BACP) For a nationwide list of qualified practitioners. Tel: 01455 883300 www.bacp.co.uk

Cruse Bereavement Care A registered charity offering free support to people who have experienced the loss of someone close. Cruse, PO Box 800 Richmond, Surrey TW9 2RG Daytime Helpline: 0844 477 9400 (Scotland tel: 0845 600 2227) www.crusebereavementcare.org.uk (for Scotland visit www.crusescotland.org.uk)

Family Therapy UK For help with family problems. www.familytherapy.org.uk

National Domestic Violence Helpline Tel: 0808 2000 247 www.nationaldomesticviolencehelpline.org.uk or email helpline@womensaid.org.uk Men's advice and enquiry line: Tel: 0808 801 0327 www.mensadviceline.org.uk

NHS Choices: counselling www.nhs.uk/Conditions/Counselling

Parentline Plus A national charity offering advice and support to anyone taking care of children. Tel: 0808 800 2222 www.parentlineplus.org.uk

Patient support groups www.patient.co.uk/selfhelp.asp, www.rsm.ac.uk/public/linkpat.php or www.medic8.com/SupportGroups/Index.htm

Relate For relationship problems, marriage guidance, family counselling and counselling for children. Tel: 0300 100 1234 (Scotland tel: 0845 119 2020) www.relate.org.uk (for Scotland visit www.relationships-scotland.org.uk)

The Tavistock and Portman (NHS Foundation Trust) Specialist mental health trust offering high-quality mental healthcare and education for adults and children. Tavistock Centre, 120 Belsize Lane, London NW3 5BA Tel: 020 8938 2337 or 020 7435 7111 (for adults and family therapy) www.tavistockandportman.nhs.uk

Trauma counselling
www.counselling-directory.org.uk/trauma.html

UK Council for Psychotherapy (UKCP) For a list of qualified psychotherapists. 2nd Floor, Edward House, 2 Wakley St, London EC1V 7LT Tel: 020 7014 9955 email: info@ukcp.org.uk www.psychotherapy.org.uk

Useful online links
www.tastudent.org.uk/html/organizations.htm

Westminster Pastoral Foundation Therapy for individuals and couples, depression, anxiety and stress, trauma, addictions and phobias. Tel: 020 7378 2000 www.wpf.org.uk

Dealing with addictions

Addiction counselling
www.counselling-directory.org.uk/addictions.html

Alcoholics Anonymous PO Box 1, 10 Toft Green, York YO1 7ND Tel: 0845 769 7555 email: help@alcoholics-anonymous.org.uk www.alcoholics-anonymous.org.uk

ASH (Action on Smoking and Health) First Floor, 144–145 Shoreditch High St, London E1 6JE Tel: 020 7739 5902 email: enquiries@ash.org.uk www.ash.org.uk

Gambling counselling www.counselling-directory.org.uk/gambling.html

GamCare 2nd Floor, 7–11 St John's Hill, London SW11 1TR Helpline: 0845 6000 133 www.gamcare.org.uk

NHS Choices: alcohol www.drinking.nhs.uk

NHS Choices: drug misuse
www.nhs.uk/conditions/Drug-misuse

NHS Choices: smoking Helpline: 0800 022 4 332 www.smokefree.nhs.uk

QUIT For help with giving up smoking. 63 St Marys Axe, London EC3A 8AA Quitline: 0800 00 22 00 email: stopsmoking@quit.org.uk www.quit.org.uk

Debt advice

Citizens Advice Bureaux
www.citizensadvice.org.uk, or check your telephone directory for your nearest branch.

Consumer Credit Counselling Service Helpline: 0800 138 1111 www.cccs.co.uk

Credit Action 6th Floor, Lynton House, 7–12 Tavistock Square, London WC1H 9LT Tel: 0207 380 3390 www.creditaction.org.uk

Money Advice Trust 21 Garlick Hill, London EC4V 2AU Tel: 020 7489 7796 www.moneyadvicetrust.org

National Debtline Tel: 0808 808 4000 www.nationaldebtline.co.uk

NHS Stressline Tel: 0300 123 2000

De-cluttering organisations

Association of Professional Declutterers and Organisers UK For a national list of de-cluttering consultants. www.apdo-uk.co.uk

Bye Bye Pigsty Tel: 07955 247800 www.byebyepigsty.co.uk

Clear of Clutter Tel: 07930 983452 www.clearofclutter.com

The Clutter Clinic Tel: 07834 338568 www.clutterclinic.co.uk

Cluttergone Tel: 01279 792000 www.cluttergone.co.uk

Stuff U Sell Collects items and sells them for you on eBay, minus 20 per cent commission and collection charge, depending on location. 8 Commercial Way, Abbey Road, London NW10 7XF Tel: 0800 046 1100 email: enquiries@stuffusell.co.uk www.stuffusell.co.uk

unclutter.com www.unclutter.com

Healthcare and health advice

Cochrane Reviews The Cochrane Collaboration is an international network of healthcare professionals, policy makers and patients who prepare, update and publish balanced reviews of research to answer specific health questions. www.cochrane.org/cochrane-reviews

Diabetes UK Information and support for people with diabetes. Diabetes UK Central Office, Macleod House, 10 Parkway, London, NW1 7AA Tel: 020 7424 1000 email: info@diabetes.org.uk www.diabetes.org.uk

The Hale Clinic Europe's largest complementary health clinic offering a wide range of complementary therapies and an advisory service. 7 Park Crescent, London W1B 1PF Tel: 020 7631 0156 www.haleclinic.com

The Herb Society The UK's leading society for increasing the understanding, use and appreciation of herbs and their benefits to health. Sulgrave Manor, PO Box 946, Northampton NN3 0BN Tel: 0845 491 8699 www.herbsociety.org.uk

KidsHealth The most visited site for information on children's health and development. www.kidshealth.org

National Institute of Medical Herbalists Includes national directory of medical herbalists. Elm House, 54 Mary Arches Street, Exeter EX4 3BA Tel: 01392 426022 email: info@nimh.org.uk www.nimh.org.uk

Neal's Yard Remedies Natural organic health and beauty products, herbal remedies and ingredients. Tel: 0845 22 31456 www.nealsyardremedies.com

NHS National Institute for Health and Clinical Excellence (NICE) Independent organisation responsible for providing national guidance on the promotion of good health and the prevention and treatment of illness. www.nice.org.uk

Overcoming jetlag Download Virgin Atlantic's jetlag-fighter app (written by Dr Chris Idzikowski) for your mobile phone (small fee applicable). www.jetlagfighter.com

Parliamentary and Health Service Ombudsman Tel: 0345 015 4033 www.ombudsman.org.uk

Patient Advice and Liaison Service (PALS) Contact your local hospital or search www.pals.nhs.uk/officemapsearch.aspx

Tired all the time/chronic fatigue syndrome Useful websites covering all aspects of chronic fatigue syndrome: www.nhs.uk/conditions/chronic-fatigue-syndrome/Pages/Introduction.aspx or www.nlm.nih.gov/medlineplus/fatigue.html

Legal problems

Acas (Advisory, Conciliation and Arbitration Service) Free advice and information on employment rights and rules for employers and employees. Helpline: 08457 47 47 47 www.acas.org.uk

Consumer Direct Tel: 08454 04 05 06 (higher rate call charges may apply) www.consumerdirect.gov.uk

Hedgeline For problems regarding hedges. www.Hedgeline.org

National Mediation Helpline 0845 60 30 809 www.nationalmediationhelpline.com

UK Mediation Tel: 01773 822222 www.ukmediation.net

Life coaching

International Coach Federation www.coachfederation.org.uk

Life coach directories www.lifecoach-directory.org.uk or www.findalifecoach.co.uk

Meditation and mindfulness

Learn Mindfulness Free lessons online plus CDs and books. Tel: 07903 343893 www.learnmindfulness.co.uk

London Meditation Centre www.londonmeditationcentre.com

London Shambhala Meditation Centre For Mindfulness-Based Stress Reduction (MBSR). 27 Belmont Close, London SW4 6AY Tel: 020 7720 3207 www.shambhala.org.uk

Meditation is Easy www.meditationiseasy.com

MeditationExpert Useful resource on meditation techniques and stress relief. www.meditationexpert.co.uk

Samye Ling Retreat A peaceful Tibetan Buddhist centre offering meditation classes and retreats, open to people of all faiths and none. Eskdalemuir, Langholm, Dumfriesshire, DG13 0QL, Scotland Tel: 013873 73232 www.samyeling.org

The School of Meditation 158 Holland Park Avenue, London W11 4UH Tel: 020 7603 6116 www.schoolofmeditation.org

Mental health

The Happiness Project Promotes happiness and offers an 8-week happiness course. Two Birches, The Harris Estate, Laleham Reach, Chertsey, Surrey KT16 8RP Tel: 0845 430 9236 www.happiness.co.uk

Mind The leading mental health charity for England and Wales, dedicated to promoting and protecting good mental health. 15–19 Broadway, Stratford, London E15 4BQ Tel: 0845 766 0163 or 020 8519 2122 www.mind.org.uk

Positive Rewards Useful website that promotes positive mental health, with advice on mental training and hypnosis therapy. www.positiverewards.com

Nutrition

Brain Bio Centre (owned by parent charity Food for the Brain Foundation) Supports mental health problems with optimum nutrition. Avalon House, 72 Lower Mortlake Road, Richmond TW9 2JY Tel: 020 8332 9600 email: info@brainbiocentre.com www.foodforthebrain.org

Food Standards Agency An independent government department set up to protect the public's health and consumer interests in relation to food. Includes up-to-date details of recommended government guidelines on nutrition. www.food.gov.uk

The Institute for Optimum Nutrition Provides nutrition-therapy education. Avalon House, 72 Lower Mortlake Road, Richmond TW9 2JY Tel: 020 8614 7800 www.ion.ac.uk

Personality testing

The Myers & Briggs Foundation Information on the Myers-Briggs Type Indicator® – a form of psychometric testing based on Jung's theories about personality types.
email: coordinator@myersbriggs.org
www.myersbriggs.org

Online personality tests
www.discoveryourpersonality.com or
www.personalitytype.com

Retirement

Getting ready for a life after work
www.getreadyforretirement.co.uk or
www.retirementexpert.co.uk

SAGA Dealing with wide issues around retirement. www.saga.co.uk

SAD and light boxes

Electronic Healing For light boxes (and other healing products). 48 Surrenden Crescent, Brighton BN1 6WF Tel: 0844 804 2130 www.electronichealing.co.uk

GB Bulbs For full-spectrum lighting. 115 Oxford Road, Abingdon, OXON, OX14 2AB www.gbbulbs.co.uk

SAD Association For information and support. Seasonal Affective Disorder Association, www.sada.org.uk

S.A.D Lightbox Company Unit 2, Aston Hill, Lewknor, Watlington, Oxon OX49 5SG Tel: 0845 095 6477 www.sad.uk.com

SAD.co.uk For light-therapy products. Tel: 08445 090 444 www.sad.co.uk

SAD.org.uk UK voluntary organisation offering information and advice about seasonal affective disorder and helpful light boxes. www.sad.org.uk

Sleep centres and organisations

British Snoring and Sleep Apnoea Association For snore-attenuating ear plugs. Tel: 01737 245638 www.britishsnoring.co.uk

The Edinburgh Sleep Centre 13 Heriot Row, Edinburgh EH3 6HP Tel: 0131 524 9730 email: info@edinburghsleepcentre.com www.edinburghsleepcentre.com

Online sleep links Links to sleep centres in the UK and other useful sleep-related links. www.neuronic.com/bss.htm

The Sleep Council High Corn Mill, Chapel Hill, Skipton, North Yorkshire BD23 1NL Tel: 0845 058 4595; freephone leaflet line: 0800 018 7923 www.sleepcouncil.org.uk

Stress management

Acupuncture
The Acupuncture Society Tel: 0773 4668 402 email: acusoc@yahoo.co.uk www.acupuncturesociety.org.uk

British Acupuncture Council Tel: 020 8735 0400 www.acupuncture.org.uk

British Medical Acupuncture Society Lists doctors qualified in acupuncture. London office tel: 020 7713 9437 email: bmaslondon@aol.com www.medical-acupuncture.co.uk

Anxiety UK Help and support for those living with anxiety disorders. Zion Community Resource Centre, 339 Stretford Road, Hulme, Manchester M15 4ZY Helpline: 08444 775 774 www.anxietyuk.org.uk

Biofeedback

Aleph One Ltd For relaxometers and biofeedback machines, also books and CDs on stress management, relaxation, behavioural problems and anxiety. Tel: 01223 811 679 email: info@aleph1.co.uk www.aleph1.co.uk

Complementary Healthcare Information Service: biofeedback www.chisuk.org.uk/bodymind/whatis/biofeedback.php

Relax UK Ltd For biofeedback equipment. Tel: 01206 767300 email: info@relax-uk.com www.relax-uk.com

York Mind-Body Health (biofeedback) www.york-biofeedback.co.uk

Getting You There Offers a tailored approach to stress management for individuals and for companies wishing to support their staff's wellbeing. Tel: 0752 3198772 email: success@gettingyouthere.co.uk www.gettingyouthere.co.uk

Health and Safety Executive Includes support and advice on dealing with work-related stress. www.hse.gov.uk/stress

Hypnosis and hypnotherapy

The Association for Professional Hypnosis and Psychotherapy Tel: 01702 347691 www.aphp.net

The Hypnotherapy Association UK Tel: 01257 262124 email: theha@tiscali.co.uk www.thehypnotherapyassociation.co.uk

Hypnosis directory www.hypnosisdirectory.net

Hypnosis information www.hypnosisinformation.co.uk

UK Confederation of Hypnotherapy Organisations Tel: 0800 952 0560 email: petermatthews@manageyourstress.co.uk www.ukcho.co.uk

International Stress Management Association PO Box 491, Bradley Stoke, Bristol BS34 9AH Tel: 01179 697284 www.isma.org.uk

Living Life to the Full Free online life-skills course aimed at helping people to help themselves. www.livinglifetothefull.com

NHS Choices: stress management www.nhs.uk/LiveWell/stressmanagement/Pages/Stressmanagementhome.aspx

NHS Choices: treating stress www.nhs.uk/Conditions/Stress/Pages/Treatment.aspx

Relaxation for Living Institute 33 Newman St, London W1T 1PY Tel: 020 7439 4277 www.rfli.co.uk

Stress Management Society Tel: 0800 327 7697 email: info@stress.org.uk www.stress.org.uk

The Stress Release Centre Counselling, stress management and relaxation courses. Also stress management books and relaxation CDs. 47 Novello Street, London SW6 4JB Tel: 020 7736 4922 email: susanbalfour@releaseyourstress.co.uk www.releaseyourstress.co.uk

Stresswise Tel: 0845 056 8977 www.stresswise.com

Time-management tips www.time-management-guide.com or www.markforster.net

Volunteering

Available opportunities www.timebank.org.uk

BTCV (conservation work) www.btcv.org.uk

Community Service Volunteers (CSV) Volunteers receive training as they do volunteer work. www.csv.org.uk

Deciding what to do www.Do-it.org or www.volunteering.org.uk

Mentoring and befriending www.mandbf.org.uk

Platform 2 For 18–25 year olds. www.myplatform2.com

Reach Online For those who want to volunteer in the UK and have professional skills. www.reach-online.org.uk

Voluntary Service Overseas (VSO) www.vso.org.uk

index

FOR EDDISON SADD

Project editor Tessa Monina
Senior editor Ali Moore
Art editor Jane McKenna
Picture research administration Rosie Taylor
Proofreader Nikky Twyman
Indexer Marie Lorimer

Managing director Nick Eddison
Editorial director Ian Jackson

FOR VIVAT DIRECT

Project editor Rachel Warren Chadd
Art editor Simon Webb

Editorial director Julian Browne
Art director Anne-Marie Bulat
Managing editor Nina Hathway
Trade books editor Penny Craig
Picture resource manager Sarah Stewart-Richardson
Pre-press technical manager Dean Russell
Product production manager Claudette Bramble
Senior production controller Jan Bucil

Colour origination FMG
Printed and bound in China

This paperback edition published in 2012 in the United Kingdom by Vivat Direct Limited (t/a Reader's Digest), 157 Edgware Road, London W2 2HR.

First published in 2011

Stay Calm Stay Healthy is owned and under licence from The Reader's Digest Association, Inc. All rights reserved.

We are committed both to the quality of our products and the service we provide to our customers. We value your comments, so please do contact us on **0871 351 1000** or via our website at **www.readersdigest.co.uk**

If you have any comments or suggestions about the content of our books, email us at **gbeditorial@readersdigest.co.uk**

Book Code: 400-632 UP0000-1
ISBN: 978 1 78020 140 5